With a compassionate and sensitive
current research, this book matches i
provides the best kind of education. T
insightful stories from personal exper
and practical knowledge.

—JOHN ARDEN, PHD

Author of fifteen books, including Mind-Brain-Gene: Towards Psychotherapy Integration
*Former Director of Training for Mental Health for the
Northern California Region in the Kaiser Permanente healthcare system*

In *Loving Our Students on Purpose*, Bernii Godwin and Danny Silk provide, in an
accessible volume, insights into optimizing the relationship between educators
and their students. The authors confirm that through witnessing and listening
to our students we open the often-shut portal to mutual trust and co-regulation. The authors back their intuitions with a neurobiologically based strategy,
consistent with principles of Polyvagal Theory, that will shift the educational
experience from emphasizing the need to control the student to the mutual
benefits of a shared journey of curiosity and accomplishment.

—STEPHEN W. PORGES, PHD

*Distinguished University Scientist at Indiana University,
Professor of Psychiatry at the University of North Carolina,
Professor Emeritus at the University of Illinois at Chicago and the University of Maryland,
Originator of Polyvagal Theory and author of multiple titles on the subject, including* The Polyvagal Theory:
Neurophysiological foundations of Emotions, Attachment, Communication, and Self-Regulation

Power emerges from secure relationships, whether one is a student, teacher,
or parent. In *Loving Our Students On Purpose*, Bernii Godwin enthusiastically
applies Danny Silk's lessons to the classroom, unlocking secrets that teachers
can use to move students from traumatic disruption to joyful responsibility
for learning. The authors share rich examples from students, neuroscience, and
psychological and educational theory that bring to life their primary discovery,
that when teachers devote time and energy to building psychologically safe
relationships with their students, they form a secure bedrock from which students can experiment, explore, and ultimately acquire the knowledge, skills, and
attitudes they need to succeed. Imagine if all teachers applied what Godwin and
Silk have grasped and embodied: our world would be populated by graduates
who know who they are and feel secure enough to risk failure to transform
societies with wisdom and compassion.

—GEORGE THOMPSON, MD

*Volunteer Clinical Associate Professor of Psychiatry at the UMKC and University of Kansas Schools of Medicine,
international speaker and consultant, and co-author of* Polyvagal Theory and the Developing Child

Loving Our Students on Purpose is an extraordinarily timely book that seamlessly integrates neuroscience, contemporary psychology, and rich personal experience into a highly practical approach to reinvigorate the teacher student connection. Bernii and Danny charts a path out of the often-default fear-based culture towards a sustainable culture of love and connection that can permeate all levels of the education system. We owe it to ourselves and to the future of our children to invest in these ideas, and fortunately Bernii makes this easy through illuminating case studies that bring the concepts to life. It's heartening to see how many of the concepts that I hold dear in my work in resilience comes together here to explain in depth how valuable it is to move away from fear and into a space of safety, vulnerability, acceptance, and trusting connection, leading towards a new relationship with students that can be truly life-changing.

—JURIE ROSSOUW

CEO & Co-founder of Hello Driven CEO
Author of The Neuroeducation Toolbox: Practical Translations of Neuroscience in Counseling and
Psychotherapy

For many generations, teaching has defaulted to coercive methods of control, some more subtle than others, in an attempt to get the best out of students. Today we have a well-founded neuroscientific understanding of learning and development that shows us a more effective way to educate our children in an environment of love, safety, and responsibility. Godwin and Silk bring together a powerful combination of the science of connection, co-regulation, choice theory, and applied neuroscience for educators in an easy to understand and very practical handbook. If you want to know how your students are "wired" and how to nurture a culture of effective learning, I guarantee *Loving Our Students on Purpose* will give you the science and the application you will need to transform your classroom.

—MATTHEW DAHLITZ

Author of The Practitioner's Guide to the Science of Psychotherapy, The Psychotherapist's Essential
Guide to the Brain, The Teacher's Essential Guide to the Brain, *(co-author)* Founder of the International Journal of Neuropsychotherapy, The Neuropsychotherapist, and The Science of Psychotherapy

A practical book for anyone interested in helping children develop well! Integrating Danny Silk's Loving on Purpose approaches, along with ideas and concepts from other authors and educational sources, this book is loaded with stories and everyday examples that highlight well-being for children. It is a book that creates connection with the reader through its conversational tone and the use of the author's personal narratives, personal reflections, and individual case studies. Combining basic neuroscience knowledge with practical well-being strategies builds knowledge and important understandings for every teacher and the students they teach.

—KAREN FERRY

Registered Counsellor, Neuropsychotherapist, Education, Wellbeing & Behaviour Consultant and Co-author of The Teacher's Essential Guide to the Brain

Most people know that children don't care how much you know until they know how much you care. Bernii Godwin and Danny Silk's unique book gives a broad ranging account of why this is so and how to live it out in the classroom. A comprehensive introduction to the LoSoP program, this book will guide anyone looking to see the world of education through its next, much needed, evolution.

—CLAIRE WILSON

Author of Grounded: Discovering the Missing Pieces in the Puzzle of Children's Behaviour, *TEDx Speaker, Therapist, and Founder of GROUNDED GrownUps®*

Loving Our Students on Purpose is a resource that belongs on every teacher's desk throughout the world. Godwin and Silk have teamed up to provide an easy to use tool for professionals in all areas of the education industry to navigate student behaviour, wellbeing, parent communication and school culture. The programme breaks down theoretical and applied neuroscience concepts relevant to understanding the developing child and uses real life narratives to exemplify how teachers and school leaders can foster connected classroom environments that balance relationships with boundaries. LoSoP is not another program for your teachers to learn; rather it is an internal reflection process focused on developing and maintaining a safe and loving school culture that can be embedded into the hearts of the teaching teams and their assistants, allied health and wellbeing staff, executive and board members. LoSoP is a great tool to increase student and staff retention, job satisfaction and joyful responsibility in your school community.

—DR. LYNNE DONELEY

Executive Director/Principal Research Officer, Associated Christian Schools, State Executive Officer QLD, Christian Education National

Loving Our Students on Purpose is a highly accessible and a compelling read, striking a fine balance between current research into neuroscience, personal response, analogies and metaphors, all of which accumulates along the way a tool kit of understandings and resources as the reader builds new ways of seeing themselves and the classroom dynamics. Schools will welcome this comprehensive and empowering model for its wide application in many scenarios where difficult conversations are present, as with parents and staff in relation to discipline, trauma, friendship, special needs and well-being. Godwin speaks with the authority of one who has worked alongside vulnerable students, been employed by school leaders, social workers, and school systems and is able to harness her advanced knowledge from social work and neuroscience. This will likely hold a place among the professional reading shelves of educators who are seeking sustainable solutions that bring positive change.

—DR. JENNIE BICKMORE-BRAND

Dean of Education, Eastern College Australia
Adjunct Associate Professor Alphacrucis University College

Mackay Christian College was privileged to have Bernii Godwin and her consultation team present at our staff retreat day at the start of 2022. This was a day filled with "ah-ha" moments for all the staff, teaching and non-teaching, as she led us through Danny Silk's materials on the importance of relationships both for us as people and as professionals in the education industry. The *Loving our Students on Purpose* material, which is the synergy between *Loving our Kids on Purpose* and *Keep Your Love On*, should be a part of all school curricula in a world that is struggling with who and what schools and education are. I unreservedly recommend Bernii Godwin and her team for their role in reminding all of us the true purpose of education.

—DR BARCLIE GALLOGRAY

Principal, Mackay Christian College, QLD Australia

An absorbing and magnetic read. Loved it. Bernii and Danny eloquently weave practical personal experience together with eternal truths and the latest neuroscience research. If you want to grow personally and/or develop professionally by transforming your understanding of your students' development and their valuable needs then I highly recommend this insightful addition to Danny Silk's Loving your Kids on Purpose.

—DARRYL MULHOLLAND

Head of School Y7-12, YMCA SAS, and Vocational School

Bernii's passion for inspiring connection and relationship between students and teachers, teacher aides, social workers, and school counsellors is found in her many years of experiences, data and research, as well as her heart for social change, development, and empowerment. Working with Bernii for many years was a joy and made me not only a better, more connected teacher, but wife, daughter, and aunty.

—ALANAH BRAUN

Year Level Coordinator and Secondary School Teacher

I used to think I understood how to show my students that I loved them, with connection always being my number one teaching priority. *Loving Our Students on Purpose* has given me direction to know how I may be unknowingly causing disconnect and ways to fix this. I feel empowered as I've now been provided with the language to use to show that I care, without making my students' problems my own.

—RACHAEL ABBOT

Primary School Teacher

Bernii's compassionate heart for students combined with her deep understanding of neuroscience yields this brilliant primer for educators looking for practical wisdom. In this book, Bernii & Danny show how to create an environment where not only learning happens, but where both teacher and student feel safe, empowered, connected, and powerful.

—DR MARGARET NAGIB

Clinical psychologist & author of Souls Like Stars: Renew Your Mind, Heal Your Heart, Unveil Your Shine; Sozo for Professional Counselors: Integrating Psychology *and* Inner Healing to Restore Individuals to Wholeness and Soul Making: A 12 week Group-Based Sozo Experience

LOVING
OUR
Students
ON
PURPOSE

For information about school wide training or individual coaching in the application of Loving Our Students on Purpose please contact:
- www.godwinconsulting.com.au
- admin@godwinconsulting.com.au.

Cover Design by Ashley Beck
Interior Design and Layout by Printopya LLC

ISBN: 978-0-9888984-6-2

Printed in the United States.

DISCLOSURE STATEMENT

Working in education over the past twenty years in various roles has given me scope to collect patterns through repeated stories in the lives of students and staff. To that end, this book is a compilation of stories that reflect those similarities and patterns in my professional experiences. This means that no character, name, or identifying details are accurate to any one person, but a hybrid of multiple experiences combined into fictional characters. Any person's resemblance to real or living persons is just a coincidence and further evidence that society cannot continue to ignore that our communities are facing similar challenges across countries, educational facilities, and generations.

Standards of practice change over time, and no technique or recommendation is guaranteed to be safe or effective in all circumstances. This book is designed to provide general information for professionals working with children within the education context and is not a substitute for appropriate training or professional supervision. The authors cannot guarantee the complete accuracy, efficacy, or appropriateness of any particular recommendation in each respect. As of time of publishing, the links and resources listed in these books were available. The authors are not responsible for any content that appears on third-party websites.

NOTE ABOUT STYLE AND TERMINOLOGY

Loving our Students on Purpose has been designed to go into every school, in all the world. As such, Danny and I have reflected our cross-country dynamic by editing using USA standards for style and spelling, whilst the school terminology reflects the Australian sector. A reference tool to general year levels and terminology for specific countries has been provided.

Age	Australia		USA		UK	
	School	Grade/Year	School	Grade	School	Year
3-4	Kindy (not compulsory)		Preschool		Pre-school	Nursery
4-5	Kindy Pre-Prep (not compulsory)		Pre-kindergarten	PreK/4K	Primary School (infants)	Reception
5-6	Prep	P	Elementary	Kindergarten/5K	Primary School (infants)	1
6-7	Primary School	1	Elementary	First	Primary School (infants)	2
7-8	Primary School	2	Elementary	Second	Primary School (juniors)	3
8-9	Primary School	3	Elementary	Third	Primary School (juniors)	4
9-10	Primary School	4	Elementary	Fourth	Primary School (juniors)	5
10-11	Primary School	5	Elementary/Middle School	Fifth	Primary School (juniors)	6
11-12	Primary School	6	Junior high/Middle School	Sixth	Secondary School	7
12-13	Secondary-Middle School	7	Junior high/Middle School	Seventh	Secondary School	8
13-14	Secondary-Middle School	8	Junior high/Middle School	Eighth	Secondary School	9
14-15	Secondary-Middle School	9	High School - Freshman	Ninth	Secondary School/GCSE	10
15-16	Secondary-Senior School	10	High School - Sophmore	Tenth	Secondary School/GCSE	11
16-17	Secondary-Senior School	11	High School - Junior	Eleventh	6th Form College	12
17-18	Secondary-Senior School	12	High School - Senior	Twelfth	6th Form College	13

Age	New Zealand		South Africa		Canada	
	School	Year	School	Grade or Form	School	Grade
3-4					Preschool	
4-5			Pre-Primary School (Not compulsory)		Pre-Kindergarten	
5-6	Primary School	1	Junior Primary	Grade 0/ Reception	Kindergarten	
6-7	Primary School	2	Junior Primary	Grade 1	Elementary	1
7-8	Primary School	3	Junior Primary	Grade 2	Elementary	2
8-9	Primary School	4	Junior Primary	Grade 3	Elementary	3
9-10	Primary School	5	Senior Primary	Grade 4	Elementary	4
10-11	Primary School	6	Senior Primary	Grade 5	Elementary	5
11-12	Intermediate	7	Senior Primary	Grade 6	Elementary	6
12-13	Intermediate	8	Secondary School	Grade 7	Junior High-Secondary	7
13-14	Junior Secondary	9	Secondary School	Grade 8	Junior High-Secondary	8
14-15	Junior Secondary	10	Secondary School	Grade 9	Junior High-Secondary	9
15-16	Senior Secondary	11	Senior Secondary School	Grade 10	Senior High-Secondary	10
16-17	Senior Secondary	12	Senior Secondary School	Grade 11	Senior High-Secondary	11
17-18	Senior Secondary	13	Senior Secondary School	Grade 12	Senior High-Secondary	12

TABLE OF CONTENTS

DEDICATION

ISAIAH.

I hope that every teacher you have treats you with love, respect, and connection, fuelling your joy of learning as you take on new adventures. May your generation and the ones to come after you know what it is to manage yourselves well, take risks, clean up your messes, and restore relationships. You will forever have your own special place in my heart. I love you.

ACKNOWLEDGMENTS

Jayden, when I started to write *Loving our Students on Purpose*, I had no idea that the journey of healing and loving well would bring me into connection with you. How blessed I am to share in our adventures, connection, growth, and messes. I love you. Thank you for your patience as I keep growing in my love and breaking through to new levels of connection as I learn to love myself in greater measures.

Andrew, Zerinah, and Jazhara, you guys are my chosen family. Thank you for opening your home as a place of safety and comfort, friendship and fun. More than anyone else you have walked out this journey of moving from weary to powerful alongside me, no matter how challenging it became at times. Thank you for your unconditional love poured out.

I am incredibly grateful to Danny & Sheri Silk who many years ago suggested, "You should write a book about this," on a visit to Australia. I am honoured by the trust you have put in me to apply your material and expand on it into a new sector—education. Your tenacity to achieve the seemingly impossible together and your ability to love each person through the struggle is evident not only in my own experience but also in the stories of those around you.

Allison, thank you for your guidance, kindness, and patience as you have walked alongside me in the writing and editing journey. You have eloquently captured my heart, voice, and vision within each page. Thank you for your integrity and encouragement throughout the entire process. A huge thank you also goes to Ashley for the beautiful external and internal graphics, you have an incredible gift for capturing a feeling or thought with artistic design.

To my mum—through hours of scribing, you collated the first draft, helping me form and reform concepts as the vision of *Loving our Students on Purpose* became clearer. Thank you for your time, honesty, and encouragement whilst I have pursued this project.

Special thanks goes to Professor Stephen Porges, who generously shared his wisdom reviewing the application of polyvagal theory. In addition, thank you to Dr. John Arden, Dr. Lou Cozolino, Dr. Margaret Nagib, Dr. George Thompson, Dr. David Collins, Claire Wilson, Jurie Rossouw, Matthew Dahlitz, and Karen Ferry who provided a thorough review of key sections on applied neuroscience for educators.

There have been many exceptional humans who have come alongside me as professionals, leaders, and mentors. Each of you has played a significant role in shaping my personal and professional development and I am so grateful for your input into my life. Specifically I would like to thank Aaron & Wendy, Royree, Andrew Z, Dave S, Dony J, Johannes, S, Peter J, Neil R, Gary C, Lynne D, Henny, Misha and Jennie BB. Plus a special thank you to Gavin & Bill.

And to my readers, thank you. May you be blessed as you unite to eradicate fear and punishment from our education systems, transforming our communities, and our world, through inserting love and hope into the lives of our students and families.

INTRODUCTION
By Danny Silk

THE MOST EXCITING REVELATION of this book is the simple power of making a connection. Somehow, so many of us learn to be married, raise a family, run a classroom, and live our lives without mastering the tools required to form, nurture, and protect healthy relational connections. The power of the connection between a teacher and a student is life-changing!

I can speak to this power firsthand. Back in the 1900s, when I was a child—October of 1978 to be more specific—I was sitting in an algebra class wrestling between pushing into solving for "x" and completely checking out in my discouragement and frustration. My teacher, Les Duntsch, leaned over next to me and checked in on my lack of progress. I hated school, but I liked this teacher. He helped me get going again and then said something that would change my life.

A little background on this student Mr. Duntsch was talking to:

> I left home at age 16.
> I lived with my girlfriend my last two years of high school.
> My high school GPA was 0.865.

I took three local college night classes my senior year to meet the graduation requirements.

I am the first in my family to graduate high school.

All of my closest friends dropped out of high school.

I don't know how much Mr. Duntsch knew about these realities in my life, but unexpectedly he leaned into the connection he had been building with me, a perpetually failing student, and said, "I see something special in you, Danny. You are going to do things that will surprise the world one day. I can feel it! I hope you see it one day, because it is real."

I felt a smile come across my face and I could sense the heat in my cheeks as I blushed. I wanted to believe what he was saying, but I couldn't yet see what he could see. Yet in that moment, Mr. Duntsch reached into my life and flipped on a switch—a switch connected to hope. I hoped there was something inside me that would help me win in life. I hoped that I could learn to make it through all this resistance in my world. I hoped that I could "change my stars."

To my surprise, I did make it to graduation the following year. The school called me at my place of employment and told me to go ahead and show up for graduation in a few days because I passed my final English exam. My stars were starting to change.

Eight years later, now married with a one-year-old child, I returned to school at a local junior college. I only enrolled in one class because I was terrified—I just knew I was going to discover that reading, writing, and arithmetic were too much for me. I was twenty-six years old and still had never read a book cover to cover. But upon finishing the course, I received an "A" grade. I was stunned! I must not have had a learning disability after all. This must be what happens when you try.

It took me seven more years to finish my Master of Social Work degree with an emphasis in Marriage and Family. I finished that journey with a wife, three children, a full-time job as a social worker, earning a GPA of 3.75. The week my degree arrived in the mail, I drove to my hometown about an hour away, went to my high school, and found Mr.

Duntsch. I handed him the envelope and watched his face. He tipped his head in curiosity, pulled the diploma out of the envelope, and held it. Then he looked at me, his eyes welling with tears, and reached out for a hug. While in the embrace, he whispered in my ear, "I told you you had something special in there, Danny. I'm glad you found it."

I had indeed "changed my stars," in no small part thanks to what Mr. Duntsch poured into my young life. I don't know who said, "People will do more for those they love than those they fear," but I wholeheartedly agree and know it to be true. My wife, Sheri, always tells people that her goal in life is to get her children to fall madly in love with her. That way she will always be able to influence them in life.

When a teacher creates a control-and-punishment culture in their classroom in an effort to find some sense of order so they can do their job, they often lose the joy that led them onto the path to become a teacher in the first place. They diverge from the goal of becoming someone to look up to, a trusted guide into the joys and challenges of learning, and instead become caught in cycles of power struggles and disconnected relationships. Disrespect and irresponsibility operate at unacceptable levels in their classroom, and anxiety fills the place where they hoped to be an inspiration.

Loving Our Students On Purpose is both a map and a toolbox. It's a map that shows the "why" and "where" of getting to a loving, connected classroom culture, and a toolbox to show you "how" to get there. Among these tools is the application of neuroscience and psychotherapy, which shifts old paradigms and shines hope toward new frontiers of successful learning. The effects of social, family, and institutional breakdowns are no longer as powerful and discouraging because we can see that we still have the ability to meet the deepest needs of the people who are in our room despite these setbacks and deficits. Understanding the design of our brains to form connections, and to learn in the safety provided by connection, guides us in how to inspire our students to learn, grow, and reach their potential. With the right tools and the right goal, teachers are poised to change a student's life like few forces on the planet. This book is a healing process in the right hands. I'm glad that you found this tool that will help you create a classroom that you want to be in, and a place that creates learning in the most effective ways imaginable.

—**Danny Silk, MSW**
Author of *Keep Your Love On*
Founder of Loving On Purpose

1

THE PROBLEM

I GRADUATED SECONDARY SCHOOL[1] with one certainty about my future: *I never wanted to step foot in a school again.* Though I loved learning and achieving, my innate perfectionism and introversion caused my school experience to be marked by fear of failure, risk avoidance, isolation, and shame over feeling that I always came up short of my own high expectations. I begrudgingly enrolled in university at the end of secondary because everyone at our school was required to do this, but midway through my first semester, I dropped out, overwhelmed by the huge campus, the complex task of timetabling lectures and tutorials, and the sheer number of strangers in every courtyard, library, or lecture hall.

There's no telling how long I might have allowed my fear and insecurities to hold me back in life and keep me in this pattern of self-defeating survival mode if I hadn't been interrupted, just a few months after dropping out of university, by a phone call that drew me straight back into the education system... and ended up igniting my life's passion and purpose.

The call was from a family friend, Mrs. Roberts, and she sounded desperate. "Bernii, Rebecca was caught on school camp smoking marijuana with her friend, Tayla. They have externally suspended them both for ten weeks. I convinced the school to let them stay enrolled for the term and

---

[1] High school for my American friends and colleagues.

5

consider their reengagement if they can keep up with the work and pass their exams. We were hoping we could hire you as their tutor."

I had years of experience as a youth leader and children's camp leader. *How hard could tutoring two girls be?* I agreed.

The term got off to a great start. I met with Rebecca and Tayla each day and got familiar with their course materials. The girls seemed motivated to get back to school and started work on their subjects. I found I made a great drill sergeant—bossing the girls around, setting tasks, and maintaining high expectations.

By week three, however, things started to unravel. The excitement of a new term, the relief of being back at school and in routines, and the curiosity about the term's material all wore off for the girls and for me. I was already getting tired, and worst of all, Rebecca and Tayla were getting to know me and finding the cracks in my armor.

By week four, Rebecca was crushing hard on a boy. When she wasn't texting him, she talked about him nonstop. Tayla was more than happy to encourage her friend to talk about her budding romance. Incomplete work began piling up, and I started to feel embarrassment that the girls were making me look incompetent as a tutor. When they had exhausted talking about boys, they started asking me about my personal life and crude adult questions—anything to get out of work. I tried redirecting them, yelling at them, emotionally manipulating them, and bribing them with rewards, but nothing worked. My patience wore thin, my humiliation escalated, and the girls saw my bitter resentment simmering just under the surface. Soon, their goal appeared to be making me lose control. They stopped doing work altogether and simply ignored me. I felt powerless, inadequate, angry at their disrespect, and most of all, I felt like a failure.

The final straw was when Rebecca flatly began to tell me no. No, she would not do her work. No, she would not stop talking about boys. No, she didn't care about school. No, she would not put her phone away as I told her. No, no. no. What do you do with a no? Well, I knew exactly what I would do with a no. If they didn't want me there, then I had better things to do. I rang Rebecca's mother, got in my car, and went shopping, leaving Rebecca and Tayla to teach themselves. Once again, I decided I was done with anything school-related.

Mrs. Roberts phoned me that night, begging, "Please, we need your help."

"They won't listen to me," I said flatly, no longer angry, but resigned to the fact that I had failed. "They won't do their work. You are wasting your money paying me to babysit. I think they both have a lot of potential, but I don't know how to get through to them."

"Please," she asked again. "We believe you are the right person to work with the girls. I know you will get through."

"Okay," I agreed skeptically. "But one more day like today and I am out."

"That's fair," said Mrs. Roberts gratefully. "Let's start again on Monday and give them a chance to think about what they are going to do."

What difference could one more day make, anyway? I had no doubt in my mind that Rebecca and Tayla had no intention of doing schoolwork and this final attempt was an exercise in futility. However, by the time Monday arrived, I had made a decision. I would at least be honest with the girls and let them know how they affected my heart before we parted ways.

We started the day sitting together. Both girls were subdued and had clearly been spoken to by their parents.

"Rebecca, Tayla," I said, looking each of them in the eyes, "This is not working for me. I am not having fun, and I don't think you are either. If you would like to graduate middle school then I am here to help. If you only want a babysitter, then your parents might need to find someone else. I was hired to help you stay enrolled at school and go on to finish senior. What do you want to do?"

"I want to go back to school," said Rebecca.

"Me too," Tayla quickly added.

"Okay," I nodded. "First, help me understand what happened at school camp."

The girls looked at one another, eyes downcast.

"We just wanted to have a bit of fun," Rebecca began. "We didn't think about the consequences. We had never smoked marijuana before."

"It was my fault," Tayla blurted out. "I brought it to camp and shared it with Rebecca. I am so sorry," she said, turning to face Rebecca.

Both girls started to cry, confessing how scared they felt when they were caught, and, after the school had called in their parents, the disappointment of realizing they'd hurt the people they loved the most. They told me how they had been publicly shamed by other students who found out, the friends they had lost because they had been branded "bad," and the rumors being spread about them.

Rebecca and Tayla were feeling hurt, scared, and rejected by their peers. Their desire to return to school came directly from two sets of parents who loved them enough to see past their poor choice and give them a chance to make different ones in the future. As the girls opened their hearts and were vulnerable with me, I felt compassion and grace flood in. These girls needed someone who would believe with them that they could make different choices in their own lives. I was not in control of them, but I could be in control of me and the love I offered to them, which in turn would support them as they learned self-control through a healthy attachment with me.

"I want you to finish school too," I said. "So, what needs to change for us to get there together?"

"We need to catch up on the missed work and study for exams," Tayla offered.

"That sounds like a good plan," I agreed. "What do you need from me?"

After a few moments' thought, the girls told me they needed a place to put their phones, a schedule where they could see breaks coming up so the work would not feel overwhelming, access to snacks, and the ability to work on the subjects they wanted for the session. I responded that these seemed reasonable, adding, "I am here if you have questions or need help. Otherwise, I will let you work quietly. If any of us are not feeling great on a day, we need to feel safe to say so and work together to encourage one another."

The girls agreed, and, to my amazement, worked for the rest of the day. This continued the next day, and the next, and soon became our new normal. In the break times, we started to get to know one another. They asked good questions about relationships and friendships, and I showed genuine interest in their lives. The more connection we built, the more work got done. It was soon week seven and they were studying for exams. To my amazement, the school recognized me as their supervisor, and I watched over them with pride as they passed all of their exams and assessments. Following this successful term, the two girls returned to school to complete their senior years.

THE OLD WAY ISN'T WORKING

My time with Rebecca and Tayla drove home a powerful truth that has become the cornerstone of my journey in behavior education: *I cannot control anyone toward success. I am not, nor would I ever be, in control of any other human but myself.*

Going into that tutoring experience, I had no tools except what I had experienced as a student myself. Bribery, yelling, and demanding compliance were what I had observed from most of my teachers. However, a few teachers had demonstrated another way. In secondary school, there were two teachers in particular who seemed to know that my success was my own responsibility. They never tried to control me—they simply cheered me on. This experience, combined with what I had just seen work with Rebecca and Tayla, fueled a desire in me to see how students' positive choices could be influenced by connected relationships—a desire strong enough that I overcame my previous determination to stay away from school. I decided to return to university and study human behavior and criminology.

Whilst I was in my first year of university, I was hired by Rebecca and Tayla's school to work in the primary school[2] special needs department. It didn't take long for me to discern the desperation, weariness, and hopelessness that lay on many of the teachers and permeated the school culture around the problem of how to deal with poor student behavior. Again and again, I observed the system or individual teachers react—as I initially had with the girls—with anger, punishment, control, shaming, or bribery to survive their day with "that student" or "that class." There was a running joke in the staffroom about Wednesday "wine and whine" nights, where teachers would commiserate about how kids are just more disrespectful these days and we should "bring back the cane." I frequently heard desperate parents pleading that there had to be a more effective way to deal with kids' bad behavior, but no one seemed to have any real solutions.

Now having spent two decades working in many schools across all levels, I have discovered that the struggle, frustration, and weariness I observed in that first year are endemic in educational culture. I have met frequently with individual teachers and heads of school to support them in their frustrations, only to hear the same list of complaints:

- disrespect
- homework/disorganization
- non-compliance
- back-chatting
- bullying/friendship fights
- physical conflicts
- low self-esteem/well-being
- talking/calling out
- damage to property
- serious acts of misconduct
- inappropriate technology use
- parent behavior
- teacher exhaustion

---

[2] Elementary school.

Many teachers I meet describe feeling frequently powerless in the face of students' behavior, humiliated in front of their classes, and trapped by systemic pressures. These wonderful teachers, who entered the profession because they loved passing along the passion of learning to kids, feel hopeless and despondent. Unless they find another way, they will walk away from their first love, teaching.

The struggle is real. Lower primary teachers are often confronted with students who are not appropriately toilet trained, have limited communication skills, and often have recently separated parents negotiating the terms of their school engagement and attempting to draw the teacher onto "their side." These students instinctively behave their emotions, resulting in hitting, biting, spitting, breaking items, running away from staff, throwing tantrums or having meltdowns, and fighting over who gets to be first in line.

These same students are also dealing with the challenge of learning behavior standards different to those they have learned at home. At home, they have been drilled to always reply, but at school when they answer a question from a peer, they get in trouble. They have been taught to acknowledge their parents who yell from another room, yet when a teacher yells from their desk, students are expected to be silent. They have been taught to run to the toilet immediately when they need to go, yet now they are in trouble for leaving the classroom without permission. Many children are raised to talk through their day ("we put the right shoe on, we put the left shoe on"), but at school teachers get frustrated that they process every thought aloud. At home, they can go to the bathroom or get a drink whenever they want, they do not always have to share their toys, and play-fighting is often encouraged, as are role-playing games with guns and swords. Their "normal" has been upended, and lower primary teachers first need to help them to learn the differing expectations of home life and school life.

As students move into upper primary, students are learning more about how they interact with the world around them. Appropriate hormone development throws students' bodily reactions into turmoil, resulting in emotional, behavioral, and social challenges like friendship conflicts, physical fights, and in some cases, low self-esteem. Students who are struggling academically may also begin to intensify their fight-or-flight reactions in the classroom as a response to both the environmental stress and their inability to successfully self-regulate, with the unconscious goal of reducing the teacher's expectations to complete work. School systems increase their expectation for academic results and parents put pressure on teachers to "manage" friendship conflicts and technology use. When that fails, because each parent wants their child to be seen as good and the other bad, the conflict seeps into their adult relationships and often onto social media as well.

School systems expect that parents and teachers are responsible for controlling children, even though the processes and environmental context at home are vastly different to school. Additionally, students come from a variety of backgrounds, including realities such as single-parent and broken homes, grief and loss, environmental disasters, substance abuse, domestic and family violence, disabilities, language barriers, and so much more. Just attending school for many students is a success that goes unnoticed. For many of the students I have worked with over the past twenty years, school is their safe place—the place they go to let their guard down and be a child.

As students move into secondary school, the incidence of inappropriate social media behaviors, disrespect, intimidation, serious misconduct, and harmful acts toward other students, as well as significant well-being concerns, increase. Parents often appear to step back with the presumption that their children are "becoming adults." This coincides with students entering the teenage hormonal stages, reducing their responses to grunts, and withdrawing from their family members. The expectation on teachers triples as parents hope that this teacher is "the one" who will get through to their child. Heads of school are put under immense pressure to put Johnny in Mr. Bank's class, because he is a male teacher and Johnny needs a strong male in his life. But Johnny can't be in the same class as Tony and Rodney, whose mothers also want their boys in Mr. Bank's class for the same reason, because they are a bad influence.

Many teachers argue that students' behavior is getting worse and there is no respect anymore. I would argue that over the past twenty years in schools, I have observed very little change in student behavior. What I *have* observed is that different teachers have different styles for setting up and managing their classrooms. There are some teachers who have settled and connected classroom cultures, and others where students appear to be one step away from juvenile detention. I have observed the same cohorts over a ten-year period move from teacher to teacher, and as they do so they go from thriving and settled, to out of control, and then to settled again. I have observed individual students go from failing to passing or passing to failing.

It is true that many students are coming to school from complex and broken homes. It is true that there are students and parents involved in substance abuse and even crime. It is true that kids are not always kind and bullying in the playground or on social media can have long-term impacts on a child's development as an adult. It is also true that many parents are looking for a better way—the tools of control and punishment they were handed by their parents do not seem as effective on their children as they thought they would be.

Many schools I visit have a policy of behavior management stating that the school will respond to a student's poor behavior with increasing intensity to ensure they respond to punishment with compliance. These fear-based tools replicate many of the criminal justice tools used in the prison system or for societal control, including isolation, privilege removal, penance, community service, yelling and telling, merit and demerit points, bribery, and public shaming. These external management tools do not promote connection or thriving due to lack of safety and engagement. Nor do they encourage students to develop the internal sense of responsibility they will need as adults. Unless we want to keep repeating the same outcomes and perpetuating staff burnout, schools simply cannot keep using fear-based punishment tools like in the past.

MY SEARCH FOR A BETTER WAY

Maya Angelou said, "If you don't know where you've come from, you don't know where you're going." In other words, knowing what has influenced your own behavior is the first step in being able to influence a different future reality. This has been especially true in my journey to move away from behavior management and become trained in behavior education. It all started with me looking back and identifying the primary experiences that formed me, first as a student and then as a professional working in education. When I did so, I noticed two powerful factors that positively influenced both my behavior and that of my peers: *connection* and *responsibility*. (I couldn't help noticing that these were the two factors that proved most effective with Rebecca and Tayla.)

As early as ten years old, I found I was innately curious about the "naughty kids," much like the child who frequently brings home a wounded bird to nurture back to life. I remember one time we had a new girl, Alex, who was rumored to have been expelled, transfer to our class. The other students teased and withdrew from her, but I sat next to her on the bus to swimming. One day, Alex locked herself in the bathroom crying, which caused quite the stir among the staff and students. I started to wonder why she would behave that way. I wondered how the school's decision to suspend her would help her overcome the challenges she had with her peers. I talked my mum into letting me befriend her. Somehow I knew that what she needed most was the thing being withheld from her: *connection.* We stayed friends until she moved for secondary school, and I never saw her exhibit any other behavior issues.

Connection was also a powerful motivator in my own life. Despite severely disliking school, if I had a good connection with a teacher, I did anything for them—even play sports! If I did not have a good connection, however, I could be the most disrespectful student in the room. I remember Mr. Ramsey, my Japanese teacher in Year 8. Mr. Ramsey only stayed a few years at our school; rumor was, he walked away from teaching. When he left, I was devastated. Studying Japanese was never the same again. I did not give my loyalty to another Japanese teacher and honestly I remember very little of it now, but I can't forget the way Mr. Ramsey had made Japanese come alive and easy to learn—it was not work, it was fun. I often think of Mr. Ramsey when I work with students who are adapting to their different teachers and am thankful for the contrast he showed me in my dreadful teen years.

I had other amazing teachers who connected with me and inspired my learning. Mr. Edwards taught me to enjoy learning and that "how I learn" impacts other people. Specifically, I learned that if I was good at a task, some students became competitive or even jealous. If I worked too quickly, I would be asked if I was okay, and even (once) questioned privately about abuse and people pleasing. I learned it was less conspicuous to do a good job, but not to try and be the best or the fastest, as this would also draw unwelcome attention. Mrs. Blackshaw and Mrs. Hurle showed me that books could be exciting. I hated to read until upper primary school, but thanks to them, suddenly I could not put a book down. In secondary, Mrs. Vale and Mrs. David believed in me and endured correcting my dyslexic errors in many English and history drafts. They showed me the joy of interactive learning in relationship with my teacher that prepared me to excel at university, and on the cusp of adulthood, they role-modeled a balance of leadership and friendship. In their classrooms, I always felt valued, challenged to explore greater depths in my learning, and safe to take risks. Risk-taking in learning, as you will see, is an incredibly important skill for students to develop, but also one of the first that the system of control tries to erase.

As for *responsibility*, it was Mr. Larry, my multi-strand science teacher, who unforgettably demonstrated to me how powerful an influence this could be on behavior. Every day, one student in our class, Jordan, would literally do nothing aside from turn up to class and disrupt the teacher. It not only frustrated Mr. Larry, but it started to frustrate our whole class because we would miss out on experiments. One day, Mr. Larry surprised us all. He simply told Jordan that he was not welcome to participate in our class anymore; instead, he could bring his own entertainment and sit up the back. Of course, Jordan thought he hit the jackpot, so he brought in some car magazines to the next class and Mr. Larry simply went on with his teaching. It did not take too long before the novelty wore off, however. About three weeks later, Jordan was sitting in the front row participating in the science lesson.

The following year, I was in Jordan's group for senior camp. Straight away, the camp leader made him the team leader, and it was like he became a whole new person. Jordan went on to be a school prefect and was the first in his family to complete secondary school. I could not help but notice that the change started with Mr. Larry communicating a boundary. He basically stopped working harder on Jordan's learning than Jordan was and gave full responsibility back to him. The message he sent was, "I will teach you when you are fun to teach. You decide." Mr. Larry understood free will and that Jordan had a choice to learn or not to learn.

My lessons in connection and responsibility continued as an undergraduate student studying my bachelor's in human services and criminology. After some time working in primary education at Rebecca and Tayla's school, I sought a placement in a juvenile detention center. Very quickly, I learned that my passion lay in primary crime prevention, which required children to learn how to manage their freedom and take responsibility from a very young age. I returned to the educational system, working in alternative education with students who had been asked to leave our local public schools, which meant the entire class had not only been expelled but were currently banned from all public schools. Our job was to prepare them to re-enter the school system or the workplace in six months.

While working in alternative education, I came across *Loving our Kids on Purpose* by Danny Silk and *Love and Logic* by Jim Faye and Foster Cline.

These tools, which I will describe more fully in this book, put words to what I was experiencing and observing about connection and responsibility, and provided me a language to share with other school staff and parents. These tools *worked* with these students, and the success stories of individual lives ignited my desire to see all teachers everywhere have access to another way.

I returned to university to complete my Master of Social Work and learn all I could about human behavior and development. During this time, I completed a practicum at the local hospital in the maternity social work department. There I received a solid grounding in perinatal and early child development and complex systems that impact a child's pathway to success, starting at conception. Working directly with families of domestic violence, substance abuse, grief and loss, sex work, mental health, child protection, and a range of complex issues provided a breadth of knowledge and insight into the needs of family systems.

Later, I returned to school social work, where I was able to interweave the broad depth of information I had gleaned into the individual student outcomes to support young people on the pathway to their own success. When students were referred to me for behavior or well-being concerns, I prioritized building connection and safety with them before supporting them to develop skills in responsibility. By taking the time to get to know the students, I was able to use this connection to move them toward success. Danny Silk often describes how connection can either be fragile like a tissue or strong like a leather strap. Where the connection is tissue-like, it is as if the student and I are both holding either end of the tissue and one slight disagreement can cause a tug that would tear the connection. Alternatively, where the connection is strong like a leather strap, a tug results in the student moving with me and trusting me with their success. For example, if I asked a student to honor the school uniform policy and take their hat off and we had a weak connection, I often received back-chatting and disrespect. If we had a strong connection, I could simply walk into a room and the student would take their hat off.

So, I made a choice that my goal in every interaction was connection first, and only then from a place of strong connection would I move toward developing internal responsibility skills with a student.

My academic journey continued as I sought answers to the cyclic needs in schools, students' individual lives, and communities. I went on to complete a graduate certificate in neuropsychotherapy, honing my understanding of the brain, how it communicates with other people, builds safety, and opens learning opportunities. Applied neuroscience confirmed what I was observing in classrooms and student relationships—specifically, that creating safe environments void of fear and punishment, environments where students feel connected and empowered as they take responsibility for their own learning, increases the brain's ability to learn, take risks, and develop resilience.

NEW TOOLS

Over my career, I have worked as a teacher aide, youth worker, and social worker for the public school sector, alternative education, and various religious education facilities. I have spent many years inside prep-to-senior classrooms, supporting students with both diagnosed and undiagnosed disabilities or behavior concerns through one-on-one and group development. I have sat with innumerable students as they process complex life and well-being issues that are impacting their ability to focus on school attendance or work. I now have the privilege of speaking to teachers about behavior education and neuroscience for education in private education and public education, from kindergarten through to secondary, in both school-based and distance education. This is me—once the girl who wanted nothing to do with school, I've become a bit of a nerd with a passion for equipping and educating teachers, the one profession that teaches every other profession.

If you are a teacher, then your journey through school, university studies and practicum placements, and a professional teaching career has provided you with a tool bag. Each day you reach into that tool bag, and those are the things you present to your students. Each of us has been influenced by our teachers' paradigms—just as we discover we were influenced by Mum or Dad when we hear them come out of our mouths toward our own kids. I am sure you can tell stories from your placements where you saw your mentor teacher yelling or telling a student that they were right and the student wrong. You may have also said, "I will never be like that." But unless we learn and practice new tools, the moment a student makes a poor choice in front of us, all we find in our tool bags are the old rusty ones that don't really work. Our perception of love, authority, respect, obedience, the goals of teaching, the practice of relationships, and the way to treat students—so much of that is downloaded before we have time to catch it. Though we said we would never be like Mr. Strict or Miss Get-Out-Of-My-Class, it is not long before we sound like them—usually by week three of the term. If we do not intentionally replace what we experienced as a school and placement student, then it is downloaded onto our normal, our template.

Remember back to your years as a student. If they were like mine at all, those were years characterized by memorizing and reciting information on cue, threats of detention or litter duty, standing outside the classroom or even in the rubbish bin (Mum, you know what I'm talking about), being singled out and humiliated so that you join the pack, and, if things got bad enough, seeing the cane brought out. I remember teachers yelling, sticky-taping mouths closed, throwing things at students, breaking rulers, using emotional blackmail, and asking parents to provide a double consequence at home—all in the name of teaching students respect and honor.

We only know how to respond to students with what we have been given, which means despite our best intentions, we end up perpetuating the same classroom culture of yelling and threats designed to break a student's will, and the staffroom culture of jokes about bringing back the cane and complaints about disrespectful comments from students.

Some of us are also going broke spending our hard-earned money on junky toys, pizza parties, or the latest student engagement gadgets to bribe our students into compliance.

Our students are getting trained with the equipment that we had, and unless we make a change, they will be training the next generation to keep using the same rusty tools. It can be heartbreaking looking back on our early years of teaching and not understanding what else we could have done. As a student aide I used to sit in classrooms and watch many students' wills break. Unfortunately, it was usually their will to learn, engage in class, or connect with their teacher that was broken, not their will to act out. This was especially common when working with special needs and behaviorally challenged students; the tools schools were offering just were not working.

As I mentioned earlier, it was in alternative education that I came across Danny Silk's *Loving Our Kids on Purpose* (LoKoP) program, which incorporates techniques from *Love and Logic* by Foster Cline and Jim Faye. Designed for parents, LoKoP is an amazing tool kit that coaches parents in a different way to approach being a powerful parent. It teaches what Mr. Larry demonstrated, which I have since seen proven true throughout my career—the only person I can control is myself, and each of my students will respond when they too are empowered to control themselves. It is imperative that our school systems and classroom cultures empower students to learn how to control themselves without the requirement of an external control mechanism. We can influence students' behavior choices by creating a connected classroom culture in which they want to participate.

Ultimately, choosing to empower our students with the freedom and responsibility to make their own choices sends them the message of love. As Danny Silk often says, "You cannot have love if you do not have freedom and you do not have freedom if you do not have a choice." Put simply, love requires freedom and freedom requires a choice; therefore, love is a choice.

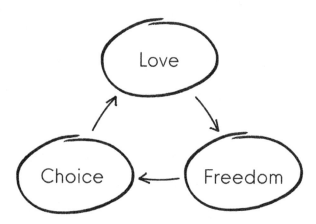

The foundation of training and teaching our students starts with this: How will we demonstrate love by creating a free space where our students have choices? Most teachers do not factor in freedom with students. The tools to offer our students freedom to think, decide, and manage themselves in our presence may not be in our tool bag, because the people who taught most of us believed it was their job to control us towards good things.

In this book, I want to offer you some new tools that will free you from the expectation that you have to play every role in the lives of your students. You will learn how to use boundaries well and take back control of *you* as you become a powerful teacher. I want to free you from fear-based punishment options and give you tools to build relationships and facilitate connected classroom cultures in your school. These tools will empower you to never argue with a student again as you transform your understanding of students' development and needs. You will experience the transfer of control to your own internal state in every scenario and you will never be taken by surprise by a student's behavior. As a result, you will be guided into the development of your own secure identity that will culminate in clear boundaries, restore connection with your students, and set them up to make choices to thrive in their learning.

Imagine for a moment a classroom where students are happy to take responsibility for their own academic success journey. Where students come to you for advice and apply your wisdom, where other staff are baffled by the peace in your classroom and within you. Imagine the phone ringing and the class going silent automatically simply because they love you and are connected to your heart. Imagine a school environment that has strong connections and student/parent relationships where problems are addressed together, information is transparent, and young lives are transformed. Imagine getting to the end of the school year and celebrating with your students rather than being stressed and burned out. Imagine your students and parents working hard on their lives so you can focus on teaching the students you love.

There is a better way to deal with student behavior. Join me in the pages ahead, and I will show you all I have learned about this better way, and how to practice it.

2

THE LoSoP PHILOSOPHY

I ONCE KNEW ONE teacher who dealt with poor behavior in his classroom by keeping a list of "bad" students' names on the whiteboard each day, thereby shaming them publicly to the class. After class, he would call their parents to dob (Aussie slang for "tell on them") and ensure a strict punishment ensued. His students were terrified of him, and many became afraid of their parents due to his behavior.

This teacher's classroom was a classic example of a fear-driven culture where success looked like complying in order to survive. I have observed many of these classroom cultures, where the teacher uses either anger and shaming, or prizes, bribes, and manipulation games, to manage students' behavior. Some appear at first glance to be full of silent, obedient, and compliant students who are behaving themselves quite well. However, it doesn't take very long to discern that this "good" behavior is not an expression of responsibility or genuine care, but is more like a form of Stockholm syndrome. Like captives broken into submission, these students are cowering from punishment, performing for prizes, and emotionally managing one another's social status based on their academic grades, talents, or "good" standing with the teacher—all out of self-preservation. It is common for me to speak with a parent who has simply accepted, "This year is a write-off. My child simply has to survive the rest of this year with Miss Moody. Hopefully they will be able to catch up next year."

Not all students are so successful at learning how to please these controlling teachers and avoid punishment, however. These are the "bad" students. One particular student in this teacher's class, Ben, saw his name written on the board on many occasions, and was subsequently punished by having his beloved tennis lesson or technology access taken away. Distressed about losing what he considered precious, and having no safe person from whom to elicit support, Ben was primed against down-regulating his emotions. Rather, the increase in stress hormones and decrease in contextual cognitive functioning often caused him to escalate to a meltdown characterized by swearing and increased aggression, leading him to be perceived as defiant. A vicious cycle ensued in which Ben would make a poor choice, be ejected from the room, return later to be ridiculed, branded, and rejected by "perfect" peers who were afraid of the teacher turning on them next, and then go home and receive further punishment from his parents, who were embarrassed by him and wanted to "support" the teacher to inflict justice. Feeling disconnected and afraid, Ben learned to hide who he was, lie, cheat, steal, and isolate to try to survive school and eventually his parents.

Ben was one of the first students with whom I attempted to apply the Loving Our Students on Purpose philosophy. I met him when he was approximately five years old, and worked with him over ten years. As our connection developed, he would come to me crying, desperate to be found worthy and terrified of both his teacher and his parents. He described how his parents were fighting over how to deal with him. On several occasions, his mother held a knife to her throat whilst blaming Ben for "making her" want to kill herself.

The primary truth I emphasized to Ben was that he could not change his parents, their reactions, or his teacher's relationship style. He could only manage himself, and that was going to be hard enough. Ben had developed significantly fast reaction skills to escape the experience of shaming, punishment, and fear. These skills would take time to replace, much longer than it took for him to learn them.

Slowly, over many years, Ben developed a plan for how he could manage himself in the classroom and at home, regardless of his parents' or various teachers' reactions. Ben found that he had incredible skills in communication and debating, which previously got him into a lot of trouble for arguing. He also learned how to recognize and manage his own emotions before they escalated to a meltdown or tantrum. Some years, Ben had the benefit of interacting with teachers who fostered connected classroom cultures. During these years, his behavior improved as his sense of safety was restored and he sought to connect with his teachers and peers. Other years, he was required to participate in fear-based classroom cultures. However, with the support of our connected relationship to come back to, he was able to continue making positive changes.

Eventually, Ben's parents started to observe the changes in him. Curious, they came to meet me and ask for help. I recommended that they complete the *Loving our Kids on Purpose* parenting program. Not only did this lead them to restore their heart toward Ben and Ben's heart toward them, they also made noticeable strides toward repairing their own relationship as a couple. This secure relationship provided a safe connection where Ben could feel supported, even as he encountered disconnected, fear-based techniques from some teachers.

WHAT IS LOVE?

The Loving Our Students on Purpose (LoSoP) philosophy is based on a set of beliefs about human nature, human purpose, and human thriving. As the title indicates, this philosophy is all about *love*.

Love is a word we use in many ways and contexts, so it's important to define it. In the LoSoP philosophy, love means doing what is best for someone because we respect, honor, and care for them. Love is not about getting something from someone, but about giving. It is fundamentally others-focused rather than self-focused—it puts "we" before "me."

LoSoP is committed to the belief that doing what's best for others is what brings out the best in us. It also invites others to bring out their best in response. There is no higher or better motivation for our behavior. Love is the superior driver of all learning, growth, problem-solving, achievement, and productivity.

So what does it mean to do what is best for others? The LoSoP philosophy is built on four key principles that guide us in the practice of loving students—and all people—well.

LOSOP PRINCIPLE #1:
OUR GOAL IS CONNECTION

The first and primary goal of love is *connection*. As Brené Brown has established in her research, human beings were made for and thrive through the experience of connection. She defines connection as "the energy that exists between people when they feel seen, heard, and valued; when they can give and receive without judgment; and when they derive sustenance and strength from the relationship."[1]

In *Dare to Lead*, Brown encourages teachers to focus on connecting with their students and making their classrooms a place where connection can grow safely—a place where students are free to let down their defenses, be themselves, and truly be seen. She explains that a child's future trajectory, along with their desire to be curious in their exploration of the world, can be completely modified if they find a place to belong.[2] Louis Cozolino likewise asserts that safe, loving connection is paramount to creating an environment that predisposes a student to increased aca-

---

[1] Brené Brown, *The Gifts of Imperfection: Let Go of Who You Think You're Supposed to Be and Embrace Who You Are* (Center City, MN: Hazelden Publishing, 2010), Kindle Edition, 19
[2] Brené Brown, *Dare to Lead* (London, UK: Penguin Random House, 2018).

demic success through neural thriving.[3] Applied neuroscience correlates with Brown's findings that the experience of safety is a key priority as students seek first to maintain connection rather than survive the environment or relationship with their teacher or peers.

LOSOP PRINCIPLE #2:
LOVE IS A POWERFUL CHOICE

Connection doesn't just happen—it is something we cultivate through our *choices*. Love is not just a feeling. It is the powerful choice to treat others in a certain way, whether or not they are loving us in return. This kind of powerful choice is something we will only be able to make consistently through cultivating a high sense of personal freedom, responsibility, and agency. This is what moves us to be internally motivated and focus on controlling and managing ourselves and our choices first and foremost.

Teaching students to be powerful, responsible, and internally motivated toward love and connection begins with becoming those things yourself. Your example of self-control and pursuing the goal of connection, more than your words, is what will lead and invite students to imitate you.

LOSOP PRINCIPLE #3:
FEAR IS THE ENEMY OF CONNECTION

The idea that we need to create a *safe place* for connection points to the truth that certain behaviors and experiences are not safe for connection. Brené Brown's definition of connection indicates what some of those things might be. Wherever people are feeling *not* seen, heard, or valued, where they *can't* give and receive without judgment, and where they *don't*

---

[3] Louis Cozolino, "Our Social Brains," *The Neuropsychotherapist*, November 8, 2014, Volume 8, 22-32.

derive strength and sustenance from the relationship, they are not experiencing a safe place.

Another way to understand unsafe places for connection is to recognize when people's behavior is being motivated by fear, rather than love. As I described in Ben's story, teachers who motivate their students with fear can elicit both "good" and "bad" behavior from them. The problem is that neither leads to genuine connection because the fear motivating both behavior styles points them toward the same goal: self-preservation. The goal of self-preservation is the exact opposite to the goal of love and connection; it puts "me" before "we" and moves us away from others rather than toward them. It orients us to avoid pain rather than approach people and problems. Fear-driven environments are hostile to connection.

One of the greatest things fueling fear in the classroom, and every social environment, is the false belief that we can control or be controlled by others. In fact, this is exactly the belief that fear-based behavior management tactics are designed to teach. So many of our educational systems and teaching strategies intentionally operate with an "outside to inside" approach that guides our students to make decisions by weighing whose reaction they are most afraid of—their school, teacher, parents, or friends. "Who is going to be mad at me? Who is going to punish me if I cross the line or do something wrong?" This actively discourages students from feeling powerful and responsible in making choices, and instead encourages them to feel and act powerless in the face of external forces.

An "inside to outside" approach, in contrast, focuses not on avoiding social punishment, but on protecting social connection from a place of personal integrity and love. Students who are trained in a connected classroom culture learn to approach their choices with questions like, "I have some responsibility to take—what is my part in this situation? What are my choices? How will they work out for me?"

As we'll explore further in the next chapter, there is distinctive neurological, cognitive, and emotional development that takes place when humans move beyond the level of survival, where instincts prevail over rational choice in the presence of threats, and experience the safety, nurture, and tools that empower them to think, reflect, and make choices in the pursuit of something good they want—love, connection, and belonging. Setting up a connected classroom culture in which students are given the opportunity, through choices, to cultivate a positive teacher-student relationship allows students to replace *pain-avoidance* tools with *approach* tools, leading to thriving.

LOSOP PRINCIPLE #4:
BUILDING AND PROTECTING CONNECTION
IS A LEARNING JOURNEY

The Loving Our Students on Purpose philosophy affirms that our primary goal is not simply that students learn to stop problematic behaviors. Ultimately, we want them to *learn to love.* We want them to be empowered to manage their freedom and make great choices toward the goal of building and protecting meaningful connections with all the important people in their lives—parents, peers, and teachers.

When our goal is teaching students to love, we recognize that punishment is not only ineffective but counterproductive to helping students deal with their mistakes and poor choices. However, responding to poor choices without punishment doesn't mean giving them a pass. In fact, both punishment and passivity are ways of abdicating our responsibility and opportunity as teachers to provide students with the modeling and wisdom they need to learn how to do better. Our students only learn when we:

1. Present them with the real *consequences* their poor choice is having or will have on themselves and those around them.

2. Invite them to take responsibility for their choice and its consequences, and set appropriate boundaries communicating that responsibility is expected and required.

3. Partner with them as they take steps to repair connection and adjust their behavior moving forward.

So how do we begin implementing the Loving our Students on Purpose philosophy? It starts with a commitment to making two critical steps in our approach with students.

Step 1: Stop Showing the "Yellow Truck"

Every one of your students is going to make mistakes and poor choices. That is their occupation. As Danny Silk puts it, kids are professional mistake-makers. It is what they do. They wake up in the morning and think, *I wonder what I am going to learn through the mistakes I make today.* There is never a day that I go to school and no poor choices occur. Even on the school holidays, we get contacted by students or parents who are navigating how to love their child through their poor choices. Every day, another poor choice. It does not go away—these people just keep being people.

Yet as much as we know this to be true, we still find it shocking. *Are you kidding me? Are you really doing this, again, today? I cannot believe you made a mistake. I cannot believe you spoke in class, again, today!* Mistakes are messy, painful, disappointing, frustrating, saddening. But the biggest problem is that they can make us feel scared and powerless. Danny calls this pushing our "big, red button." When our students push that button, it's *our own* fear that wants to start calling the shots.

The moment we feel powerless in the presence of a student's poor choice, the temptation is there to grab for power through control, intimidation, and punishment. Before we know it, if we're not careful, we go into "yellow truck" mode. In *Loving our Kids on Purpose*, Danny shows a photograph of a huge yellow Tonka truck squishing a little red ute to the ground. It is absolutely clear which vehicle has all the power and which does not. The little ute has been yellow trucked![4]

I think every teacher and parent can relate to this scenario. I'm putting my own hand up. This is exactly the approach I used with Rebecca

---

[4] Danny Silk, *Loving our Kids on Purpose: Making a Heart-to-Heart Connection* (Shippensburg, PA: Destiny Image, 2008), 55.

and Tayla at first. Everything I was doing in reaction to their poor be-havior sent the message, "It is my job to control you. I am responsible to make you stop doing bad things and only do good things. So I am the yellow truck, you are the red truck. I have all the power, you have no power. Do what I say or I am going to hurt you. "

For some reason in schools we think that it will work to try to strip students of power. And yes, for a short time it seems to be working in prep when I can force them to sit at an isolated desk away from their friends. By the time the student is fifteen, however, they will most likely walk out of the classroom if I try it. In all my years in schools, the num-ber-one reason for a tantrum type conflict of *any* age, including staff, is moving someone's desk/seat without that person's buy-in! That's all it takes for my illusion of power to unravel in a moment.

For teachers laboring under the false belief of control, it is painful when they start to discover they do not control the next thing that comes out of a student's mouth, the next thing they do with their hands, the next thing they learn. Nor do I. It is amazing how many emails I get from staff acknowledging they cannot control a student and asking me to try to control them instead. My answer is the same every time. I do not control this student. I can only continue to work with them to develop their own internal responsibility over time, but the relationship between the teacher and the student needs to provide a safe environment where the student can try out the new skills I'm imparting to them.

Step 2: Start Showing Your Heart

The only way we can teach students to control themselves is by first con-trolling ourselves and not allowing fear to determine our response. In *Dare to Lead*, Brené Brown emphasizes how critical it is as leaders that we grow in self-awareness of our emotions and how they are influenc-ing our behavior. All leaders will experience fear, she asserts, yet fear is simply an emotion behind behaviors. Therefore, we must deal with our own instinct to react to fear with self-protective behaviors before we can guide our students toward their own emotional awareness and internal sense of responsibility. The extent to which each of us will undertake this journey, Brown notes, lies in the courage to be vulnerable and apply an "inside to outside" approach on ourselves.[5] We must cultivate a mindset that says, *I do not control you. On a good day, I control me. That's where my focus is. No matter what you do, or what your learning process is today, I am going to control me. My love is going to stay on towards you.*

This commitment points us to the goal of a connected classroom—building heart-to-heart connections in which each person is powerful (internally motivated) and responsible for their part of the connection. Of course, the real challenge in forming heart-to-heart connections is that you can't build them without *exposing your heart.* After having the courage to be vulnerable with ourselves about what's going on inside us, we must be vulnerable with our students.

So many teachers try to pretend that they do not have any emotional response to their students' craziness, but that is a total lie. They think, *I am not going to let my students control me.* But their self-protective reactions reveal the truth—they are so scared of these people that they are not themselves. Instead of reacting out of pain, we must bravely, responsibly, and vulnerably show our students how they are affecting our hearts. When we do this, we allow them to feel the weight of who they are and the impact of their choices in this relationship. They have power to influence their environment, and only by seeing the reality of that power can they recognize the responsibility that comes with it.

As I described, it was when I chose to be vulnerable with Rebecca and Tayla about how they were affecting me that everything changed in our relationship. The goal shifted from control to connection, creating a safe place, and inviting them to be vulnerable in turn about what was actually going on inside them. Exchanging the truth in our hearts laid a foundation

---

[5] Brené Brown, *Dare to Lead.*

of trust—we became partners in a common goal instead of opponents in a power struggle. The responsibilities settled where they needed to be in the relationship—the girls were making choices and managing themselves toward that, and I was there to support and cheer them on.

Showing vulnerability doesn't mean falling apart or putting *too much* responsibility on the students for how their behavior is impacting the classroom. It doesn't mean reversing roles and asking them to be the adult in the relationship. It means giving them honest feedback that their behavior is affecting those around them in a negative way, communicating how you need them to adjust, and giving them the chance to choose that for the sake of protecting connection, rather than out of fear.

The beauty of establishing this heart-to-heart connection is that it enables us to lead with love. The Holy Grail of this kind of leadership is getting to the point where your students can simply look into your eyes, know how they are affecting your heart, and adjust their behavior accordingly. Obviously, I'm not talking about giving them an "evil eye." But as the proverb goes, the eyes are the windows of the heart. When you are connected heart-to-heart, you learn to look in those windows and perceive what's happening inside. This presents each person in the relationship with a choice. Is your connection with your students strong enough that they will adjust their behavior when your eyes show them how they are affecting you? Will you look into your students' eyes and adjust your behavior because you see how it is affecting their hearts?

Wouldn't you love to answer the classroom phone and have such a strong bond with your students that all you need to do is give them eye contact, and they instinctively and collectively take ownership of their choices and adjust their noise level? This is what we are after, teaching our students the value and power of relationship and love. It is not about compliance or obedience. Those things happen, but not because they are the goal; rather, they are the symptom of the heart-to-heart connection. In a connected classroom culture you and your students are getting good at sending the message "I will protect this connection" back and forth.

Step 3: Establish the Core Commitments of a Connected Classroom Culture

The Loving our Students on Purpose philosophy leads us to deal with students like we never have before. Creating a connected classroom culture based on self-control and responsibility gives us the opportunity to move from an external relationship to an internal relationship. Our thinking shifts from the teacher being a punisher and controller enforcing students' behavior to an internal, relational leader who provides freedom and choices as they love each student, even as they make messes and clean them up.

To achieve this connected classroom culture, here are a set of commitments to teach and establish with your students:

- We will always make connection the goal of each relationship. Disconnection and punishment are never an option. When disconnection occurs and trust is broken, clear boundaries will make it safe for connection to be restored.
- We will celebrate every success, no matter the size, and will always seek to send the message to each person that they are valued, known, and worthy.
- We will always demonstrate trust in relationships by being transparent and volunteering what's going on inside to stay connected to one another. We will protect one another's information and prioritize safety in this relationship.
- We will value responsibility and always take responsibility for our half of the relationship. We will never seek to blame or fix you. With love and respect between us, we will get there together.
- We will work hard at our love and actively express love in how we speak and treat others. We will never turn our love off toward each other.

As in all things, it's essential that you lead by example in keeping these commitments. Through your powerful choice to demonstrate love and pursue and protect your connection, you invite your students to do the same.

3

NEUROSCIENCE OF FEAR, CONNECTION, AND FREEDOM

A CONNECTED CLASSROOM CULTURE that actively cultivates love and lowers the fear of punishment gives our students the best chance to enter their optimal learning zone and grow as powerful, responsible, connected people. In the next three chapters, I'm going to introduce you to some of the neuroscience that supports this claim.

We'll start in this chapter by looking at the structure of the brain and how it needs the experience of safety and connection to develop high-level cognition and learning. In Chapter 4, we'll consider the role that the nervous system plays in perceiving both safety and threats in the environment. Then in Chapter 5, we'll explore how safety and connection meet the specific basic neurological and psychosocial needs that form a person's sense of self.

I recommend putting on your "nerd" hats for these chapters, as it will get a bit technical and some of the terminology may be new. But stay with me, because once you grasp the concepts, it's beautiful to see how applied neuroscience provides a theoretical and scientific framework that reinforces the Loving our Students on Purpose philosophy. Let's dive in!

THE TRIUNE BRAIN

We all have a brain. You have a brain, and your students have brains. And they work, too! What we need to remember is that our adult brains are more developed and have experienced more of life to apply context in every situation, and that we had patient adults around us as we navigated the brain development journey. We now get to be that person to our students.

Neuroscientist Paul MacLean came up with a simple model of the brain to help us understand the development process.[1] Despite it being challenged as overly simplistic, it opened important conversations for exploring neural development.[2] MacLean refers to his model as the *triune brain* because it has three distinct parts—the reptilian complex, the limbic system or paleomammalian complex, and the neocortex or neomammalian complex.[3] Further, MacLean contends that each of these three systems develops and operates from the bottom up, thus resulting in the earlier, primitive complexes effectively overriding more advanced cognitive processes when survival is threatened.

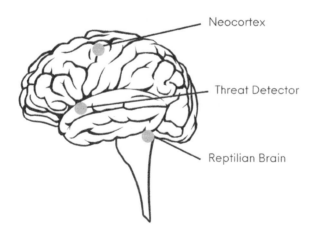

Neocortex

Threat Detector

Reptilian Brain

---

[1] Paul D. MacLean, *The Triune Brain in Evolution: Role in Paleocerebral Functions* (New York: Plenum Press, 1990).
[2] P. J. Rossouw, *Neuropsychotherapy: Theoretical Underpinnings and Clinical Applications.* (USA: Mediros, 2014).
[3] A. Montgomery, *Neurobiology Essentials for Clinicians: What Every Therapist Needs to Know* (New York: W.W. Norton & Company, 2013).

The *reptilian complex* (think instinctual, dinosaur brain) is fully developed at birth and governs the physiological aspects of survival by increasing blood flow and thereby oxygen to this section of the brain. This section of the brain is often thought of as the primitive brain or responsive brain, and is most commonly referred to as the "survival brain" because it regulates our heart rate, breathing, blinking, and other basic survival needs.

The *limbic system* is partially developed at birth, but it requires cues from the environment as it develops to make it operational. The limbic system refers to a cluster of systems that regulate emotions, including the thalamus, hypothalamus, amygdala, and hippocampus, and is thus referred to as the emotional or "impulsive brain." The limbic system is much more responsive to developing memories that result from negative experiences than from positive experiences, as it instinctively seeks to ensure survival and support the predominant reptilian brain. It is within the limbic system where you will locate two almond-shaped amygdalae, which when "juiced up" or stimulated signal the reptilian brain to initiate the flight, fight, or freeze response. As a result of this chemical reaction, our emotions typically become displayed outwardly. Many years ago, one of my students named this his "silly brain," and aptly so, because when activated, the amygdala compromises one's ability to apply cognitive wisdom. Wow, do our students do many "silly" things throughout the day!

The last part of the brain to develop is the *neocortex*. At birth, it is undeveloped and largely unoperational. This part of the brain is responsible for executive function and can down-regulate other functions; in other words, it helps us to "make sense." It is accurately referred to as the "smart brain," as it is from within this part of the brain that we develop high executive functions such as focus, empathy, problem-solving, and context. This is the last part of the brain to evolve and will only be fully developed when your students get to about twenty-five years of age, and in many cases even older. So, as I remind parents, this part of the brain still has a lot of development ahead and won't be fully functioning until ten years after school. (Not only that, some of our teachers and parents are themselves still experiencing brain development.)

Dr. John Arden provides a different and more evolved perspective to the simple triune brain model.[4] Rather than a bottom-up approach (or top down or side to side), Arden suggests that it is all areas of the brain interacting simultaneously and in balance with one another that encourages healthy neural functioning. Arden recognizes the misunderstanding that occurs in the triune model's reference to the limbic system or "emotional brain," in that these terms do not fully explain the purpose and function of this region, nor are they used by neuroscientists. Rather, he focuses on the importance of understanding the amygdala as the "threat detector." It is largely responsible for assessing the environment, determining the level of threat or danger, and activating a response. It also functions as a relevance detector, helping determine if there is something personally relevant to you in the environment.

Your amygdala is part of a network of neurons called the Salient Network, which includes parts of your cortex such as the Anterior Cingulate and Anterior Insula. Emotions are generated by this network and motivate you to act. They are sometimes activated with loneliness, anger, or under threat, but can also be activated with excitement in a non-threatening environment. Therefore, an environment that stimulates stress can be triaged either as threatening or manageable, or as "dirty" or "clean" stress. For example, when the school principal walks into a classroom, a teacher's threat detector could draw on memories of a previous experience with a principal who yelled at her in front of her class and assess this entry as threatening, thus signaling danger and activating a stress reaction. This reaction may result in less cognitive functioning (reduced focus on the students and lesson) and more concentrated vigilance toward auditory danger signals (i.e., students talking) and the principal's

---

[4] John Arden, "Mind-Brain-Gene: Toward Psychotherapy Integration." [conference presentation] Digital Webinar (USA: IAAN, 2022)

non-verbal cues or movements, and even inhibiting memory of the lesson. This is dirty stress.

Alternatively, for a teacher who has a positive relationship (and memories) with their principal, their entrance into the classroom may be triaged as non-threatening. In fact, it may signal an exciting opportunity to engage the student in an impromptu interaction or give the teacher a confident platform to demonstrate their teaching skill as they draw on their executive functioning. This is clean stress, and can be helpful in extending the teacher's skill through positive growth from helpful feedback.

Although it is essential that we teach our students skills of executive functioning, when we are working with children, we need to remember that their more primitive neural pathways communicated by their survival brain and their threat detector are going to react first. Since these are the more developed parts of the brain, we generally see children instinctively resort to them when they experience fear or a threat to their perceived survival. It should therefore be a school-wide agenda to teach students how to understand and engage their brain, recognizing the successive stages of appropriate development that evolve in complexity over their lifespan, along with the relevant life experiences associated with those stages. For example, a five-year-old being taught to regulate their displeasure at having to share the bike path at kindergarten will have a lower ability to engage their smart brain compared to a learner driver learning to share the road. So, it is important that we meet each student where they are developmentally and take them on a journey, because what we teach them today is becoming neural-wired context in their prefrontal cortex, which may inform the choices they will make in their futures.

COWS AND NEURAL LOOPING

One of the things I actually enjoyed about high school was participating in agriculture subjects. We had a wonderful little farm at the back of the campus with ewes and lambs, chickens and ducks, alpacas and cows. To the excitement of all the students, the farm also had been gifted a cow and the cutest calf we had ever seen. The farm was my happy place. One of my tasks was to feed the animals before and after school. I loved the quiet of the farm, the excitement of the animals when they saw me carrying feed buckets, and the time away from the bustle of regular school life. I comfortably interacted with the animals as I moved between their different enclosures.

One day, my Ag science teacher was checking on the mama cow and her calf whilst I was doing my feed rounds. We were both in the cow's enclosure when she suddenly became agitated and unhappy, pointing her long horns in preparation to charge and puffing angrily as she beat the ground with her hooves. I looked from the cow to my teacher's eyes, where I saw fear pulsating through every vein.

"Run!" he screamed.

There was no time to think or consider my options. The cow was charging now, and it was a very small enclosure. We both sprang into action and scaled the six-foot fence with hardly a second to spare. Landing on the other side, we just stood there stunned, looking at one another, back at the fence, and back again.

"Maybe you should try out for high jump," my teacher joked. I just stood there speechless, my whole body alive with adrenaline.

Not too long ago, my mum became the proud owner of a property where cows were brought to have their calves. From the safety of the veranda, I enjoy surveying the green pasture dotted with newly birthed calves. They are, after all, still cute. Instinctively, however, I stay out of the paddocks while the cows and their babies are there. If I do wander down to the fence line, I am sure to take the mama cow something extra tasty to snack on—a peace offering from that first encounter in high school. Even though I have never been charged by another cow, and I know better than to come between a cow and its calf, my threat detector informs me that possible danger lies ahead, and I have to work hard not to instinctively go into flight mode when I am around cows.

I imagine you have similar experiences you can think of from your own life. Your heart rate is pulsing, your energy is high, you are ready to leap onto the roof of the building to get away from a perceived threat. So, what has happened in my brain to develop an unreasonable yet repetitive pattern of cow aversion?

Very simply, the development of neural pathways is encouraged or discouraged by environmental stimuli that our brain judges to be safe or unsafe. In a safe environment, the survival brain and impulsive brain remain calm, allowing the smart brain to fire effectively and make decisions, evaluate situations and environmental stimuli, make sense of experiences, and then categorize them in a way which allows us to adjust and make positive choices about our lives.[5] This is why my mum, in contrast to me, will lovingly visit her "girls," as she refers to her cows, and has no fear of their potential behavior. She has had a positive experience with cows, so when she sees one, her brain remains calm, and even gets excited.

Because I have not had a positive experience, cows signal a potentially unsafe environment to my brain. In an unsafe environment, the impulsive brain is triggered, increasing blood flow to the amygdala within the limbic system and decreasing blood flow to the smart brain, thereby impacting our ability to think clearly due to upregulated stress.[6] Thankfully, when this happens, our bodies are also primed to respond, providing the swift reaction we need to ensure our safety.

Just think about the many experiences in a school environment that might send fear or stress signals (aside from angry cows) to our students—exams, due dates, being asked a question in front of the class, being looked at by a peer and then seeing them whisper to the person nearby, speeches, being required to participate in sport or music or drama, dissecting a toad, going to the bathroom alone, talking to so many unknown adults like the canteen or admin (and yes they are absolutely

---

[5] A. Montgomery, *Neurobiology Essentials for Clinicians: What Every Therapist Needs to Know* (New York: W.W. Norton & Company, 2013).
[6] M. Dahlitz, *The Psychotherapist's Essential Guide to the Brain* (Park Ridge, QLD: Dahlitz Media, 2017).

lovely staff, but to some students talking to strangers is incredibly difficult), and the list goes on. School environments are full of stress signals being navigated by developing brains every minute of every day.

What is more, the memories stored in the limbic system are more enhanced by negative experiences than positive ones. This is why when I see a cow, I instinctively draw on the one negative memory that threatened my safety rather than the many positive cow interactions I have had. This experience of becoming "stuck" reflects *neural looping*, in which the limbic system relies on these negative memories to provide feedback and context to future choices. In brief, neural looping occurs when the amygdala sparks up the hippocampus. In other words, when the impulsive, threat detector (amygdala) fires up the memory center, it activates a loop which stimulates the impulsive brain further.[7] When this process continues to recur, the person becomes stuck in their experiences and consequent behavioral reactions. The student who avoids attending school on days when they are due to present in front of the class because they feel physically sick is likely responding this way due to such a loop. The negative experience of feeling nervous and sick has become a fast memory that their brains, which are geared toward their survival, use to initiate a freeze response (or a fight/flight response first at home with Mum, who is trying to get the student out of bed).

Dr. Peter Rossouw states that in general, for a person to learn they need many repetitions.[8] The more complex a concept or task is, the more repetitions it requires to learn. However, Rossouw suggests that whilst the brain makes new connections in a split second, it remembers according to *intensity*. Therefore, a traumatic experience that occurs very quickly can result in an immediate learned behavior.

Rossouw outlined an experiment done with mice who were expected to navigate a maze. The mice had all but one whisker cut to ensure equal

---

[7] Dahlitz, *The Psychotherapist's Essential Guide to the Brain*; Robinson, N. *Christine: An Adolescent and Social Anxiety Disorder.* In Rossouw, P. J. *Neuropsychotherapy: Theoretical Underpinnings and Clinical Applications.* USA: Mediros, 2014: 73-90.

[8] P. J. Rossouw, *Neuropsychotherapy: Theoretical Underpinnings and Clinical Applications.* (USA: Mediros, 2014).

navigation (don't worry, their whiskers grew back). It took each mouse an average of thirty repetitions learning to navigate the maze before they could make it to the food without having to "locate it" themselves because they had learned where it was. But there was also a catch. In the maze, there was a section where each mouse was required to jump over a gap to continue their journey toward the food. The mice need their whiskers to help them navigate the distance of the jump. Many of the mice were able to determine the length of the gap, make a successful jump, and then repeat this jump each time. But for those mice who missed and fell into the gap, it was a different story. The second time these mice approached the gap, their negative memories provided a feedback loop that they were in danger, so they simply turned around without even attempting the jump a second time. These mice were motivated by survival.

This experiment highlights that a painful or traumatic experience can very quickly trigger learning—but is it helpful learning that will set a student up to thrive, or is it neural learning toward survival? Think of your students. When you ask them to attempt a new extended math concept or try a new technique in the performing arts or a sport, when they are given a chance to try again, who is turning around and refusing a second attempt, and who is forging ahead jumping across to new learning confidently?

This experiment is also a good example of what occurs in a student's brain when you introduce punishment into the classroom culture. "If you do A, I will inflict pain to ensure that next time you will obey." No one would argue that this type of approach has an immediate or a fairly fast effect. However, punishments also have concerning consequences, such as disconnection in relationship and the development of mistrust, which activates survival instincts. We don't want our students always in survival mode around us—that isn't fun for anyone.

The good news is that students who become stuck in a particular fear-based response can, with the right support, also become unstuck and develop new thriving networks. To explain this principle, psychologist Donald Hebb founded the *theory of consistency*. This is the notion that "neurons that fire together, wire together," which contends that repetition creates neural pathways that reinforce behavior, regardless of whether it is positive or negative.[9] Neuroscientist Michael Merzenich, who researches brain plasticity, suggests that the converse is also true—"neurons that fire apart, wire apart."[10] The loop or experience of being stuck can be suitably broken through changing the neural pathway, much like a circuit breaker. In other words, our brains are good at establishing patterns and habits of thinking and behavior, but they are also capable of learning new patterns and habits if we give them the necessary information and repetition to change.

Clinical psychologist Melissa Glenwright provides an excellent metaphor to understand how people become stuck and unstuck through neural looping. Using the metaphor of a highway, Glenwright explains that through repetition, a specific path or neural connection becomes stronger. The stronger it becomes, the more likely the person will take the same path in the future, eventually creating a "superhighway." To break this cycle, the person needs to start creating a new pathway or "road." At first this may be more like an off-road bush track, but via repetition the track will eventually become a road and slowly develop into a superhighway itself, thus increasing the likelihood that the person will choose that pathway in the future. The old highway will eventually break down from disuse (in the form of glial cells), which will reinforce the new learning superhighway.[11]

TANTRUMS, MELTDOWNS, AND REGULATING EMOTIONS

Two of the most misunderstood behaviors we support students with at school are meltdowns and tantrums. From a brain perspective, meltdowns and tantrums are distinctly different. Meltdowns result when a

---

[9] L. Cozolino, *The Neuroscience of Psychotherapy: Healing the Social Brain (2nd Ed.).* (New York: W.W. Norton & Company, 2010).

[10] C. Henson and P.J. Rossouw, *BrainWise Leadership: Practical Neuroscience to Survive and Thrive at Work* (Sydney: Learning Quest, 2013).

[11] Melissa Glenwright, "How Samantha used neuroscience to build a pathway out of social anxiety disorder," in P.J. Rossouw, (Ed.). *Neuropsychotherapy: Theoretical Underpinnings and Clinical Applications* (USA: Mediros Pty Ltd., 2014), 353-369.

child's brain becomes so over-regulated that they move into a fight/flight/freeze reaction that is out of their control. During a meltdown, no logical thinking or common sense can be conceived, and it takes time—often longer than twenty minutes—for the adrenal chemicals in the brain to start dispersing and the person to appear to "wake up or come to."[12] When a child is having a meltdown, the primary goal is to help them come back to a regulated state where their smart brain can come back online.

A tantrum, on the other hand, is a learned behavior. The child uses anger, screaming, or emotional withdrawal (a silent tantrum) to manipulate or control another person or the situation to get what they want, and they can start or stop the tantrum depending on the reaction they are getting. (Tantrums are a great time to use the "fun or no fun" tool, which we will cover later.) Often a child discovers how effective tantrums are in their early formative years, when they do not get what they want, engage the tantrum tool, and their caregiver gives in to stop the behavior. The toy, the ice cream, accessing their parent's phone, taking sides in an argument, placating rather than allowing a place for supported self-soothing—all of these can create a dynamic in which a young person learns how to get what they want. Unfortunately, they learn how to do it in a way that violates the rights of others, can be disrespectful and dishonoring, and can sabotage the development of trust and connection in relationships. However, it's important to understand that children are not consciously manipulating or controlling you with a tantrum—they are not applying higher executive cognition to ensure their needs are met. Rather, using tantrums is typically an unconscious behavior, which through repetitive experiences has been reinforced by the caregiver's responsive behavior. The goal in working with a child who throws tantrums is to guide them in unlearning this behavior and replacing it with a new pattern of respect and self-control.

Meltdowns and tantrums can look similar, however, so the first step to taking the right approach is determining where the behavior we're seeing is

[12] Stephen W. Porges and Deb Dana, *Clinical Applications of the Polyvagal Theory: The Emergence of Polyvagal-Informed Therapies* (New York: W.W. Norton & Company, 2018).

coming from. I worked with one sweet boy with Asperger syndrome, Tom, who became easily overstimulated, especially by change. Change for Tom could quite simply be the teacher wanting him to move on to a different task. This seven-year-old's brain however, would be fixated on perfecting a current task to please his teacher, whom he experienced as often angry toward him, and with the change in instruction, Tom would be suddenly thrown out of control. Misreading Tom's meltdown as a tantrum, the teacher would conclude that he was trying to manipulate and control her to get his own way, which increased the teacher's sense of powerlessness and anger. This in turn reinforced Tom's fear of the teacher, increasing his strive toward perfectionism. Together Tom and his teacher became stuck in a loop of misunderstanding and reactivity.

Think about this for a minute. If Tom did have a remote control and the power to control the teacher, wouldn't he choose, "Give me longer to complete this task," or "Help me get it done quickly," or "Love me while I finish the work I am proudly accomplishing from your first request"? Instead, when the teacher became angry, Tom ran for his life as his survival instincts kicked in. Of course, a young student missing from the classroom and running around the school is a serious safety concern (especially because there are cows about), so the first thing we did to stop this situation from escalating was teach Tom to run to the safety of the school's behavior education unit, the Living Room, where he could be supervised and supported whilst his threat detector had time to reassess the level of safety (down-regulated). Once Tom made it to the Living Room, which usually took all of his cognitive functioning, he felt safe and let go of the last of his self-control by throwing what could have been perceived as a mammoth tantrum, but was actually his brain detoxing the stress chemicals and releasing its energy in a safe place (much like the child who holds it all together until they get home and then becomes emotional). When the screaming and destruction calmed down, Tom would look around at the upturned couches (that he couldn't actually move when he was calm) and the toys and books everywhere, and started to clean up his mess.

Each time, we came alongside Tom after the meltdown and talked through emotional regulation. Slowly, he started to adjust his behavior. Where he once ran and hid on the back-school ovals, he began going straight to the Living Room. Where he once threw a tantrum when asked to clean up the mess he made (yup, he would throw a tantrum after a meltdown), he started to clean the mess up himself. These improvements were slowly being built into his smart brain for future context. This doesn't mean he stopped experiencing meltdowns, but he began building a vaster awareness of what triggered his meltdowns and how to respond as he continued to grow his capacity for problem-solving and executive functioning.

Our students need repetitive support at all ages to learn to recognize and regulate their emotions. This requires teaching students to extend their emotional language beyond the basic "sad, mad, glad, bad" descriptors. All children (and adults) will benefit from developing an emotional vocabulary. The feeling wheel, which you can easily find online, is a helpful tool to do this.

Next, students need support to regulate their various emotions. Some tools for doing this effectively in primary school include programs such as *The Zones of Regulation*,[13] Sue Larkey emotional regulation course,[14] Life Academy Kids,[15] BrainGrow[16] or HeartSmart.[17] Using visual aids such as those created by My Learning Toolbox help students to learn about their emotional, physical, and psychological reactions when they start to be triggered, escalate, erupt and then move into recovery mode.[18] By working on these activities, students develop a personalized language and tools that reflect their own individual reactions, and learn to reduce the likelihood of survival-seeking in the future.

---

[13] www.zonesofregulation.com
[14] www.suelarkey.com.au
[15] https://kids.loplifeacademy.com/
[16] https://braingrow.com.au/
[17] www.heartsmart.school
[18] https://www.mylearningtoolbox.com/

For younger students, I recommend tools such as *The Red Beast* storybook by Al-Ghani.[19] This simple story describes the phases a young person goes through when their threat detector has been activated and how they are supported to restore their equilibrium. Many students, especially those diagnosed with Asperger's, further benefit from applying stories like *The Red Beast* to social stories, which can be developed in video or book form for future viewing. Not sure how? Google it. Social stories are a great tool for the whole class to engage in.

In secondary school, personal development programs such as Life Academy Kids, the Shine and Strength Curriculum, Bridgebuilders, or Truwell school well-being program are just some of the many programs accessible to schools.[20] Be aware that regardless of the program, one of the greatest influencers of skills in emotional regulation is found in the role-modeling and connection that the student experiences in relationship with you as their teacher. Thus, the greater your emotional awareness and capacity, the greater your students' will become.

Through participating in these activities, students will begin to verbalize their thoughts and feelings, as well as increase their ability to interpret other people's intent, thereby increasing the likelihood they could identify and express their needs. We will consider core survival needs further in Chapter 5, but here the point is that when we support our students' growth in emotional awareness and regulation, we help them remove guessing from the relationship and instead learn to provide a clear target for the other person to aim at.

For example, a student distressed by a pet's illness may arrive at school disheveled, unfocused, and be easily distracted, constantly talking to peers or checking her phone. A teacher who observes the disengagement may set a limit by confiscating the student's phone. In her emotive, upregulated state, the student may simply act her emotions and lash out by arguing

---

[19] K. Al-Ghani, *The Red Beast: Controlling Anger in Children with Asperger's Syndrome* (UK: Jessica Kingsley Publishers, 2008).
[20] https://www.truwell.org/; https://empoweringlifeskills.com.au/bridge-builders/; https://hillsong.com/contributors/contributor/shine-strength/

with the teacher or refusing to hand over their phone. Alternatively, in a connected classroom culture, a student who has been taught to recognize and verbalize her emotions would be more likely to inform the teacher at the start of the lesson about her situation and request access to her phone for an update from her parent (expressing a need). The teacher, wanting to be fair and consistent to the class, may negotiate an alternative whereby the student can check her phone, but that it is to be located on the teacher's desk. The extent to which teacher and student remain connected and communicate effectively is significantly enhanced by regular healthy expression of needs, which when met, bring comfort and reinforce trust. This is part of the trust cycle, which I'll expand on in Chapter 5.

SWITCHING THE BRAIN ON

There are some simple tools you can use when you start to notice your students, the class, or even your own emotions are escalating. A key thing is to remember that the smart part of the brain needs to be switched on. The moment it's switched off and the threat detector is juiced up, that person is not going to be making good choices.

One great way to help students turn their smart brain on is to get them to stop and do some deep breathing. Deep breathing aids in mood regulation, strengthening our mental resilience, and is a weapon against depression or anxiety.[21] Further, the rush of deep breathing can restore the body into a state of positive action rather than stress response, whilst also boosting the immune system. Apps such as the Wim Hof Method[22] may be helpful. However, my top tip is to teach your student how to use a 3cm length of straw. Before you roll your eyes, I have never in twenty years had a student abuse the privilege and create a spit-ball projectile— our connection is simply not worth violating. Not only does using a straw

---

[21] Caroline Leaf, *Switch on Your Brain: The Key to Peak Happiness, Thinking and Health.* (USA: Baker Book House, 2015).
[22] www.wimhofmethod.com

promote deep breathing, but their mouth is also too busy to talk (win-win!). Breathing exercises typically suggest:

- Mind clarity: inhale for 4, exhale for 4
- Relieve stress: inhale for 4, hold for 4, exhale for 4, hold for 4
- Deep relaxation: inhale for 4, hold for 7, exhale for 8
- Calm down: inhale for 4, exhale for 6

Breathing deeply requires the oxygen to be taken in through the nose and filling the lungs (outwardly this appears as filling the stomach, rather than a high breath filling the chest) before breathing out through the mouth. A great way to know if you are doing this correctly is to sit up straight and place both of your hands facing inward toward your belly button and touching gently. As you breathe in, your fingers should come apart as your belly swells, then, as you breathe out, your fingers should return into position. From littles to older students, I teach them about taking a deep breath, holding it for four taps on their knee under their desk, breathing back out for four taps, and repeating that five times. This gives the body an opportunity to redirect the blood flow back to the smart brain and away from the emotive brain's stress network (of course, it is important to ensure that the student you are working with does not have a respiratory condition, such as asthma, that might be affected.)

Another helpful technique to help turn the smart brain back on is for the teacher to stop the whole class or individual and consider their five senses (touch, taste, smell, sound, see), naming five experiences currently relating to each sense. We call it "The 5 in 5." It's an easy way to regroup, start cognitive thinking, and reduce the overactive limbic system. It's good for us as adults to do this as well when we feel we are getting a bit anxious, as it helps to ground us. I find this especially helpful to do for myself whilst a student is having a meltdown. Sometimes they even stop and join in.

LEARNING TO APPLY CONTEXT

Teachers are in a fantastic position to support students to develop smart brain (prefrontal cortex) functioning, including critical thinking, focus, empathy, rationality, and problem-solving. Providing regular opportunities to practice these skills in a safe environment will increase the likelihood of the student drawing on these tools in the future. Remember, repetition will result in the construction of a superhighway response. Do you want your classroom to reinforce the development of a superhighway that transports your student toward emotional regulation and joyful responsibility, or to reinforce the need to survive school and self-protect from connection with teachers?

As I mentioned earlier, children's primitive brain regions, their survival brain and threat detector, are far more developed than their smart brains, so this is what we must expect and prepare to see. More often than not, students will act out their emotions, behaving in ways that do not reflect context, logic, empathy, and problem-solving when things happen to them. That is why chastisements such as, "But I have told you a hundred times," or "We spoke about this last week," are superfluous. Even for adults experiencing chronic stress, when something real or perceived scares us, blood (and oxygen) rushes to our primitive limbic system to signal our threat detector and our ability to consider our options and react effectively becomes limited. When fear is heightened and the primitive brain structures are engaged, none of us is using our smart brains to think thoughts such as, *How can I talk through this situation with the teacher more respectfully?* or *How can I tell my friend how I felt about the rumor they spread about me?* Instead, we react to ensure our survival. The difference for us as adults is that we have had the opportunity to learn from these experiences to apply context, logic, and empathy more consistently in many situations. As teachers, we have the opportunity to pass this learning on to our students.

One of the most common scenarios I observe, whether it be with senior students or preppies, is when a student becomes upset or angry because a teacher has moved their seat or removed their technology device. They view these as their little area of personal control, like their bedroom, and the idea that someone would take away their freedom and move them awakens their "red beast"—anger. I see students melt down or throw tantrums over this time and time again, followed by the stand-off with the teacher. Every time, it reminds me of *me*.

A number of years ago I had an office, and the decision was made by someone above me that it was time for my office to move. I received an email telling me about the decision and instructing me to move immediately. I was hurt and angry. No one had spoken to me and asked my thoughts. To me, the demand was unexpected, unreasonable, and dictatorial. How dare they move me out of my office without considering the impact this would have on me or my productivity? Another part of me started to question my performance. Perhaps I had done something wrong or they had just realized that I was not up to the task? I stomped my feet, had a bit of a tantrum, and said a whole lot of things not worth mentioning. It was not my finest hour, or month.

Feeling like I had no say in the matter and acting like a victim, I begrudgingly moved my belongings and wasted a lot of personal energy working through the emotions of confusion, disconnect, mistrust, and hurt triggered by my insecurities and fear. I was moved to an office that immediately increased my stress, created more work, and placed me in the pressure cooker of behavior education. And guess what? It was the best decision anyone could have made. Why? Because from within that location, the consistency of the behavior team grew, and as a result, school-wide consistency began to emerge.

I would never have made the decision to move offices on my own. I would, however, have complied if I was included in the decision and allowed my voice to be heard. You see, I can handle a no, but it is important to me to feel heard and understood. The experience, however, gave me empathy toward many of our students who daily react to having something forced upon them, like being made to move their seat or having their device taken away. Even with a fully functioning adult brain, unexpected changes in my environment that threaten my sense of safety and control will affect me. Kids also want the freedom to control their lives. (As we will see in Chapter 5, this need for control is critical to their sense of self.)

In the aftermath of this experience, I began to use my adult brain to reflect and ask myself questions. What could I have done differently to manage me? How could I have managed myself in that situation better so that I did not react with a tantrum? In reality, moving offices is not such a big deal. My reaction was not very professional and it certainly was not very respectful or honoring. In my fear-fueled reaction, I had made a mess, and once I calmed down, I needed to clean up the mess. If I had taken time to ask clarifying questions and sought discussions rather than withdrawing in shame and anger, I would have seen the bigger picture, that the leadership team wanted to strengthen the behavior education team to increase school-wide engagement during a season of significant and unsettling change for the school.

Fast-forward a few years. Another decision was made for me to move offices. Same situation, but this time I was far more prepared. I had not only already thought through the situation and confessed my mistakes caused by my anger in the earlier experience. I had also experienced a significant amount of joy from being in the new office space, which had positively impacted my team, and I had strengthened my connection with those making this decision. My prefrontal cortex had developed context to refer to when future similar experiences arose. This time when I was told to move my office, I felt a strong measure of trust that the decision maker had my best interests at heart and that it was safe for me to have a conversation with them so that I felt that any concerns were heard. Next, I prepared my team, because the move would impact them directly. We took a moment to celebrate the change and I bought a new desk that was set up before the end of the day. I had applied context from my previous experiences in which I had learned that change, whilst uncomfortable (and this change was very uncomfortable), could be positive. This enabled me to react from a position of trust and connection.

Ideally, this is the connection we want to have with each of our students, one of trust even during times of uncertainty, which can sometimes be out of our and their control. Sometimes, like in my example, we must make a decision that is out of our student's control. Perhaps it is time that you move a student's seat—I am not saying you shouldn't do it. In those moments, going in aware that this decision could trigger a student's threat detector (perhaps they will feel embarrassed or separated from peers) and that they may make a mess is important. We do not need to be afraid of the messes. We are not afraid of a student "behaving" right there in front of us because we have a plan for how we will manage ourselves and a process to help students clean up the messes they make, much like I had to do. This creates a classroom environment where students do not feel that they are fighting for their lives, but experience the safety needed for them to discover how to repeatedly turn on their smart brain, apply context and critical thinking, and respond from trust and connection.

Again, the big problem with using fear, threats, bribes (veiled as rewards), and intimidation is that *they appear to work*, at least in the short term. That is why we keep choosing to use these tools despite the long-term implications on the developing adult. Juicing up the amygdala and getting people worked up makes us feel like we can control our students, but it is not conducive to long-term goals of connection and it is certainly not conducive to helping students develop the confidence and smart brain skills necessary to make good choices into their future. Yes, being upset and angry could get a student to be quiet in the moment, but it may also make it more difficult for them to take a risk at some future time when they are learning a new skill. When students feel safe they become bold, and when they become bold they become curious and creative, all of which are essential to the posture of learning.

Every behavior or skill we want our students to learn requires the boldness to show up, try things, take risks, adjust, and try again. Learning how to speak up for ourselves, for example, is a very healthy and necessary skill for young people to develop, as it is essential during adulthood. One day, they will be in the workplace or in a relationship where it is vitally important for them to be able to speak up for themselves and communicate their needs effectively. This skill will protect them from violent relationships, enhance equal opportunities in the workplace, and may influence large financial negotiations.

The challenge is that students start learning this skill when they are children and don't yet know how to speak up respectfully. Our job is to guide them in honing this skill. This is why whenever I meet with parents, I assure them that when their angel starts learning to argue back, they do not need to fear—this will become a great skill and tool. When a ten-year-old argues back with their limited logic, language, and emotive immaturity, what they have done is reached into their toolkit and pulled out a tool that immediately everyone (except them) in the interaction realizes is a rather blunt and ineffective tool. Blunt tools can cause more injuries than sharpened ones because they are less accurate. As my husband and Chef Jayden has taught me, sharp knives are safer because you don't have to apply much pressure for them to easily glide through the food. In other words, they are more effective. When a chef selects a tool, such as a knife, it is a deliberate choice related to the task required. It is kept sharp in preparation for that exact moment, and through lots of practice and repetition, the chef has developed the skill they need to use this tool to be effective in their craft, stylish in their presentation, and safe in their use. Whilst they are developing, our students get opportunities to practice and sharpen tools like this every day with their fellow students and with the various adults who work in schools, not to mention their parents. It will most likely take many mistakes and deliberate sharpening to learn how to do this well and to do it respectfully. But as long as they are consistently guided towards the goal of respectful communication—largely by us modeling respectful communication—they will get there.

What compromises this learning process is when we introduce disrespect in the form of fear, punishment, control, and manipulation, because this erodes safety, triggers the survival brain, and causes us to use our tools as weapons of self-defense rather than tools for self-control and connection. Our hope is that as our students graduate senior school, they leave not with an arsenal of weapons to keep others at a distance or try to make people behave in certain ways, but with a utilities truck full of tools they know how to keep sharpened, apply in the right situations, and use with grace as they navigate the world of relational connections as adults. This is why, in all our interactions with students, parents, and each other, we must be committed to discarding the illusion of control (weapons) and moving forward into a paradigm of healthy self-control (tools). As Danny Silk says, "The today you are building is the tomorrow you will live in." This means that each student's experience with you informs their perception of all future teacher-student and classroom culture relationships. What legacy are you building today?

4

POLYVAGAL THEORY AND THE NEUROPSYCHOTHERAPEUTIC PROCESS

AS WE HAVE SEEN, safety and connection are critical to brain development. But there's a lot more to the story when it comes to understanding how our brains are actually perceiving and responding to the experience of safety and connection, or the lack of it. To get a fuller picture of what is going on at the neurological and physiological level of this experience, we need to look at what is going on in our nervous system when we encounter either safety, love, and connection, or danger, fear, and self-preservation.

In case you haven't had a recent refresher on the nervous system, I'll start with a brief summary. (If you haven't yet put on your "nerd" hat, I recommend doing so now!) The primary components of the nervous system are the brain, spinal cord, and nerves that branch throughout the body in a complex and finely tuned network. The brain and spinal cord constitute the *central nervous system*, and the nerve network, which contains both sensory nerves that collect data from our physical interaction with the environment and nerves that stimulate our organs and muscles to function, is called the *peripheral nervous system*. The brain is like the supercomputer that receives and sends messages through the peripheral nervous system to govern and direct everything our body does.

Part of the peripheral nervous system is the *autonomic nervous system* (ANS), which is responsible for controlling all the bodily functions that don't involve conscious awareness—keeping our heart pumping, our lungs breathing, our digestion working, and regulating our body's temperature. Within the ANS is the *sympathetic nervous system* (SNS), which prepares the body for the stress response to perceived threats ("fight or flight"), which is balanced by the *parasympathetic nervous system* (PNS), which prepares the body for rest and recovery from stress ("rest and digest").

Dr. Stephen Porges developed Polyvagal Theory to explain how the brain takes in environmental information—particularly the social environment—through our senses, triages it via the *vagus nerve*—the primary nerve in the ANS—through the limbic (threat detector) and reptilian (survival) complexes, and primes the body to respond physically to safety, danger, or a life threat. The vagus nerve has two primary branches originating in the *dorsal vagal complex* (DVC) which governs the "freeze" or immobilization response, and the *ventral vagal complex* (VVC), which governs pro-social responses like social communication leading to co-regulation (spontaneous interaction, play, learning and laughter). Both branches of the vagus nerve connect to the rest of the sympathetic and parasympathetic nervous system.

This triage process centers around two primary unconscious questions: "How stressful is my current experience?" and "How safe is my current environment?" In other words, our brains are constantly scanning to determine where our current level of stress falls on a scale of safe to dangerous or life-threatening, and scanning our environment to see if it will offer us protection or provision to help us cope with that stress.

Dr. Porges explains that the physical response to our brain signaling safety, danger, or life-threat involves three circuits in our autonomic nervous system, which combine into six states as the VVC engages with the SNS or the DVC:

Neural Circuit	Response Signaled	Fear State (Avoid)	Love State (Approach)
Ventral Vagal Complex	Homeostasis (Safety)	Disconnection	Connection
Sympathetic Nervous System (VVC+SNS)	Mobilization (Danger)	Fight/ Flight	Play & Learn
Dorsal Vagal Complex (VVC+DVC)	Immobilization (Life Threat)	Freeze/ shut down	Intimacy

What this table shows is that our social behavior can be enabled or disabled by changes in our physiological state, which is dependent on our nervous system's evaluation of safety in our environment. When we or our students perceive our environment as unsafe, we display inhibited social behavior and social disengagement, which decreases our mental and physical health. In this fearful state, when our ANS receives information that the body and external environment is in danger, it will engage our sympathetic nervous system (SNS) and initiate the fight/flight sequence from within the limbic system (threat detector)—or, if the received signal suggests a compromised safety level that is triaged as life-threatening, it will engage the dorsal vagal complex (DVC) through the reptilian complex (survival brain) to inhibit mobilization through the freeze (immobilization) sequence.

However, when we or our students perceive that safety is assured in our environment, then our ANS, via the VVC, will engage the DVC in a completely different way, stimulating us to reduce overworking, increase intimacy, and increase rest and calm to the body, or it will engage the SNS to initiate playfulness and positive risk-taking. In a safe environment, we are more likely to display positive social behavior, even when facing danger or a threat, which also increases our health. This is why Dr.

Porges argues that our autonomic state is optimized during safe social interactions (trust and connection), and disrupted during states of defense due to perceived danger or life threats.

Our brains are constantly evaluating the "window of tolerance" between our current level of stress and perceived safety in the environment. If our ANS takes in the information related to our current situation and informs the SNS and DVC that we are able to manage the situation despite some mild stress, we remain in our window of tolerance and can self-regulate effectively. Tolerable stress is necessary and beneficial for increasing our resilience and learning, as it primes us to focus and activate synaptic connections. A student with an exam date looming, for example, may experience slightly elevated stress that increases their motivation to study. If studying is a familiar experience, they have the ability to draw on previous context and determine they can tolerate this short-term pressure, study, and receive a pass mark, thus remaining inside their window of tolerance.

However, if stress is detected and the environment as insufficiently safe, the student moves outside that window of tolerance and triggers the fearful "fight or flight" or immobilization responses. For example, for a student who frequently fails despite feeling like they studied hard, an exam date may trigger their defense mechanisms and either cause them to become energetic entering the exam room, causing conflict with the teacher and potentially being asked to leave the room (SNS fight or flight), or refuse to attend school altogether (DVC immobilization).

Both of these scenarios are common to learning in the classroom. The more positive experiences we have on the edge of our window of tolerance, the more our ANS is encoded that we are safe when similar experiences happen in the future. We are thus able to apply context from our prefrontal cortex to adapt to the stress of everyday situations and return to the adaptive self-regulation stage. As a result, our window of tolerance can be expanded as we learn how to self-regulate, a skill which our students are learning through co-regulation experiences with us (more on co-regulation in a moment).

There is an interesting phenomenon that can occur for students (or adults) who have experienced chronic stress or trauma. These students can unintentionally trigger their defense response as an expression of feeling safe. A core reason for this is that trauma is often inflicted by what should be a safe, trusted person or in a safe environment. Thus, when their body goes into a state of trust and safety, instantaneously there may be a reaction that they are actually "unsafe." The body may send the message, "I was fooled once, but I won't be fooled again." The student may psychologically want to feel safe, but their unconscious physiological reaction acts to protect them, demonstrating that intention and reaction don't always align. One student may clearly communicate their desire to attend school or a part-time job, yet their physiological reactivity communicates that they are in a state of defense when put into those situations. In this case various post-traumatic therapies may be engaged to help the brain and body down-regulate in a safe environment.

NEUROCEPTION AND CONNECTEDNESS

Now that we know more about what's going on in the brain and nervous system in response to stress and safety, let's look at what social cues encourage us to feel safe to approach social behaviors that create connection. Dr. Stephen Porges and Deb Dana, LCSW explain that there is a "neural love code" that generates the experience of "connectedness," which forms the building block of all relationships.[1] According to Dr. Porges, connectedness is the ability to mutually, through synchrony (in step together) and reciprocity (back-and-forth responding), engage with others to regulate physiological and behavioral states—that is, to co-*regulate*. Simply put, as I experience safety and trust, our connectedness grows. When I experience fear, however, disconnection enters the relationship.

[1] Stephen W. Porges and Deb A. Dana, *Clinical Applications of the Polyvagal Theory: The Emergence of Polyvagal-Informed Therapies* (New York, NY: Norton, 2018), pp 47.

Building connectedness, Dr. Porges argues, requires four progressive steps:[2]

$$\text{Safety} \longrightarrow \text{Proximity} \longrightarrow \text{Contact} \longrightarrow \text{Bonds}$$

To connect, we first require safety in our relationships. At any level, if safety is compromised, we must return to that primary step to restore connection. Once safety is assured, we move into closer proximity by reducing physiological distance. Now that we are closer, we can experience physical contact with the other person (e.g., offering a handshake), before finally establishing a social bond.

In modern culture, one of the most common ways we violate connectedness is through our use of technology to communicate. Technology does not increase opportunities for safety, proximity, contact, or social bonding. Rather, when we email or text another person, it is no longer in real time, thus violating synchrony, and in the unpredictable waiting for a response, reciprocity is violated. This is the same problem that emerged in an experiment Porges describes, in which a counselor asked the client a question, then turned his head aside when the client began to answer. The result of that violation of connectedness was that actual fights broke out in the counseling room.[3] It is important to understand that connectedness in the classroom can be affected by things as simple as sitting behind a desk at a computer or moving around the room whilst students are isolating on their devices. When we are focused on objects or content, we are less aware of social behaviors and other people, including our students. This explains why we observe people bumping into others without awareness when walking through the playground or shopping center whilst they are interacting on their phone.

---

[2] Stephen W. Porges, "Clinical Application of Polyvagal Theory." [conference presentation] Digital Seminar (Wisconsin, USA: PESI Inc, 2019).
[3] Stephen W. Porges, "Clinical Application of Polyvagal Theory."

Safety in proximity must occur prior to physical contact, and is assured primarily by *feature detectors*. Feature detectors are how our nervous system perceives safety, danger, or a life threat. These include face-to-face interactions and expressions, vocalization (including intonation), body posture, listening, reciprocity, and gestures. Face-to-face interactions are considerably important, because it is the nerves around our eyes that communicate exuberance and safety. As such, the upper part of the face is significantly responsible for communicating cues of safety. Consider the crow's feet that develop after years of smiling and laughter. The lower half of the face, however, primarily has to do with survival, and can often be used as a tool of aggression. Under stress, the upper part of the face can become "flat" as the person shuts down, and this reduction in expression therefore communicates potential threat to anyone in their presence. The orbital muscle around the eye and cheek, which are communicating safety, are also connected to the middle ear, which impacts auditory processing such as listening and responding. This explains why you can sense that someone has heard you through looking into their eyes. So, if we want to increase our student's ability to hear us, we must first communicate safety in our face-to-face features.

When the body's nervous system decides to behave in a certain way based on the observable feature detectors, this is called *neuroception*. Neuroception is the neural process of evaluating risk without awareness, or unconsciously. In actuality, many of our reactions are unconscious and expressed as reflexes (physiological states) within the body.

Dr. Porges refers to the observations of Claire Wilson in her book *Grounded: Discovering the Missing Piece in the Puzzle of Children's Behaviour*, which reflects a true story about a teacher, with numerous worries in her home life, arriving at school one morning after a particularly stressful journey. She did gate duty, then taught her morning classes. At lunch time, she observed that students from each of her classes were lined up outside the Head's office. Why? Because under strain, the teacher's face displayed less safe feature detectors, resulting in students neurocepting (unconsciously perceiving) the teacher being unsafe and physiologically responding to ensure their survival by reducing listening and hearing (i.e., following instructions) as their bodies become primed to engage defense mechanisms.[4] Porges also notes that teachers and professionals who have used Botox treatments equally report increased incidents of being misunderstood and increased disconnection. When there is a disconnection in face-to-face interactions (through technology use or "flat" facial effect, etc.), there is a disruption of connection, which reduces opportunity to co-regulate and potentially triggers internal states of defense.

Dr. Stephen Porges and Danny Silk both argue that in situations where safety and connection are compromised, we must get the safety and connection back before we can implement any form of effective learning, growth, or change. Dr. Porges clarifies that being safe is not the removal of a threat, but the removal of *fear* of the threat. The nervous system is not satisfied with the removal of the threat—it wants cues to enable us to feel safe. Increasing safety in connectedness can be done by engaging in neural exercises that include face-to-face interactions, singing (which uses all the muscles in the face and ear), wind instruments (which requires deep breathing), breathing exercises, posture, listening, and interactive play that includes synchrony and reciprocal behavior (turn-taking).

All of these exercises enable us to co-regulate with our students and make them feel safe, even despite being in a situation that includes fearful stimuli (e.g., a classroom of other students). Through the experience of co-regulation with others, our students learn the skills implicit to self-regulation. This is what Danny Silk describes as becoming powerful people who can manage freedom responsibly.

Play is an especially effective way to help our students co-regulate with us and each other, as it can be harnessed as a tool to build emotional resilience in students. Play creates low-risk opportunities for expectancy, expectancy violation, and repair. Consider the baby playing peek-a-boo

---

[4] Claire, Wilson, *Grounded: Discovering the Missing Piece in the Puzzle of Children's Behaviour*, (CHEW Initiatives, 2018), Kindle Version.

with their father. The baby is assured by the friendly face of the father, feels threatened by the loss of facial contact, and then experiences safety being restored through the unveiling of the father's face and shared humor. Humor, interestingly, includes the violation of expectancy, which is what makes it funny to share with someone who is building resilience. For a student without emotional resilience, however, humor increases the experience of fear. As Dr. Porges has observed, group play in schools (and friendship conflict responses) can increase student resiliency by including face-to-face opportunities to experience low-risk rupture and repair in relational connectedness.

Perhaps the most powerful tool we can draw on to establish safety and connection with our students is to offer a *loving presence*, which Pat Ogden describes as a loving atmosphere that favors healing, and involves giving nonverbal cues such as gentle facial features or tone, open body language, empathy and compassion, soft muscle tone, or soft eye contact that result in the neuroception of safety.[5] All of these ways of displaying a loving presence cause our students' *mirror neurons* to light up. Mirror neurons respond to acts that are perceived to carry intent or purpose. They do not cause merely "mirrored" behavior; rather, mirror neurons respond to the recognition of a predictable sequence, such as raising a hand to smack or stiffening your jaw when you feel anger. The mirror system learns by experience and becomes the tool we elicit to help us understand the intention of others.[6]

For this reason, when interacting with students, I find it essential to use a predictable sequence of intent to mirror a loving presence. This looks like me showing a calm face, using a gentle, respectful voice and tone, displaying open body language, and meeting students on their level, regardless of their behavior. It may be physically getting down on the ground to look into the eyes of a prep student or lowering the volume of

---

[5] Pat Ogden, Stephen Porges, & Deb Dana, *Clinical Applications of the Polyvagal Theory: The Emergence of Polyvagal-Informed Therapies*, (New York, NY: Norton, 2018).
[6] Matthew Dahlitz, *The Psychotherapist's Essential Guide to the Brain* (Park Ridge, QLD: Dahlitz Media, 2017).

my voice. All of this allows students of all ages to be able to predict my movements and help them understand my intention to make them feel safe and connect with them. In short, I am building trust by providing consistent cues for how I will behave around them and removing unpredictability that comes from a reactive temperament, sarcasm, misplaced teasing, and public shaming.

Mirror neurons are especially stimulated when we look into the face of another person and make sense of the perceived expression.[7] Our neural networks, based on our own experience when we make those expressions, become activated to inform us of the other person's intent. For example, when a student smiles at you, you begin to smile back, even if it is subtle. This informs the student of what we may be experiencing and therefore allows them to predict intent. "The teacher is happy with me." So too, if you are not aware of yourself, a student who feels anxious that they will look silly answering a question in front of peers may reflect these internal processes to you as the teacher, resulting in an increase in your own anxiety that you don't know enough and look silly in front of the students you are teaching. Knowing yourself allows you to apply context and remind yourself that you know your content, so that you do not somatically react to the internal dialogue of thirty faces staring up at you.

Mirror neurons alone are not the holy grail of developing empathy and learning; rather, it is the connectivity of mirror neurons within the system, which can be affected by various factors. Again, communication may be affected by something as simple as a child interacting with a male teacher who has a beard covering his lower face, or with a female teacher whose latest Botox treatment renders her mouth or eyebrows static. Beards, Botox, and face masks compromise one's ability to read basic non-verbal facial communication, which is primary to neurocepted safety. It's also important to be aware that, in addition to other factors, autistic children and adults have delayed mirror neuron systems, which

---

[7] L. Lundquvist & U. Dimberg, "Facial Expressions Are Contagious," *Journal of Psychophysiology*, 9, 1995, 203-211.

reduce their capacity to learn through observation, attune emotionally, offer empathy, or understand metaphoric language.[8]

Regardless, when we offer a predictable sequence of behaviors that communicate love and connection, safety can be neurocepted by our students, making them more likely to engage with us. The whole process of creating safety and building a good, strong connection through love and empathy is called "right-to-right brain attunement."[9] This neural connection enables you and your students to feel safe to express emotions, allowing each of you to manage your half of the connection whilst the other person can explore their options.

Only after our students have neurocepted safety and we have achieved right-to-right brain attunement can we begin the process of replacing old logic with new logic at the neural level.[10] As Danny puts it, only once we are connected can we then start the process of problem solving or conflict resolution, which requires higher order executive functions. Each student's ability to apply context, reasoning, and problem solving—that is, to use and develop their smart brain—is growing incrementally from engagement with the environment throughout their schooling career. In short, students need to experience safety first in their environment and in their connection with their teacher, and then cognitive learning can ensue.

AMY: A CASE STUDY IN APPLYING NEUROPSYCHOTHERAPY

One of the best ways to grasp Polyvagal Theory and all of this information about our nervous system, safety, and connectedness is to see how it can be applied therapeutically to help students who are struggling with habitual fear responses to the stresses and lack of safety they perceive in

---

[8] Dahlitz, *The Psychotherapist's Essential Guide to the Brain*.
[9] Arlene Montgomery, *Neurobiology Essentials for Clinicians: What Every Clinician Needs to Know*. New York: W.W. Norton & Company, 2013).
[10] Dahlitz, *The Psychotherapist's Essential Guide to the Brain*.

the school environment. For this purpose, I am going to walk you through a case study that is actually a representative composite of many students I have worked with over the years.

One of the most common reasons I am asked to meet with a student as a social worker is due to immobilization (freeze), which typically looks like work or school refusal, or even suicidal ideation. Essentially, the young person has "checked out" and disengaged because at an unconscious level, they have come to perceive attending school, or even leaving the house, as life-threatening.

The very first question I am looking to answer with a student having this experience is, "How is your connection?" As we have seen, a student who feels safe and connected will seek social engagement through decreasing proximity, making contact, and developing a social bond. Thus, I am looking at the connections in the student's personal and educational life. In all instances where a student is immobilized, the social bonds are missing for various reasons. As Danny says, the first problem that always needs to be solved is getting connection back.

Amy was one such student brought to my attention by her father, Lenard, who was concerned that she had been absent from school for more than a term. Lenard was specifically anxious about how Amy's absence would be considered a failure of his parenting skill, especially in the eyes of his parents, with whom they resided. Lenard strongly disagreed with the medical certificate Amy had acquired from her GP, which stated that she needed the time off school due to anxiety. Lenard described Amy as "seeking attention" and said she should "suck it up" and just go to school.

To intervene successfully, my first task was to co-regulate with Lenard and down-regulate his sympathetic nervous system, which was initiating a fight/flight sequence. This presented as a clenched jaw and fists, fast speech, chaotic thinking, and distress. By mirroring a calm demeanor that incorporated empathy, I pointed out that demonstrating his desire to get Amy support would actually reflect positively on his parenting skills.

As Lenard neurocepted safety with me rather than judgment about his parenting, I was able to provide him with psychoeducation about Amy's physiological experience of safety and trust. Over a period of several months, I continued to add to this education during brief interactions with him during home visits or phone calls. Helping Lenard feel safe in his own self-construct as a parent, as well as aiding in his understanding of the triune brain and vagal system, increased his connection and empathy in relationship with Amy, resulting in Lenard becoming the primary attachment figure in Amy's support network. Stephen Porges asserts that parents' behavior changes when children become more reciprocal. Throughout the process, as Amy engaged her social engagement system, Lenard responded by strengthening his connection and bond toward his daughter. In other words, his heart was turning towards her as her heart turned towards him.

Amy was a seventeen-year-old completing her final year of school. She lived with her parents and brother in a comfortable neighborhood and had been enrolled at the same school for all of secondary school. She enjoyed dancing and movies with her friends when she felt physically able to attend, but when I started meeting with Amy, she was currently unable to leave the house to engage in school or social activities.

I first met Amy at her family home. She appeared well dressed and of healthy weight; however, I was aware that she had unexplained stomach pain and frequent illness. In that first encounter, Amy displayed limited muscle movement and a flat facial expression with minimal eye contact. She gave one-syllable replies in a flat tone, but she also articulated her desire to "be normal and attend school."

This is a very common experience with students who experience school refusal. They actually want to attend, but they are physiologically unable to. Many of these significantly disengaged students are then forced into proximity with strangers in clinics or at the family home without establishing the safety necessary to assure that this proximity can lead to a secure social bond. For this reason, my initial focus was on meeting Amy's need for safety. I asked her to select the most comfortable place to speak, and she chose a large picnic table in the garden, where we sat at opposite ends. I offered empathy and sensitivity to this being her personal space, which rewarded me with the briefest eye contact. I knew I was being sized up.

Next, I aimed to increase Amy's comfort by applying an approach articulated by Melissa Glenwright—using closed questions to build rapport.[11] I kept the questions to safe topics, like Amy's dog and the present garden, which released pressure from Amy needing to think quickly or too deeply. Peter Levine also recommends this technique, explaining that shutdown clients benefit from decreased compassionate or reflective dialogue and soft eye contact to reduce the experience of shame, which is often concurrent.[12] Sure enough, I observed Amy's homeostasis restore as she took and released several deep breaths, thereby discharging stress, then looked around her garden before entering right-to-right brain attunement with me, demonstrated by increased soft eye contact and more descriptive details in her responses.[13] Nevertheless, I remained conscious of her muscle tension, locked jaw, and flat facial effect throughout the encounter.

Amy then surprised me by moving to sit at the same end of the picnic table with me, thereby creating proximity. She began to describe a history of conflict between her family members that typically occurred during the morning routine to get ready for school. She also described a history of anxiety in social interactions such as sport competitions, school assessments, or going to movies with peers, where she would experience nausea and vomiting prior to the event. As a result, Amy often excused herself from attending. Amy stated that she had few friends. The few girls who attempted to reach out to her she ignored, not having the energy or inclination to explain what she could not even explain to herself. It

[11] Melissa Glenwright, "How Samantha used neuroscience to build a pathway out of social anxiety disorder," in P.J. Rossouw, (Ed.). *Neuropsychotherapy: Theoretical Underpinnings and Clinical Applications* (USA: Mediros Pty Ltd., 2014), 353-369.
[12] Peter A. Levine in S.W. Porges and D.A. Dana, *Clinical Applications of the Polyvagal Theory.*
[13] Arlene Montgomery, *Neurobiology Essentials for Clinicians.*

appears that when preparing for school or social interactions, Amy was being triggered into a "freeze" response, which immobilized her from any further action.

Amy appeared to have limited understanding of what caused her to freeze. She was only aware that she constantly felt nauseous. It was imperative to explain to Amy the neurobiological construct of her physical reactions, as understanding why she reacted in certain ways would provide her a sense of orientation. Over a number of sessions, I explained the triune brain, neuroplasticity, and the window of tolerance as applied in polyvagal theory. Amy appeared to grasp that she had been flipping outside her window of tolerance, but through our therapeutic connection, she had started to have experiences in which she was pushing gently on the edges of this window, which would allow her to slowly, with support, increase her tolerance of emotions and cognitive processing. This looked like returning to school, though not initially to classes, and using an alternate study and exam location.

Amy could articulate that her primary goal was to experience daily functioning without feeling nauseous or anxious. Her secondary goals were to continue participating in sport, attend social functions, and graduate senior school. Due to daily nausea and fear of her family's reactions, Amy's perception was that school and social interactions were dangerous. Homeostasis, according to Klaus Grawe, however, requires the alignment of goals and perceptions.[14] Thus, providing a neutral location (a withdrawal room at school), surrounded by a loving presence (a consistent social worker), Amy was able to start attending school more frequently.

Amy was progressing well and reengaging in the classroom by morning tea daily, until one day when I was required to suddenly disrupt her homeostasis. I received a non-negotiable direction to ensure that Amy was in an unanticipated school assembly. Despite her agreement exempt-

---

[14] K. Grawe, *Neuropsychotherapy: How the Neurosciences Inform Effective Psychotherapy.* (New York, NY: Psychology Press, 2007).

ing her from social activities at school, this was an unexpected requirement that I did not have the authority to overrule.

I had less than five minutes to prepare and transition her into the assembly space. Upon hearing the news that she was required to attend the assembly, Amy's pallor turned gray, her face took on that familiar flat affect, and she started sweating—all signs that her sympathetic nervous system was revving up her flight/flight response. However, she maintained constant eye contact with me, suggesting that through the earned secure attachment with me, she was neurocepting the message that she was safe. I immediately assisted her in employing mindfulness techniques, including breathing (see Chapter 3) and grounding. Grounding refers to the internal sense of centering, can include stabilizing oneself in the spiritual, physical, professional and locational.[15] To assist Amy to ground herself, we first employed locational grounding by visualizing the specific room she was going to, what the layout would be, who the teachers were, where her closest exits are and what route she would take back to her safe room after the assembly. Then we took a moment to pause, and connect with our breathing, visualizing clean air coming in, and stress or tension falling away from the soles of her feet as she exhaled. Then I drew attention to Amy's feet feeling secure and stable on the ground despite the range of difficult emotions. Physically, we mirrored to one another an upright posture with a confident stride, sharing solidarity in our facial expressions as we headed to the new location.

When we arrived at the assembly room, Amy entered with the other students and I was required to leave. Immediately after the assembly, Amy returned to her safe room, and I knew it was critical to help her repair the damaged connection, as there was the significant potential of re-traumatizing Amy by abandoning her to excessive levels of distress. I arranged for her to spend the remainder of the day in the safety of the withdrawal

---

[15] Shari M. Geller & Leslies S. Greenberg, "The Mind-Brain-Body Connection, or How Emotional Styles Influence Health," In S.M. Geller & L.S. Greenberg, eds, *Therapeutic Presence: A Mindful Approach to Effective Therapy* (Washington, DC: Magination, 2012) 109-131.

room. Unfortunately, this proved insufficient to help Amy bounce back after this experience. Amy had overshot her window of tolerance due to being unable to regulate her fear response, and subsequently refused to attend further classes for three weeks. Sadly, one assembly unnecessarily re-traumatized Amy.

I returned to making home visits to help Amy re-engage at school. We slowly re-established previously successful reengagement pathways, starting with safety, before we could move on to proximity, contact, and social bonds. From many observations working with students who experience a similar freeze (immobilization) response, each reengagement takes longer to facilitate. Stephen Porges documented similar effects of fear in the guinea pig project, which identified that not only could a frightened mammal suddenly drop their heart rate to induce immobilization, but when frightened frequently, the mammal could take longer to come out of the tonic immobility.

After restoring safety in the connection through home visits, Amy returned to school—first to meet me on campus for support sessions, then progressively to attend some scheduled lessons, and then slowly returning to attending all subjects class by morning tea. She took responsibility for her own exposure, communicating with me as she lengthened her time in the classroom. To their credit, her teachers did not request any further unexpected assemblies or school activities. Amy revised her goals until she was attending all of her lessons by the end of the school year and graduated.

5

THE SAFETY STOOL

THE TRIUNE BRAIN MODEL and Polyvagal Theory give strong support to the critical importance of establishing safe, connected environments where students aren't in survival mode and their smart brains can learn and develop. However, there is an even deeper reason for creating these environments. More than supporting our students in their journey to develop higher cognitive and critical thinking skills, safety and connection support the development of their sense of *self*.

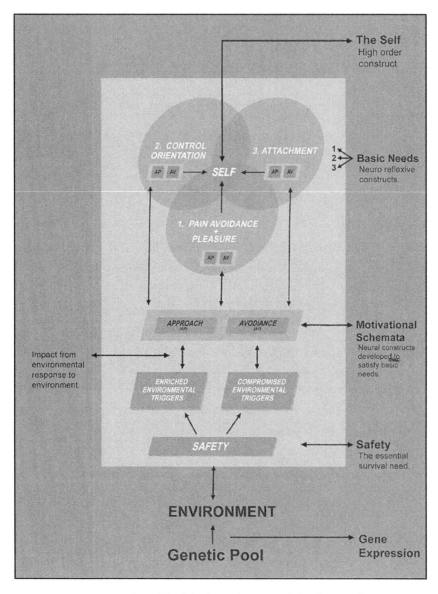

*Integrated model of the base elements of the theory of
neuropsychotherapy, by Dr. Pieter Rossouw*

According to clinical psychologist Pieter Rossouw's integrated model of the base elements of the theory of neuropsychotherapy, the experience of *self* is a higher-order construct that develops because of three basic needs being met or not met effectively.[1] These needs are:

1. Attachment
2. Control/Orientation
3. Pain Avoidance/Pleasure Seeking

We're going to dive in and look more closely at the nature of each of these three needs, but first, we need to understand Rossouw's concept of *approach* vs. *avoidance*.

From birth, a child's sense of self begins to develop through the classic interaction of nature (genetics) and nurture (environment). Inevitably, they encounter various forms of stress, which Rossouw terms *incongruence*, which trigger these basic needs for attachment, control/orientation, and pain avoidance/pleasure seeking. In a safe, enriched environment where these needs are met, the child learns to perceive these stressful experiences as *manageable incongruences* (that is, the stress falls within their window of tolerance) and to respond to them with some form of *approach*. Approach behaviors are what we saw happening in the "Love State" column of the table of six Polyvagal responses in the last chapter—connection, play, learning, and intimacy. To repeat the same example I used there, a student who experiences the stress of a pending exam as tolerable or manageable does so because they perceive they have the skill to manage it. Their need for control/orientation is satisfied, and thus they will feel confident and motivated to get to work and study hard. On a chemical level, their body's arousal response to stress downregulates, while serotonin bumps up and blood flow increases to their smart brain, thereby encouraging neural proliferation (new learning) and supporting them in being successful at their task.[2] The safe environment also allows such positive experiences to

---

[1] P. J. Rossouw, *Neuropsychotherapy: Theoretical Underpinnings and Clinical Applications* (USA: Mediros, 2014). Graphic used by author's permission.
[2] Rossouw, *Neuropsychotherapy.*

be repeated, thus encouraging approach behaviors to become habitual and resulting in an increased sense of confidence, capability, and agency that will be reinforced each time they respond to stress.[3]

However, in an unsafe environment, the opposite takes place—the student learns to perceive stress as *unmanageable incongruence* (outside their window of tolerance) and reacts with *avoidance*, triggering the behaviors we saw in the "Fear State" column—disconnection, fight or flight, and freeze/immobilization. Their arousal response (generated by the emotional and survival brain and the sympathetic nervous system) goes into action, flooding the body with stress chemicals such as norepinephrine, corticotrophin releasing factor, adrenocorticotrophin hormone, adrenaline, and cortisol, which prime their body to survive while suppressing their smart brain, memory function, and even their immune system.[4] One common avoidance behavior teachers often see is when they call on a student to answer a question, and the student suddenly "forgets," freezes, or acts silly. This signals that the student has not learned to feel safe when called upon, and is reacting to this perceived threat with "fight or flight" or immobilization responses. If such experiences are repeated and reinforced, patterns of avoidance become established as the student's default response, triggering the onset of the anxious brain and potentially the emergence of psychopathology.[5]

Again, the important point here is that the way a student learns to deal with stress—either with approach or avoidance—and meet their basic needs directly affects the development of their sense of self. In safe environments where students can engage in higher smart brain functioning (problem-solving, empathy, focus, critical thinking) resulting in new learning, they establish patterns of approach that support the development of their sense of positive self-esteem, agency, confidence, and capability. In

---

[3] Rossouw, *Neuropsychotherapy*.
[4] Rossouw, *Neuropsychotherapy*; Dahlitz, *The Psychotherapist's Essential Guide to the Brain*.
[5] K. Grawe, *Neuropsychotherapy: How the Neurosciences Inform Effective Psychotherapy* (New York, NY: Psychology Press, 2007).

unsafe environments where their brains and bodies stay in survival mode, thereby compromising higher cortical functioning and inhibiting new learning, they establish patterns of avoidance that ultimately weaken their self-esteem and confidence and encourage behaviors of self-protection.[6] For this reason, helping students develop a healthy sense of self—already a high priority to most parents—should be of considerable importance to school well-being and behavior response models.

THE SAFETY STOOL

I created the Safety Stool to help students and teachers understand how individuals approach or avoid meeting their basic needs and how this impacts one's sense of self. As you can see in the illustration below, the Safety Stool correlates directly to Rossouw's integrated model of the base elements of the theory of neuropsychotherapy on page 78.

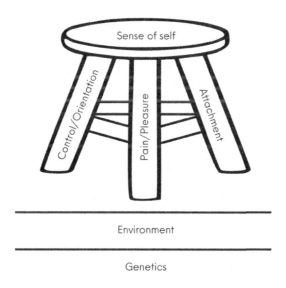

---

[6] Rossouw, *Neuropsychotherapy.*

To apply the safety stool, we start at the bottom, the foundation upon which everything we are and do rests—our genetic pool, genetic expression, and family history.

We all have families and genetics that we just cannot change. We do not get to choose our parents, biological gender, height, ethnic bearing, family bloodline and heritage, or if we are born with a genetic disability. Many of our students have family histories full of stressful experiences exacerbated by generations of limited financial skills, nutrition skills, or relational skills. Some of the families I have worked with face domestic violence, gambling, substance abuse, language barriers, cultural trauma, religious rigidity, criminal activity, mental health, and a range of other complex histories that color the way they experience or interpret interactions with others. Many combined experiences may be going on in our brains and our student's brains because of our genetics and history. Even as adults, many of us may be coming into our teaching profession from backgrounds of physical illness, disability, anxiety, or depression. All of these contribute to the foundation of our sense of self.

The next layer of the foundation is our present environment at home, at school, and in the wider culture, all of which can play a big part in defining the stability of the foundation upon which the safety stool stands. We may be attending a Christian school, secular private school, alternative school, home school, or public school, each of which has unique environmental factors to consider. We also have changing family environments and dynamics such as violence, mental health, and life skills, and dynamics in the wider culture like social media. All interactions in these environments play a part in the creation of a stable or unstable foundation for our sense of self to stand on, and in the case of children, they have no control over them. If this base is unstable at some level, or if the environment experiences a sudden quake (like a divorce), it is like putting a stool on uneven ground. Even if our stool (sense of self) is excellently constructed, it will become a bit wobbly on an uneven foundation and cause our sense of self, precariously located atop of the stool, to feel unstable.

As teachers, I believe we should apply the safety stool to ourselves as well as our students. Knowing who we are and where we have come from is essential if we are to guide our students on the journey of understanding their own sense of self. We need to become aware of what foundation our stool is standing on, and whether it is safe and secure, or unsafe and unstable. We need to consider if there is anything in our genetics or history that we or our students need support with. Do we or they need to see a doctor, a psychologist, or a psychiatrist for physical or emotional healing? We also need to look at how the current environment is affecting us and our students. Do we know something about the home environment our students are going home to each day? Is our current school or individual classroom creating the environment and culture we want to continue to be a part of, or do we recognize that fundamental changes are required?

Next, we can look at the construct of our three-legged stool, which reflects the coexistence of three basic needs—attachment, control/orientation, and pain avoidance/pleasure—has an essential role to play in supporting the seat of the stool, which is our sense of self, the way we feel and what we know to be true about ourselves. When these needs are met, our stool will be very stable, enabling us to be a powerful person as we interact with the world around us. If it is placed on some uneven ground, it may become a bit wobbly, but will probably be still functional. If any of these needs go unmet, however, we will find that our sense of self becomes unstable, wobbly, or may even threaten to collapse.

THE NEED FOR ATTACHMENT

It is commonly said that students need just *one* significant teacher, coach, or leader to come alongside them for them to succeed. While it generally needs to be an attachment that lasts longer than the twelve months a teacher typically spends with a student, it is true that one secure attachment can make an incredible impact in the life of any child, precisely because of how it nourishes and supports the development of their sense of self.

It's important to understand that each student's (and our own) ability to develop secure attachment is impacted by early childhood experiences. Specifically, this ability depends on the trust we build with our primary caregiver as an infant and how we experience trust or lack of trust through childhood into adolescence. Furthermore, according to John Bowlby, a pioneer of attachment theory, one's experience of attachment during childhood will remain relatively unchanged into adulthood.[7] For all of us, implicit early memories of interactions with caregivers continue to inform our understanding and interaction with the world.[8]

Citing Erik Erikson's theory of psychosocial development, which posits that the first task of every child in infancy is learning to trust his or her environment, Danny Silk explains that success or failure in this task centers around the "trust cycle" a child experiences with their primary caregiver.[9] It is worth noting that younger children rarely have the vocabulary to express specific needs, nor the cognitive capability to accurately determine what they need. The role of the parent is to accurately attune to the child's needs and respond accordingly to assist them to co-regulate and achieve comfort. For example when a baby cries, the parent attuned to their child responds with providing comfort through food, sleep, or hygiene. The trust cycle begins when the parent correctly attunes and responds to the child's needs. When the caregiver responds to the need and the child experiences satisfaction, the child is comforted and reassured, and the child learns that he can trust himself to express his needs and his caregiver to meet them in the future. This makes him more likely to express future needs, trusting that the caregiver will be able to meet them, and to develop a secure attachment to that caregiver. Alter-

---

[7] John Bowlby, *A Secure Base: Parent-Child Attachment and Healthy Human Development.* (New York: Basic Books. Inc, 1988).

[8] A. N. Schore, *The Science of the Art of Psychotherapy* (New York, NY: W.W. Norton & Company, 2012).

[9] Danny Silk, producer and director. *Keep Your Love On.* [DVD]. (Redding, California: Loving on Purpose, 2013).

natively, if a child expresses a need and receives either an unsatisfactory response or no response, then the need is left unsatisfied, no comfort is experienced, and mistrust begins to develop in the relationship, and the attachment becomes insecure.

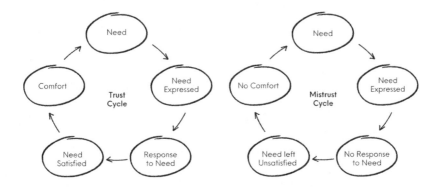

Central to this trust cycle, then, is the relationship between *attunement* and *attachment*. I referred to right-to-right brain attunement in the previous chapter. This involves two people and their two brains adjusting to one another through synchronicity, albeit subtly, as they resonate with the internal states of one another.[10] Attachment, or bonding, is the connection formed between the two brains through a felt experience—it is essentially the response to attunement.[11] Attunement therefore leads to attachment, the success of which results in the way that attachment is expressed in the relationship.

Right-to-right brain attunement and healthy attachment also sets the stage for right-to-left brain integration in the classroom. The right brain is responsible for experiencing emotions—both reactive fear responses or positive safe and secure emotions. The left brain is responsible for learning and thinking tasks. When a teacher achieves right-to-right brain attunement with his or her students by providing a safe, loving presence, this

---

[10] L. Cozolino, *The Neuroscience of Psychotherapy: Building and Rebuilding the Human Brain* (New York, NY: Norton, 2002).
[11] A. Montgomery, *Neurobiology Essentials for Clinicians: What Every Therapist Needs to Know* (New York: WWW Norton & Company, 2013).

compels the student to downregulate their stress response and instead activate both hemispheres of the neocortex (smart brain). Higher-level cortical functions such as problem-solving, reasoning, empathy, and applying context require an integration of both right-brain emotional signals and left-brain sense-making and logic. In order for this integration, which happens via the corpus callosum connecting the two hemispheres of the brain, to be successful, the student's brain must be free from negative environmental stimuli such as trauma or punishment.[12] The integration sequence begins with the right brain, because it is the emotional awareness of safety that encourages left-brain analysis, logic, and learning. This means that the transition from right-to-left brain is a process in which the student must first develop right brain attunement, bonding, and attachment with their teacher and only then transition into learning and thinking tasks. Montgomery warns that teachers who pursue left-brain integration hastily, before establishing attunement and sufficient attachment, may compromise safety and elicit a defense response. The student won't be engaging in learning until safety has been assured.

Simulating an experiment in which babies' reactions were monitored when their primary caregiver was present or separated,[13] Mary Ainsworth concluded that there are four attachment styles that develop between children and their primary caregiver. We frequently observe these styles in childcare, kindergarten, and prep classrooms at dropoff and pickup:

Secure attachment (balanced sympathetic and parasympathetic nervous systems). The babies showed some distress when their primary caregiver was absent and sought immediate reconnection upon their return. They displayed expressions of solid trust, resulting in conflict-free behaviors to satisfy their basic needs.

In the classroom, these students are observed to be attentive to the relationship with their teacher, seeking to please whilst also feeling safe to experiment and make mistakes while they explore their environment.

---

[12] Montgomery, *Neurobiology Essentials for Clinicians.*
[13] Rossouw, *Neuropsychotherapy*

In the early year levels, these students may display some distress when their parents leave them at school; however, upon seeing their teacher they transition quickly into the classroom.

Insecure-avoidant attachment (parasympathetically dominated behaviors). The babies showed no distress when their caregiver was absent and avoided reconnection upon their return. This suggests that poor satisfaction was expected from the caregiver, leaving the attachment needs unmet.

In the classroom this is often seen in students who are dismissive of the teacher altogether, reducing the possibility of emotional harm. Students display no expectation that the teacher will meet their needs and don't seek to have them met. These students take care of themselves. These students are often seen to ignore their parents entirely, running away from them at pickup time and not even glancing back when they are dropped off.

Insecure-ambivalent attachment (sympathetically dominated behaviors). The babies showed some distress when their primary caregiver was absent, yet oscillated between aggressive rejection and seeking connection upon their return. Other conflicting behavior showed up in this attachment style, such as a child who appeared disconnected also developing fears of being alone. This pattern is often the result of inconsistent parent availability or threat of abandonment.

In the classroom, these students may seek close proximity to the teacher and become distressed when the teacher needs to leave their side. These students can be clingy, and their fearful responses may become the focus of bullying behavior from peers. In alternative education, students with this style can behave very unkindly toward their teacher. For example, they can be dismissive and rejecting until the teacher's time is required elsewhere or the teacher resigns, then suddenly the student expresses intense desire to be connected with that particular teacher. These students are observed to be clingy and greatly distressed toward their parents at dropoff, yet demonstrate alternating aggression and comfort-seeking at pickup.

Insecure-disorganized/disoriented attachment (oscillating between sympathetic and parasympathetic nervous system). Upon the caregiver's return, the baby responded with bizarre behaviors such as avoidance (shunning connection, being dismissive), ambivalence (needing constant reassurance, needy), or disorganized attachments (no coping strategies). Often, children with this attachment style fail to develop meaningful relationships due to the lack of a consistent, supportive, and validating environment or experience.

In the classroom, these students are unpredictable, erratic, and can be emotionally challenging for staff. One day they are pushing you away; the next they become clingy and over-connected. Often they are sending opposing messages at the same time. The push/pull experience leaves teachers elated when the student appears to "approach connection" and then devastated when they withdraw it. Teachers are tempted to ask themselves, "What did I do? What is wrong with me?" Confusion often masks these relationships. Equally so, the parents of these students may be demonstrating similar attachment patterns in their behavior responses. These children are often impacted by trauma such as abuse or neglect, or their caregiver's preoccupation with their own problems.[14]

The experiment showed that the babies, and therefore children, considered most likely to thrive were those who were able to develop secure attachment styles,[15] and that the greatest factor contributing to secure attachment was the presence of a consistent, trustworthy caregiver who responded effectively to the child's needs.

The way a parent approaches an infant directly impacts their brain's structural development. The emotional reactivity of a parent lights up the infant's brain and passes on an emotional legacy that creates secure or insecure relationships.[16] On many occasions, I have seen children and parents who both react with the same emotionally reactive victim mind-

[14] Montgomery, *Neurobiology Essentials for Clinicians.*
[15] Rossouw, *Neuropsychotherapy.*
[16] B. Badenock, *Being a Brain-Wise Therapist: A Practical Guide to Interpersonal Neurobiology* (New York, NY: W.W. Norton & Company, 2008)

set—the apple really does not fall far from the tree. Therefore, working with a student to create neural pathways toward responsibility and ownership may require them to unwire and overcome significant learnings experienced in relationship with their caregiver. This is an extensive undertaking and will take many repetitions. Thankfully, schools are the perfect location for repetitive relational skill practice to occur.

Many students I work with, especially in alternative education, have insecure attachment styles—they have poor connectivity with parents and have had repetitive negative experiences with education staff. Recognizing a student's style and level of attachment is important, but what matters more is that I provide them with a consistent, trustworthy connection. This enables me to support the development of an earned secure attachment back to a primary caregiver or other significant figure, such as another teacher or authority figure, through applying the trust cycle consistently.

In one circumstance, I worked with a young woman named Peta who had experienced significant childhood trauma that had been exposed at school, requiring her to have regular sessions with a psychologist and with me as the consulting social worker. I learned that she was complying passively with, but not engaging in her sessions with the psychologist. For Peta to get the best possible care, I needed to assist her to develop an earned secure connection with her psychologist. One way that I could do this was by focusing on the development of our own connection, and then I could use this to transfer the connection to the psychologist. Due to my location within the school, I started by creating regular opportunities for Peta and me to be in proximity. This included scheduled sessions together but also opportunities for her to assist me with mundane tasks. The goal was to flood her with repeated positive engagements with an allied health professional. Throughout this time, I was looking for basic needs that could be met in order to produce comfort for Peta. This started with small needs at first—permission for incorrect nails for a special event, arranging to meet during a class she did not particularly enjoy, providing her with a book about photography which was her interest, saying hello when I saw her in the hallways, etc. As safety increased, we moved toward talking about the psychologist's office, what it looked like, and how she felt there. Finally, we role-played how to share the personal details that she wanted to share. Over a period of three weeks, Peta came bursting in with a smile to see me one morning and said, "I did it! I told the psych everything." Together, we celebrated what a huge step that was, and slowly over the proceeding weeks, Peta and I reduced our connection time as she earned a secure attachment with her psychologist, who would support her for years to come.

So what happened? Peta was avoiding connection with a psychologist because of a previous negative experience—an incredibly common scenario. School-based counselors or social workers are in prime positions to increase student's trust in seeking allied health support in the future. Students graduate and leave school, and it is important that when they do, they know how to access allied health and mental health support in their community as adults. Schools are not designed for students to return when they need future help—they are designed to teach students how to approach support and positive life experiences for the remainder of their adult years outside of the school environment. This includes accessing counseling and psychology.

Over time, Peta's confidence to approach connection with her new psychologist increased through many positive repetitions in connection with me. I was clear with Peta from the start that her psychologist was more equipped to support her in this next stage of her healing and I wanted the very best care for her. It was never a question of rejection or having to disconnect from me; rather, she learned how to manage connections with new support people because I had secured her trust. Eventually, as this new connection strengthened, my role was no longer required and naturally decreased. Throughout this process, I frequently spoke with Peta's primary caregiver and equally supported the development of a secure attachment between them through providing education on building trust. As a result of the secure attachments built with her caregiver and psychologist, Peta's sense of self thrived and she had a successful school journey that resulted in increased academic achievement, senior graduation, and continued psychology connection as she entered post-school life.

THE NEED FOR CONTROL/ORIENTATION

Psychologist Seymour Epstein considers control to be the most fundamental basic human need.[17] William T. Powers' perceptual control theory[18] reinforces this notion, suggesting that our cognitive and behavioral processes constantly seek for our goals and perceptions to be in alignment. When alignment does not occur, our sense of self is unsettled.

Orientation is an aspect of control that involves the ability to appraise a situation accurately to determine our options and choose actions that allow for the expression of control. Our strong propensity toward meeting our need for orientation produces behaviors that attempt to control our environment, or our perception of it, and to determine a maximum number of options available to us.

Pieter Rossouw notes that if a child experiences safety and the satisfaction of their basic survival needs and wants, their need for control will also be satisfied.[19] However, when their basic needs are left unmet despite their attempt to control the desired outcome, it activates their survival instincts. If, for example, a student trips and scrapes their knee on the concrete and cries to attract help from the duty teacher, who provides them with a Band-aid, they experience a manageable incongruence—that is, they learn that the environment does have dangers, but also that they have the ability to access protection and assistance when they encounter them, resulting in comfort and safety. If, however, the teacher responds to the child's cries by

---

[17] Seymour Epstein, "Cognitive-Experiential Self-Theory" in L.A. Pervin (ed), *Handbook of Personality: Theory and Research* (New York: Gilford, 1990),165-192.
[18] William T. Powers, *Behaviour and Control of Perception.* (New York: Aldine, 1973).
[19] Rossouw, *Neuropsychotherapy.*

reprimanding the child for running on the concrete, then the child experiences incongruence in their goal and perceives their environment as unable to meet their need. As such, a child may learn to avoid seeking assistance and comfort when they are hurt, unwell, or unsafe.

Not only that, when the child receives the message that their need for health, safety, and comfort are unimportant, this translates to, "You are unimportant," and can severely compromise a child's sense of self. Furthermore, if a child internalizes that others are more important than them, it is common for these children to focus their time, energy, and resources on "helping" their friends and getting involved in other people's lives as they cross over into codependent relationships. In short, if they cannot control the outcome of their own lives, they go to work attempting to control the outcome of other people's lives. Simultaneously, whilst they are "giving of themselves" to others, they are increasingly unable to manage the surging experiences of mistrust, disconnection, poor health, and complexities in their own life as they abdicate responsibility due to their perception that they are not in control, but are victims to the whim of others. Feeling out of control results in blaming external forces for not taking responsibility for their life, as they avoid decisions and services which would benefit them for fear of judgment, rejection, pain, and hard work. In turn, this makes them susceptible to violence, abuse, and unhealthy relational dynamics.

To meet the need for control/orientation, we look for opportunities to support children to identify their needs, consider their options, and manage their outcomes in healthy connection with their teachers and parents. Parents and teachers are therefore not acting as the rescuer and problem solver, but as an accessible tool and resource that the student can trust to approach as they resolve incongruences in their own lives.

As the example of the child with the scraped knee demonstrates, the child's need for control and orientation is closely linked with the need for secure attachment. We see this in the "trust cycle"—when a child expresses a need to a caregiver and the need is met, it equally produces trust in the caregiver (attachment) and trust in the child's own self-agency to do something that will result in their need being met (control). Conversely, when their need is not met, a child not only experiences a violation of attachment, but also of their sense of control in their environment.

Danny Silk notes that the behaviors of trust and connection that lead to secure attachment equally endorse freedom and choices within a relationship. He also adds that it is within the safety of a secure attachment that a parent or significant adult can provide a child the best and most effective guidance for making good choices.[20] Simply put, within a secure attachment, a child does not experience the threat of being controlled by someone or something else, or the need to control others or the environment, both of which are survival-driven. Instead, she can learn to control herself and use her smart brain to make good choices, which is what meets that core need for control/orientation and supports the development of healthy self-confidence. She can also willingly receive guidance and instruction from trusted adults. When attachment is lacking or insecure, however, she will naturally be looking for ways to gain a sense of control or protect herself from external controls.

This principle plays out every day in our schools. The behavior policy within a school environment plays an enormous role in informing students of their orientation and options in the classroom or on the playground. Even more crucially, the way teachers and staff teach and enforce behavior policies either enhance or discourage trust, connection, and attachment with students. Behavior policies basically fall into one of two categories—they are either informed by a fear-and-control system of punishment or a love-and-boundaries system of discipline. According to Danny, wherever fear-based control techniques are present in a culture or belief system, it triggers survival behaviors and limits thriving.[21] Here's his basic breakdown of the primary differences between the punishment and discipline approaches[22]:

---

[20] Silk, *Keep Your Love On*.
[21] Silk, *Keep Your Love On*.
[22] Adapted from Danny Silk, *Unpunishable: Ending our Love Affair with Punishment*. (USA California: Loving on Purpose, 2019).

PUNISHMENT	DISCIPLINE
Upholding the rules	Restoring the relationship
Pain is inflicted/imposed	Pain is embraced, learning to process pain
Confronting, owning, and changing behavior is irrelevant	Confronting, owning, and changing behavior is essential
Forgiveness is irrelevant	Forgiveness is essential
Stopping bad behavior	Transforming heart
Requires submission of control	Requires responsibility, self-control
Stopping bad behavior	Transforming heart
Good behavior is compliance and manipulative	Good behavior is fruit of love and character
Fear-driven	Love-driven
Goal of self-preservation (surviving)	Goal of connection (thriving)
External rules	Internal rules

Very simply, a student's basic need for control and orientation will not be met in a punishment-focused environment, but only one guided by discipline. Whichever school behavior culture is present (punishment or discipline) will likewise inform the way in which staff experience and are managed by executive leadership and even school boards who set the policies for the school. What is true is that all humans, including teachers, seek to control their options and outcomes free from oppression, control, fear of punishment, and manipulation.[23] A love-based environment, which requires high levels of freedom that come from choices, strengthens one's sense of control and subsequently one's sense of self.

Orientation and control in a school environment extends to both the students and the teachers and includes basic necessities such as holiday and event scheduling, subject timetabling, lesson planning, rules and expectations, and cultural expectations. Imagine for a moment a school environ-

---

[23] Silk, *Keep Your Love On*.

ment in which daily the lunch breaks are at different times, the subjects are unpredictable, and the rules change. Both students and teachers would enter a state of disorientation, not knowing if they were doing the right thing, unsure what to prepare, and uncertain how time will progress. A teacher planning a lesson needs clarity about the topic required, the class needs and adjustments, the teaching time, and many other details. To enter a classroom without this detail would result in a teacher potentially being poorly prepared, anxious, and feeling unsafe. Where a teacher can orientate themselves easily to the school expectations, routines, and lesson planning, they will begin to thrive and experiment. Feeling safe increases risk-taking, thinking outside the box, and exploration into creative teaching tools. Partner strong orientation and control with a positive connection with leadership, and you see teachers thrive in ingenuity and confidence. The students benefit from their teacher thriving and engage in the creative learning process as they equally take risks in their learning and development.

Too often, however, school staff experience a constantly changing environment. The most common complaints include the school growing too quickly without establishing consistent expectations, inconsistency in rule application, unpredictability of leadership to be available for support and then too involved when they do come, unclear behavior response options, frequently changing curriculum standards, and new students and staff who upset the thinly established equilibrium. Staff who are unable to orientate themselves effectively experience chaos around them, fail to secure a footing through positive leadership connections, become anxious and unhappy, and avoid creativity and connection. This, in turn, impacts the learning environment of the students. Left unchecked, staff become disillusioned, weary, and critical as they avoid being part of the solution. Eventually, burnout ensues, resulting in high staff turnover, and the cycle repeats as new staff impact the culture but are unable to orientate themselves to the unpredictable and unhappy internal culture. Not surprisingly, the students in these school cultures also increasingly display behaviors that are unpredictable, avoidant, and unhappy.

What is essential to every school environment is that when new staff or students arrive on site they have a well-developed orientation program that sets up the structure (the DNA of the school culture) on which they will cultivate the likelihood of each person approaching control and thereby taking responsibility for their own life choices. Much like a vine requires a trellis to grow in a healthy trajectory toward the sun, clear processes and procedures allow for grounding in one's self as we thrive in community and connection.

THE NEED OF PAIN AVOIDANCE AND PLEASURE MAXIMIZATION

The third leg of the stool is the need for pain avoidance or pleasure attainment. The pleasure principle was first recognised by Freud[24] in his theory of personality. Later, Epstein[25] and Grawe[26] agreed with the premise that a core human need was to maximize pleasurable experiences (joy!) and avoid painful or unpleasant experiences, whether physical, psychological, emotional, or social. Henson and Rossouw refer to it as "the mother of all needs."[27] Our neurological construct automatically classifies experiences as good or bad, providing feedback that then informs future decision-making.[28]

It is noteworthy that this leg of the Safety Stool is activated negatively and compromised when the previous two needs (attachment and control) remain unmet. This is because each of the basic needs are interconnected; thus, they can trigger activation in each other resulting in the simultaneous activation of multiple basic needs.

---

[24] Sigmund Freud, *Beyond the Pleasure Principle* (New York, NY: W. W. Norton & Company, 1959), original work published in 1920.
[25] Seymour Epstein, "Integration of the Cognitive and the Psychodynamic Unconscious," *American Psychologist*, 49, 8, 1994, pp. 709-724.
[26] Grawe, *Neuropsychotherapy*.
[27] C. Henson & Peiter J. Rossouw, *BrainWise Leadership: Practical Neuroscience to Survive and Thrive at Work* (Sydney: Learning Quest, 2013), 212.
[28] Rossouw, *Neuropsychotherapy*.

Grawe argues that one's goals and perceptions need to be aligned in order to achieve the maximal state of pleasure. With that said, how a student or person classifies an experience as good or bad depends on their current state or prior experience, and their capacity to do this accurately depends on a more primitive need—safety.[29] As an example of a state-dependent evaluation,[30] students may view playing a sport outside on a hot sunny day negatively in comparison to an indoor sport, yet positively on a cool day (and vice versa). A class speech, on the other hand, is something a student will perceive as good or bad based on their prior experience. A student who feels sick speaking in front of the class or has a memory of being laughed at by peers may classify speeches as bad (avoid), whilst his peer, who experiences a euphoric rush while presenting and positive laughter with peers, may classify speeches as good (approach). Consider the students known as the "class clowns." These students are likely to classify being laughed at for their humor as good, whilst being laughed at for not knowing the answer as a bad experience. Through repetition, they have learned to avoid the pain of being considered "dumb" by developing an option which increases pleasure through peer acceptance. Relearning taste preferences toward experiences is a complex process, but motivators such as positive self-evaluations and social compliance play a large part in influencing these changes. For example, a teenager (or adult) learning to enjoy the taste of alcohol may be motivated by desiring social acceptance, which is linked to attachment and self-esteem enhancement, and over time drinking alcohol becomes the automatic preference of the neural evaluative process.

Dopamine is the neurotransmitter involved in pain avoidance and pleasure maximization.[31] One of the roles of dopamine is to strengthen the synapses, the repetition of which increases the likelihood that the same behavior will be selected again in the future. This occurs in the

---

[29] Rossouw, *Neuropsychotherapy.*
[30] Rossouw, *Neuropsychotherapy.*
[31] Henson & Rossouw, *BrainWise Leadership.*

instance of both pleasurable and painful experiences; nevertheless dopamine will only enhance motivation toward engagement, not the experience of engaging pleasurably. It is therefore less about avoiding pain and more about motivation toward something pleasurable, even if it is the false promise of pleasure.

Especially in the classroom, students whose behavior appears to be reflecting mainly pain-avoidant choices can quickly become problematic. We must understand that these students are actually seeking a restoration of joy and pleasure maximization. Sensing a potentially distressing situation, these students' amygdalae signal the stress response, and they will do anything to engage in what they perceive as a pleasurable outcome. It's not just about pleasure, it's also about comfort. Dopamine propels us toward fulfilling what we perceive to be pleasure, yet too often we are believing a lie about what is true pleasure or comfort. For example, the pain of not being able to get a reward fuels the craving for that thing, which previously brought pleasure, again. Could this be equally true for classroom bribes as it is for the high received from illicit substance use?

One of our highest goals as teachers is to help our students associate learning with pleasure maximization. The process of mastering new ideas, concepts, and skills is endlessly rewarding, but it does involve work, struggle, and discomfort—that is, pain. We want to do all we can to encourage our students to discover that a greater pleasure lies on the other side of enduring the temporary discomfort of wrestling to understand or execute something new. If we do not do this, our students are likely to gravitate towards the seeming comfort of pain avoidance and stasis in their learning. Students may be observed to refuse to answer the teacher, quit a team sport, or even drop out of school because they sense there is greater pleasure, or at least less pain, in avoiding those activities. Quitting or saying no becomes the avenue for control, and if repeated often enough, dopamine enhances the likelihood that the student will select this option again and again. Optimal learning occurs when our students experience neural proliferation (new neural pathways). If students become more likely to avoid new experiences because they perceive true pleasure and comfort comes from "staying the same," then the establishment of new learning can be stunted. Unfortunately, these pseudo pleasures and comforts never actually bring pleasure and comfort. Yet as dopamine propels them toward it, they begin to believe the lie that it is true comfort, that leveling off where they are is "good."

For these students, focusing on developing new patterns of approach is paramount. This is where creating connected classroom cultures becomes so important. Creating healthy relationships will allow students to see the lies they have believed about where true pleasure comes from and learn a new way of connecting and getting their needs met. If these new patterns can be established and consistently repeated, they will become strengthened by dopamine as they become part of the students' new behavior toolkit. This is a key reason why a connected classroom culture, which reinforces pleasurable learning through new experiences, is a necessity if you want to influence future positive behavior choices. Pleasure and joy are essential for thriving. Without it our neural systems stay on high alert, triggering a fear response to minor threats. When we downregulate the experience of fear, our students increase in new learning, productivity, and creative thinking; simultaneously, dopamine flows as joy increases.

Substance use and addiction are commonly discussed when reflecting on the role of pain avoidance and pleasure maximization. Bruce Alexander and colleagues theorized that illicit substances are a means to numb pain, and to test this, created an experiment referred to as "Rat Park."[32] Prior to developing Rat Park, rats were given opiates in their cages and observed over time to ignore food and water in their bid for more opiates, effectively starving to death. Apparently, feeding their addiction overrode their desire for survival. Rat Park was an enriched environment in which some opiate-dependent rats were brought to live and given free

---

[32] S. H. Gage, & H.R. Sumnall, "Rat Park: How a Rat Paradise Changed the Narrative of Addiction," *Addiction*, 114(5), 2019, 917-922. https://doi.org/10.1111/add.14481.

access to opiates. Despite their opiate dependency prior to entering Rat Park, these rats largely ignored the opiates offered, and after trying it several times, settled into life in community with the other rats. Though limited in its scope, the Rat Park experiment suggests that true pleasure derived from an enriched environment and connection is a significant predictor against addiction, as these rats no longer experienced the effects of pain from a caged, isolated existence.

Ashley was a young man I knew who, after years of emotional and verbal degradation, family breakdown, and unhealthy lifestyle, became disconnected from his parents. He learned early on that his peers seemed more encouraging and, seeking the false pleasure of peer acceptance and money, Ashley dropped out of school at Year 9. Soon after, he started experimenting with substance use. Substances quickly became his tool for avoiding pain. As he grew older, Ashley's substance use expanded into dealing and criminal activity. Ashley described the substances and the people associated with drug use as the only option he knew to regulate his low sense of self, which was constantly unstable.

Hitting rock bottom, Ashley decided to approach his greatest fear—himself. With professional help and almost a year of rehab, Ashley saw the restoration of strong family connections. He also pushed through the initial pain of approaching his fears and self-perception. For Ashley, approaching pain became the vessel in which he broke free of his negative self-beliefs and started to approach true pleasure by developing strong connections, healthy lifestyle, and taking responsibility for his life. This included returning to honorable work, staying connected to mentors, and setting up a home so that he was able to get access to his son.

Many of the students I come in contact with as a school social worker mirror Ashley's story. Disconnected from significant others, these young people seek to avoid painful experiences by approaching what appear to be pleasurable ones but rather through their false pleasure create cycles of pain in their lives. It is our responsibility in the classroom to ascertain how to offer new true pleasurable experiences to our students whilst simultaneously teaching them how to process pain because life is full of unpredictable events. We don't need to avoid pain, we need our students to learn how to approach healthy pleasurable and joyful relationships and experiences. Ashley often states, "Connection is the opposite of addiction," by which he means he has discovered that the pleasure of being in healthy connection far outweighs the pleasure of addiction—much like the rats in Rat Park.

A discussion on pleasure maximization is not limited to substance use, but may also include videogames, social media, gambling, sex, and shopping, to name a few common pain distractions. All of these distractions present the allure of false pleasure through pain avoidance that creates cycles of pain and terminates learning, thus creating a dilemma between true pleasure, which may require approaching pain. Before we consider the impact of destructive tools like these, however, we must consider this—where did young people and adults learn to be deceived by the lure of "false pleasure"? The answer lies in what they have learned to rely on for *regulation*—the ability to regulate the up- or downregulated responses from autonomic arousal. When we perceive that an experience will bring distress or pain that will impact our internal state, priming us for survival, then we will apply the most familiar tools we have to assure our survival (not necessarily homeostasis).

What I commonly observe is children being taught to regulate their arousal state through *object regulation*—external tools that distract or avoid responding to emotional responses altogether. For example, a parent puts a phone in front of their child when they are upset to distract them; I have seen many teachers and teacher aides do this as well. Other methods to object regulate include food, screen time, or present bribes. Object regulation does not require meaningful trust and connection with another human that leads to the development of self-regulation tools. Soon, these children become adults who don't know how to connect with someone and ask for help, but rather avoid pain through engaging in behaviors such as mindlessly scrolling on their phone, significant hours playing videogames, accessing pornography, gambling, shopping sprees, or even the onset of eating disorders. Remember, repeated behaviors are strengthened by dopamine, which motivates the student toward the behavior regardless of whether it is a painful or pleasurable experience. Thus, these tools are reinforced as future neural pathways despite not being able to provide genuine, life-giving pleasure maximization.

Co-regulation, in contrast to object regulation, involves parents or significant caregivers being present in moments of stress (especially in the first three years of life) and responding by using their voice, presence, attunement, gestures, and intonation to assist children to feel connected and understood. It is important to note that the caregiver does not rescue the child from their emotional arousal, but meets them where they are. From within this safe connection, babies and children can start to develop skills to self-soothe strong emotions, calming themselves as they regulate their arousal state. When a child learns co-regulation through repetition (reinforcing dopamine release), then in future moments of similar stress the child will start to confidently self-regulate their own responses rather than requiring the ongoing assistance of an adult.

During secondary school, the brain undergoes significant changes. The neural processes that seek reward and pleasure overtake the development of cognitive control systems that respond with responsible decision making and planning.[33] As a result, a teenager's emotional responses bias them to seek short-term reward over long-term benefit. Co-regulation during this developmental period is especially important, highlighting the role teachers and caregivers have in stepping toward relationship with their teen rather than away, as their teen may be requesting in their bid for independence.

In the classroom, teachers apply many tools to co-regulate with the whole class or individual students. In the last chapter, I touched briefly on how breathing, mindfulness, and grounding techniques can enhance

---

[33] K.D. Rosanbalm, & D. W. Murray, "Caregiver Co-regulation Across Development: A Practice Brief," OPRE Brief #2017-80 (Washington, DC: Office of Planning, Research, and Evaluation, Administration for Children and Families, US. Department of Health and Human Services, 2017). https://fpg.unc.edu/sites/fpg.unc.edu/files/resources/reports-and-policy-briefs/Co-RegulationFromBirthThroughYoungAdulthood.pdf

co-regulation in the classroom. You may also call students to the "sacred mat," where together we cross our legs and breathe deeply, provide a transition song to move to activities or to gain focus, or take the child's hand when speaking with them. The tools teachers use are endless. The teacher who knows how to self-regulate becomes a force to enhance co-regulation with their students.

Self-regulation then is what we want all of our graduates to master. Self-regulation is just that—the ability to regulate your own feelings, thoughts, or actions associated with distress and return them to homeostasis. One of the tools students develop through consistent co-regulation is the recognition that sometimes self-regulation requires a significant other to be a part of the process. Self-regulation increases a student's ability to approach difficult problems and develop meaningful relationships. Consequently, the dopamine release related to these pleasurable experiences increases the likelihood that they will be chosen again in the future.

Object and co-regulation is not limited to our classrooms. Let's talk about our staff rooms for a minute. How common is it that after a tough day or a disrupted week, the leadership team sends a box of donuts or serves food at the enforced staff meeting to soothe the adults? Do you know of staff who are going home and engaging in substance abuse, compulsive shopping, or mindless technology use? Rather than teaching our staff that after a difficult day they should eat their feelings, school administrators would benefit from increasing opportunities for staff to engage in co- and self-regulation. This could look like self-regulation spaces where staff engage in mindfulness or meditation (such as a labyrinth reflective garden) or equipping a quiet booth with a Safe & Sound Integrated Listening System to support staff to regulate their autonomic nervous system. When higher levels of distress are involved, administrators are further encouraged to provide co-regulation through a trustworthy mentor program, quality training, and professional supervision. These techniques are far more effective than sending food to a staff room where the occupants sit around commiserating and repeating their distress, strengthening the likelihood of the experience and their emotive reaction repeating itself in the next lesson.

Every experience is either categorized as pleasurable or painful, though of course, as we have reflected, my experience and yours can be very different. The extent to which each student (or teacher) will approach or avoid pain/pleasure is impacted by many life experiences, but comes back to, "What is this student controlling for?" I am looking to understand who their closest connections are. Is it a parent, a specific teacher, or a peer who is impacting their decisions? And what is informing the behavior? Are they approaching or avoiding responsibility or connection?

LOOKING IN THE MIRROR

The same safety stool principles apply to us as adults. We all come with our own backgrounds, which may include anxiety in our past due to our mental health or experiences in past workplaces, and may, like many of our students, be coming into a cultural environment we are not used to (foundation). We may be struggling with wanting our students to like us and affirm our worth, and may even be subconsciously or consciously looking for a codependent attachment with students or even our team members, wanting them to help us to feel or look good (attachment). Perhaps our last workplace set a high standard for perfectionism and mistakes were met with punishment, thus priming us to expect that our behavior will be externally enforced (control/orientation). We also may approach or avoid pleasure/pain due to our own sense of worth or perceived needs (pain/pleasure).

I encourage you to take some time asking yourself the following questions:

- What is driving my sense of self and self-worth?
- Do I have skills in developing secure attachments or do I need support to develop this area?

- Is my goal disconnection with colleagues or students in order to avoid pain in our relationship?
- Am I trying to micromanage my environment because I do not want my team to think I am doing a bad job?
- Am I underachieving for fear that I will be asked to take on more work, or worse, am I overacheiving lest I be found out to be incompetent?
- Do my students experience a punishment or discipline-based environment?

Remember, if any one basic need is not being fulfilled, our sense of self becomes unstable and we will find ourselves acting out our insecure emotions, which is no fun for anyone. If as teachers we are acting out our emotions, this can quickly transfer onto thirty little people or teenagers who are sitting in front of us. It can spread to other staff in the staffroom and multiply very quickly, resulting in unsettled class environments, negative staff room gossip, increased stress, conflict, dissatisfaction, and eventually burnout.

It is essential for us to become comfortable working through these elements of the safety stool ourselves. When we become powerful people and model healthy, approach-based behaviors for identifying and meeting our needs, we can start to help our students unpack why they are reacting and behaving emotively and guide them toward making similar choices themselves.

As we've discussed, when students act out their emotions it can look like a tantrum, disrespect, non-compliance through to simply shutting down, or fearful compliance—all avoidance behaviors. When students never learn to recognize where these behaviors are coming from and what they actually need, those patterns of avoidance are likely to continue. They will stop wanting to be at school, wanting to take risks in skill extension, and wanting to learn, which ultimately inhibits them from thriving academically and in relationships with peers and teachers. But if we can help them recognize that they are reacting emotively and help them figure out which leg of the stool may be compromised, we can then help them build a plan to develop self-control, choose approach behaviors, and manage those feelings more effectively in the future.

Jenny was a senior student with learning disabilities. Despite being seventeen years old, she presented emotionally as a ten-year-old. Over a period of days, she became more irritable and dysregulated in her emotions. She was observed to start bringing her teddy to school, curling up in a ball, and sucking her fingers for long periods of time during the day, which disrupted her learning and her class considerably. Jenny's emotional state kept escalating and erupted into a meltdown in which she repeated the phrase "Don't send me home" over and over. Initially, her teachers, concerned about abuse at home, called me to speak with Jenny. I moved Jenny to a calm, darkened space where she could lie down, be removed from peers and well-meaning teachers, and had access to water and food. Jenny clutched her teddy, repeating, "Don't send me home." I stayed present, calm and waited. Using deep breathing and asking mindful questions about what her senses were experiencing, Jenny slowly calmed down.

Next, I wanted to explore Jenny's experience. Her teacher was pressuring me to consider abuse. However, I saw no notable patterns or signs of abuse. Aware of her regressed emotional age, I considered what her previous experiences of approach and avoidance at school were like. I took a narrative approach to get Jenny to "tell the story" of her last school. Simply put, Jenny's memory was that anytime she felt emotional, she would be sent home because she would be in trouble at school. Moreover, her secure connection was with her mother, whom she did not want to disappoint. Feeling like her school environment had become unsafe when another student touched her teddy, Jenny felt internally unable to manage her strong emotions of pain. Avoiding seeking help from a teacher and being unable to speak with her mother, Jenny's emotional state of anxiousness grew. Unfortunately, having nowhere to go in the classroom and feeling like she was out of options, Jenny transitioned into the fetal position as her internal meltdown erupted. I phoned Jenny's mother, they spoke, and a few minutes later, Jenny was sitting up eating her lunch and chatting readily.

As Jenny and I unpacked her experience, we were able to identify ways to increase her sense of safety and orientation in the classroom. She identified a quiet place where she wanted to go to self-regulate in the classroom. Jenny's love for art became a tool she could use to seek pleasure even during times of pain. She asked for teachers to be made aware not to frequently check in on her, as this escalated her anxiety. She wanted to please them, yet is fearful of their reaction. She recognized that speaking to her mother has an immediate calming effect if she was unable to self-regulate on her own. With a plan in hand, the staff and Jenny were able to navigate her success in the classroom and increase their own connection with one another.

A few weeks later, I became aware that Jenny and her boyfriend had broken up, a significant emotional event. I was interested to see how Jenny handled this in light of the plan we had made. I found Jenny sitting in her safe place. As I approached, she said, "I'm sad."

"It's okay to feel sad," I empathized.

"I would like to do some art," was Jenny's next statement. Not only was Jenny using her plan, she was approaching something pleasurable whilst processing her pain. She calmly worked on an art task before returning to class for the remainder of the day, knowing she could speak about her feelings with her mother when she got home.

JOYFUL RESPONSIBILITY

Putting aside the complex neuroscientific language, the truth remains that the degree to which students have a strong sense of self and the likelihood that they will approach, rather than avoid, new concepts is directly correlated to their experience of connection (attachment), freedom (orientation/control), and love (pain avoidance/pleasure). As I observe students, I am constantly asking questions about their safety stool. What needs are they expressing through their behavior? Is our attachment secure, our brains attuned, and our hearts connected? What are they trying to control in their environment? Are they trying to orientate themselves to the new environment of our school? Are they under the illusion that they can control me or their teachers? Is there an issue around pleasure and pain? Are they avoiding being embarrassed by having to read in front of their friends so they don't want to put their hand up? Are they making jokes so that their friends will laugh at them and they don't feel incompetent?

Our goal isn't simply to teach students information, but to coach them toward being powerful people with a stable and secure sense of self and the habits of approach to manage their emotions and meet their needs. We do this first by role-modeling what it looks like to be secure and powerful ourselves, and then by offering a loving presence with the goal of establishing secure attachment, trust, and empowering discipline in our connection with them. It is not that bad things, sudden unexpected changes, or major life events won't happen—we know they will. This is why we must teach our students how to take responsibility for their own lives and outcomes amidst difficult seasons that will inevitably come. We do this by creating safe places for risks to be taken, messes to be made, learning to occur, problems to be solved, and relationships to be restored through using tools of approach. This gives our students the opportunity to learn that taking responsibility for their own lives is a positive experience that increases happiness and pleasure and can be replicated the next time a mistake or life event happens. I call this level of maturity *joyful responsibility*.

6

THE POWERFUL TEACHER

I OFTEN HEAR FROM school leaders, teachers, and even parents the wistful hope that if they implement these strategies perfectly, then the incidence of unwanted behaviors will go down. That is like wishing that your students were adults—and none of us adults are perfect either. Loving our Students on Purpose is not about stopping children from being children. Remember, these children are professional mistake-makers.[1] Unwanted behaviors are going to keep happening. Rather, it is about developing tools to be powerful and manage ourselves whilst we guide our students as they make mistakes and clean up messes, which they get better at as they become adults. This chapter is therefore about you.

The tools we are going to be applying to the education context reflect concepts from Danny Silk's resources, including *Unpunishable, Culture of Honor, Keep Your Love On,* and *Loving our Kids on Purpose.*[2] Consider purchasing these resources for an expansion of these concepts and a broader application into different spheres of influence, such as parenting, marriage,

---

[1] Danny Silk, producer and director. *Loving our Kids on Purpose.* [DVD]. (Redding, California: Loving on Purpose, 2013).
[2] Danny Silk, *Unpunishable: Ending Our Love Affair with Punishment and Building a Culture of Repentance, Restoration, and Reconciliation.* (Sacramento, California: Loving on Purpose, 2019); Danny Silk, *Culture of Honor* (Shippensburg, PA: Destiny Image, 2009); Danny Silk, *Keep Your Love On* (Redding, CA: NewType Publishing, 2015); Danny Silk, *Loving Our Kids on Purpose* (Shippensburg, PA: Destiny Image, 2008).

and leadership. Together, these tools will assist you to build relationships that are going to decrease fear and increase connection and love, because that is what motivates us toward healthy connections with our students and creates an opportunity for them to be in the optimal learning zone, which is everyone's goal. The combination of these tools is useful for helping us understand how to first be powerful people and how then to become powerful teachers in our classroom and in our school environments.

In understanding what a powerful teacher looks like, we need to explore how "powerfulness" and "powerlessness" are expressed—and what those words *don't* mean. As Danny clarifies, if you have ever heard of someone described as powerful, you might assume he or she would be the loudest teacher in the room, the one telling everyone else what to do, making and enforcing the rules, dominating staff meetings and making the most demands on staff. However, this is not powerful. Powerful does not mean controlling or dominating. In fact, a controlling, dominating teacher is the very opposite of a powerful teacher.

Two of the most common statements that I hear from teachers are, "They are out of control," and "The system/students/parents make me feel powerless." Many teachers don't realize they can be powerful or even that they ought to be. They are trained early on that they are not responsible for their reactions. The students are, and their job is to comply and obey the school and administration rules. However, this is not accurate. For us to teach our students to become powerful people, we first need to understand how we can become powerful people and thereby powerful teachers—teachers who live fearlessly because they carry an internal culture of love, connection, and responsibility; teachers who carry joy.

The powerful teacher:

1. focuses on managing themselves
    *   whilst empowering students to manage themselves.
2. pursues the goal of connection
    *   whilst teaching students to take responsibility for their half of the connection.

Powerful teachers have a plan for how they will manage themselves and what they are going to do when a student makes a mess in front of them. Not only that, powerful teachers daily provide opportunities for students to courageously fulfill their potential without the restraint of fear. You are going to learn how to guide your students into being powerful people, because you are going to be a powerful teacher.

MY PERSONAL JOURNEY FROM POWERLESS TO POWERFUL

If you are like me, then you know how it feels to stand in front of students, colleagues, and leadership wondering, "How long will it take them to find out I am an imposter? How long before they realize I am a fraud and not actually who they think I am?" I have heard this from many educational and leadership staff, and I was there once myself.

My journey to becoming powerful started with me reading *The Business of Honor* and learning that I was indeed a valuable and worthy person.[3] To recognize myself as valuable required me to go on a journey to overcome the lie that I was of no value and therefore replaceable. We often hear this term used in the workplace: "People are a replaceable commodity." Collins Dictionary asserts that if something is "replaceable," it means you can throw it away when you are finished and put a new one in its place. It goes on to say that if you refer to someone as replaceable, you mean that they are not so important that someone else could not take their place. Replaceable could therefore be defined as someone or something of no worth, worthless.[4]

As a reflection of words spoken over me by employers, I had internalized a "truth" that I was replaceable and therefore worthless. As a result, I was driven by overachieving, performing for acceptance, and

---

[3] Bob Hasson and Danny Silk, *The Business of Honor.* (Loving on Purpose, 2017).
[4] s.v., "replaceable," Collins Dictionary, https://www.collinsdictionary.com/dictionary/english/replaceable.

fearfully trying to be all things for all people lest they learn the truth and discard me. When I was coming from a place of fear and powerlessness, I believed that the leadership, parents, staff, or students were in control of me. I handed them the keys to my life, and I received my worth from how they connected or disconnected with me. My performance-driven life came with no satisfaction, causing me to slowly develop burnout and eventually rebel as I fought to have control of my life again.

I was constantly afraid others would have no use for me, so I worked long hours, perfected perfectionism, put others on impossible pedestals, and took over-responsibility and over-caring to ridiculous levels. Sure, the students and staff I worked with looked like they were thriving, but in truth, I was working harder on many of their lives than they were. Bitterness crept in as I judged those around me to be lazy or not working as hard. I felt like I was taking all the hits. I became a celebrated, workaholic scapegoat. My self-worth was so low that I believed this was my lot in life. I could help others by being a martyr, a "worthy victim." I did not yet know that I could say no, or that I even should. In my powerless state, I could not tell what my responsibility was and what belonged to others. Any sign of conflict and I would swoop in to clean up the mess and take ownership, absolving others of their responsibility. Often, I would take the blame for others to "save" them from perceived punishment.

I remember one time a colleague asked me to support her in a parent meeting. I had taken notes on her behalf and afterward I gave my notebook to her so that she could type them up. The day got busy, and my colleague was called away from her desk. Unknowingly a group of students broke into her office and tore the notes from the parent meeting out, effectively stealing my notes. I had never had my notes stolen, highly valuing security and privacy. It felt like such a violation; however, I responded by taking the blame—they were my notes after all. I admitted the mistake to the parents, and I reported myself to my supervisor. Internally, I felt angry that my colleague did not take ownership, as she was the one who left the notebook out on the desk. Yet I felt powerless, and I took over-responsibility too far. It is easy to want to "save" others from their own mistakes, but it is not helpful for the other person who does not get to experience the weight of responsibility.

I was hurting, crushed under the weight of over-responsibility I had created for myself. I had lowered my own value and had a trail of broken-ness following me, all of which was about to be directly reflected to me with nowhere to hide. In truth, the journey to becoming powerful was a painful one and it did not happen overnight. For me, being powerless was so familiar that I did not recognize it. Even after spending ten years reading and listening to Loving on Purpose, I was still blind to my own powerless behavior. It was finally exposed when I was invited to spend a few weeks with Danny and Sheri Silk, and the Loving in Purpose team, which not surprisingly is made up of some of the most powerful people I have ever met. This environment was love on steroids. Little did I know that my broken spots were about to be exposed.

Even before I left, I was questioning, "Why me? I don't deserve this honor. They are going to be so disappointed with me." I was sending my-self so much emotional junk mail, my inbox was overflowing. It was not humility; it was a powerless mindset to think that I was so worthless I did not deserve to be a part of the LoP family. I felt guilty for taking leave from work, for being chosen over others, for the generosity shown me. I even felt shame when others cheered me on. I have on a few occasions been so fearful and afraid that I became frozen in silence. This was one of those times.

What I saw and experienced in the Silk home was transformational. I would like to say it was an immediate transformation, but in fact, it was the beginning of a two-year journey. I arrived close to midnight in Sac-ramento and immediately felt embarrassed as Danny Silk himself picked me up from the airport and lifted my bag into the back of the truck. He loved me enough to stay up late, drive out to get me, and bring me into his home. Boom, love! Over the course of those few weeks, I started to understand the gut-wrenching cry of many of my new students who literally implore, "Don't love me," because being exposed yet still loved unconditionally "hurt." It required me to face the lies I believed about myself and start to dig up some painful and unhelpful self-perceptions that had been allowed to fester over the years. It required me to let go of who I thought I was and accept a new narrative of a woman who was worthy to be loved, chosen, and cherished.

The experience of coming into a culture of love has opened my eyes to what it is initially like for many new students or families who come into a connected classroom culture. Being loved despite the lies we tell ourselves can be painful, because let's face it—we don't believe we deserve it. You will see this with many of your new students. When you keep your love on, at first they seem to hide, duck, and weave to get away. They shut down and seemingly push you away. But eventually they can't fight it any longer and they stop running and start to connect back.

On the first morning, Danny invited me to chat in the living room. I remember we got to talking about ballroom dancing, a hobby of mine, and Danny shared funny stories about Sheri and him trying to teach themselves from YouTube. Together we laughed and connected over something we had in common.

Inside, however, I was telling myself of a different narrative. Earlier that year, my dance school had hosted a gala ball. I was very excited, as it was my first ball. I had a sparkling gown, and my hair and makeup were carefully applied. I remember feeling excitement and anticipation as my dad came downstairs to see me. "You look different," was all he said. My heart dropped. It became a repetitive phrase throughout the night, and afterward when anyone saw photos the standard phrase was, "You look different." I had not realized how much I longed to hear that I was beautiful. This was my internal narrative whilst sharing how much joy ballroom dancing brought into my life. Polite smile on the outside, broken heart on the inside.

The next moment, Ady, Danny's granddaughter, bounded into the room, all smiles and full of indiscriminate kindness. She had been drawing and wanted to show us her artwork. Danny was the model grandfather, poring over her drawings, praising her, and calling out her gifting and talent. Ady beamed and confidently went on with drawing more pictures, pushing her creative limits. I smiled encouragingly as Ady held up another picture.

Inside, I was telling myself of a different narrative. As I watched Ady, I remembered how my mom, who is an incredibly talented artist, would encourage me to do art. She would buy me art supplies and speak words of encouragement that one day I would be an artist. For my birthday one year, she bought me an art kit that would be the envy of any little girl. I responded by turning my heart away from my mom. I was angry at being "pushed toward art," and rebelliously started to withdraw from experimenting with any artistic talent. If I did do something creative and was praised, I felt ashamed and embarrassed. And so, I kept my heart turned off toward myself and my family.

I had never allowed myself to experience the depth of love the Silk family lived out so naturally. Not because it did not exist in my home—it did—but because my heart was turned away from my parents and slowly, I allowed it to be turned away from more and more people. I lived in constant fear of rejection and I was so ready to be perceived as unlovable I started to act as if I was already unlovable.

As I sat in Danny's living room, I started to reflect on the hardness of my heart and where it was turned. How much pain must it have caused others when I turned my heart away from them—away from my family, away from loved ones, away from my friends? A raw depth of sorrow arose, and it was good. It was time to allow the infected splinter to be removed— the splinter was the lie that I was worthless and replaceable. I had ignored this splinter for so long—just like I once ignored a large splinter in my foot, which I did not want to get removed because I knew I would have to have a small surgical procedure, which would hurt even more. As a result, the skin had started to grow over it and an infection set in, causing pus and swelling. Eventually the pain of the infection outweighed my fear of a surgical incision and I had the procedure to get it removed. In the same way, the time had come for some heart surgery.

I have an incredible capacity for pain, so much so that I was prideful of my capacity. But love and goodness, being blessed and cared for—this really shook me up. I could understand deserving pain. It was a lot harder to accept unmerited favor and blessing, and harder still to believe that I was a valuable and one-of-a-kind person. As my time with the Silks continued and my belief of worthlessness was fully exposed, I went silent, withdrawing into myself. Unable to connect or talk, I felt even more embarrassed and ashamed.

By the time I came back to Australia, I had decided that no matter how awkward and uncomfortable it felt, I was going to turn my heart toward my dad and my mom. I was going to approach pain and break through to pleasurable connections. This started awkwardly at first, by forcing myself to share with them more information about my life. Only a week after returning home, I was heading to a social dance, dressed up and looking forward to socializing with my friends. When I got home, I noticed that my dad had waited up, and as I came in the door he said, "Here's my beautiful daughter." The walls were coming down. I started noticing all the loving ways my dad had been keeping his love on toward me and that his heart had always been turned toward me. It is the most amazing feeling in the world when your dad speaks life over you.

I was turning my heart toward my parents, and they were holding their hearts firmly toward me. I know what it is like to be the kid, the student, with their heart turned away from their parents or teacher. I have had a glimpse of the pain my parents must have felt as I kept my distance from them because I couldn't believe the truth that I am worthy to be beloved, chosen, and cherished.

Immediately upon discovering this truth, my life appeared to start unraveling. Why? Well, I had created relationships with other people around me who benefitted from my powerless behavior—my colleagues and leadership, and even my friends. Many of these relationships were characterized by me working harder on their lives than they were, taking too much responsibility, and being self-deprecating out of fear of rejection. When I stopped behaving in my normal powerless way, these people started displaying strong negative emotions to attempt to recalibrate me back to being powerless. I even had one principal demand that I "lower myself in their presence." It was not that any of these people were bad; rather, they had come to have a certain expectation of me because of my behavior, and when I changed my self-belief their expectations were no longer being achieved. Others, however, celebrated the freedom I had discovered. Some even drew courage from my testimony and took steps to becoming powerful themselves. It was in this season that I learned who my true friends were—they continued to love me for who I was, and this, I learned, did not depend on my performance.

The more I developed value for myself, the more my boundaries started to reflect my value. I actively surrounded myself with others who were already powerful people and had high value for themselves. These people encouraged me in my worth and uniqueness. Subsequently, I developed more confidence and started to consider the importance of my boundaries, which were set by my yes and my no. Setting boundaries for myself helped me to make decisions that reflected value for myself and my love of others. I actively reduced overachieving and stretching myself too thin, I became clear about what I would and would not do, I started to let other people experience the weight of responsibility in their own lives, and when they did not like this experience, I shook off any blame and refused to rescue them. Some people in my life quickly left, and through this experience I learned that as I increased my self-worth, there would be some people who wanted to stay in co-dependent, powerless behaviors and I could not do anything about their half of the connection. I grieved these friendships and connections.

This increase in worth also significantly impacted my workplaces and colleague relationships. Learning that I was not to blame or even responsible for the disturbances, politics, or conflict in the various schools

I worked in released me from the unreasonable and unachievable burden to be the "savior." I took time to discover the professional qualities and boundaries I wanted to offer in my workplace, and I clarified the type of leadership and culture I wanted to commit my time, energy, and resources to. Powerful people are generally not celebrated in a culture that thrives on powerless behavior. It was because I had a firm foundation of worth and love that I no longer fell "victim" to the rejection of a workplace and instead saw the freedom and choice I had selecting the right fit for me.

Powerless and powerful look and feel very different. When I was operating as powerless, I was left feeling distressed, unable to change my situation, and fearful. In a work culture, powerlessness is often experienced as fear of failure due to unspoken rules that result in avoidable mistakes and subsequent dressings-down framed in the guise of a "learning experience." So too, unspoken rules, unclear position descriptions, and vague policy and procedures result in fear of pushing limits, experimenting, and creativity. Powerlessness in the workplace can create the experience of being deliberately set up to fail, which results in staff shrinking back and minimizing themselves rather than fulfilling their full potential. Staff may also fear being made to disappear or told that they are replaceable—that is, worthless.

One metaphor I have found helpful is that of a puppy being hit on the nose with a rolled-up newspaper at seemingly unpredictable moments to "teach them a lesson" in compliance. Eventually the puppy flinches, hesitates, or develops anxiety about a person, place or behavior, interpreting it as "bad" whilst the owner pats themselves on the back for the puppy's compliance. This experience of punishment-based compliance is not conducive for establishing connected classroom cultures that result in powerful teachers and students. I value myself too much to keep returning to an environment in which I am constantly in fear of being unpredictably smacked on the nose.

POWERFUL VS. POWERLESS CULTURE

The goal of a culture of love is to encourage people to be powerful, vulnerable, honest and willing to confront—character traits that show up in the way we interact with our leadership, teams, and classrooms. In a powerful culture we value connection with team members, learn assertive communication, respectfully disagree, give and receive feedback, build and protect trust, clean up messes without involving punishment, and believe the best in one another.[5]

Powerful organizations and school cultures have high levels of trust, safety, peace, love, appreciation, growth, and excellence. In short, the powerful teacher and culture is more interested in character than compliance.

POWERFUL CULTURE	POWERLESS CULTURE
Cultivates character	Requires compliance
Creates a safe place for students and teachers to grow in freedom	Students and teachers are afraid to take risks, experiment, and apply new skills.
Drives the fear of punishment out of the culture.	Students and staff are increasingly afraid of punishment and being made to disappear.
Courageously confronts issues.	Offers shallow, evasive answers in meetings or have stopped meeting altogether but rather are talking behind closed doors.
Empowers students and teachers to clean up their mess.	Instead of fighting for things that we value and love, we allow fear to drive us to self-protect hiding mistakes and looking for someone else to blame/take responsibility.
We are all visibly on the same team.	We have stopped celebrating each other's achievements and may even sabotage the success of others.
We trust one another.	Most of us are avoiding eye contact, lying, mistrusting one another, and are highly uncomfortable being vulnerable.

---

[5] Carla Chud & Danny Silk, *The Pathway to Powerful: Learning to Lead a Courageous, Connected Culture*, (Sacramento, California: Loving on Purpose, 2018).

As I became a powerful person, I needed to become clear on what I valued, what I would actively pursue, and what I wanted to protect. As a powerful leader, I needed to not only be able to articulate the values and behaviors that I wanted to cultivate in my life and school, but also to model them. It is our character displayed in our actions that will create the momentum we need to establish a culture of love and trust.

As a powerful teacher/leader in a connected classroom culture, I seek to demonstrate and protect these five core values:

1. Strong Connections: We will always make connection the goal of each relationship. Disconnection and punishment will never be an option.

2. Celebrate: We will celebrate every success no matter the size. We will always seek to send the message that you are valued, known, and worthy.

3. Transparency: We will always demonstrate trust in this relationship by being transparent and volunteering what's going on inside to stay connected. Your privacy is important to me.

4. Collective Responsibility: We value responsibility and will always take responsibility for our half of the relationship. We will never seek to blame or fix others. With love and respect between us, we will get there together.

5. Culture of Love: We will work hard at our love and actively express love in how we speak and treat others. We will never turn our love off toward each other.

THE POWERFUL TEACHER ALWAYS PURSUES CONNECTION

The goal of all of our relationships is connection.[6] As we have already discussed, for connection to happen, we need a safe, secure environment.

[6] Danny Silk, *Keep Your Love On*.

When connection happens, learning can flourish. So, what is your goal? Unless you know your goal, you cannot take responsibility and be deliberate about pursuing and achieving it. Powerful teachers make connection their goal.

When someone scares us, it is easy to make distance the goal and try to push that person away. We make "protecting myself from you" the goal. There is nothing a student or another person can do to connect with you if you have already decided that distance is your goal.

"I'll change when you change."

"If they were nicer...."

"If only they would work harder..."

"If connection were their goal, then I would make it my goal too."

These are things we say that demonstrate the belief, "Someone else controls me." But you have already learned that nobody controls you. You get to control your own goal, and you get to choose connection. A conversation in a connected relationship sounds very different to one in which distance is the goal.

I remember speaking with a distressed teacher, Miss Mate, who was having frequent conflict with Sumer. Through tears, Miss Mate described Sumer's rude comments as she interrupted their Year 7 history lesson each week.

When Miss Mate had finished pouring out her frustrations, I asked, "What is your connection like with Sumer?"

Miss Mate stared at me for a while and shared that she avoided her, purposely sitting her on the other side of the classroom and even in the corridors. She walked the other way if she saw Sumer coming. Miss Mate looked so dejected.

"What do you think might happen if you moved your goal from distance to connection?" I asked gently.

Miss Mate looked at me, looked down, then looked back at me. "Sumer wants nothing to do with me," she countered.

"You are right," I agreed. "It seems like Sumer does not want to connect. But you can role-model what it would look like to turn your heart toward Sumer."

Miss Mate was hesitant, but agreed to at least try. A week later, I saw Miss Mate chatting with Sumer as the class lined up. I went over and listened. Sumer turned to me and asked, "Did you know Miss Mate has a motorbike license? I love motocross. I was just showing Miss Mate a photo of my new dirt bike."

Miss Mate was smiling warmly at Sumer, "It's a great bike. Are you ready for class, Sumer?" Smiling, they both walked into class together.

When we find ourselves in disconnect with a student, we need to go right back to the very beginning. We need to get the connection back. Where there is disconnection, fear and anxiety swoop in and take over. This is entirely the worst time to try to solve a problem, yet it is so tempting to jump ahead and try to solve a problem before we take the time to build connection. It is connection that enables the doors of the hearts of our students to open so that they can receive and value the wisdom we are throwing in there. Connection allows them to trust the ideas we are giving them, so that they will try something new and see if it works for them. As we have seen, at the neurophysiological level, building or restoring connection regulates the survival and threat detector regions of the brain, freeing the smart brain to focus on learning. Learning requires mistakes, practice, repetition, and adjustment, and as a powerful teacher, you show your students you are not fazed by this process. This is called "containment"—it sends the message to the student, "I can handle what you are showing me. I'm not going to react. I can handle your emotions and manage myself." By doing this, I demonstrate that I am powerful, that I love you, that I am able to maintain self-control and connection, no matter what is happening in front of me.

We are sending the message every single day: "I love having you in my class." This should never be a secret in our classrooms or in our school environment. We all work in different roles in schools or other child-orientated programs because we love our students, but how many of us are communicating this every day, even on those super-tough days? Remember, the students who need our love the most are usually showing it in the most unloving ways. So we need to get really good at protecting our half of the relationship. We need to get very good at flipping the love switch on and ensuring that it never gets switched off.

As a system and educational body of teachers and staff, we get to role-model healthy, powerful relationships fuelled by unconditional love. We get to give our students the experience of making mistakes in a safe place. We want our students to make mistakes. If Ady were not encouraged to experiment and make mistakes in her drawing, she would never push her limits and explore her creative potential. We want our students to explore their potential, whether it is in their art or drama creativity, their arithmetic and science experimentations, or their debating skills. It is through us that our students experience the humbling and often sometimes exposing experience of being loved with unmerited favor as we role-model this to them daily.

Little by little, we are building it up, teaching our students how to stay connected during conflict, how to step out of the role of powerless victim and how to take responsibility for their actions. We are preparing them to be incredible employees and business managers, loving spouses, and powerful parents. More than that, as your students learn how to turn their hearts to their teachers and parents, you will have the pleasure of witnessing their parents turning their hearts back toward their children. Our families will create a new normal that will impact generations to come.

It is a wonderful moment when I exit a student from receiving support. It is an even greater moment when that student comes back to share how they have gone on to develop healthy relationships and maintain a powerful mindset. Recently I had the pleasure of a past student popping by. He wanted to share how his senior year was going and his plan for further education, and he wanted to thank me. He described how he had been building connection with his parents, feeling more secure and valued as a member of the house, and enjoying a new normal of peace and love. His words were, "I don't know how to even describe the impact you have had on my whole family." These moments make it all worthwhile. I reminded him that the change came from him managing his half of the connection and encouraged him to keep being the change in his family as they create their new normal.

CHOSEN CONNECTIONS

Remember, both our and our students' brains are wired for connection.[7] When we experience connection, safety increases and our stress response down-regulates. This is what we are going after and why making your goal connection is so important. I want my students to have an experience of connection and safety that they can model all their other relationships after.

I am going to walk with you through how we make connections with our students, connections that only powerful people can make. It is vital that we understand the foundation in our relationship, connection. You cannot transfer the message that you are unconditionally valued and loved without that connection. When we lose our internet connection, our life seems to just stop, and the same is true when we have a disconnect in our important relationships.

Building, strengthening, and protecting connection is something that starts with me being powerful, and moves out from me into the environment as the people around me experience me pursuing this goal. You cannot make me love you and I cannot make you love me; rather, these are powerful choices we each make. It is foundational to healthy relationship to understand that there is a choice involved, a responsibility for building our vital connections with other people. I call these *chosen connections*.

---

[7] Louis Cozolino, "Our Social Brains," *The Neuropsychotherapist*, 8, 2014, 22-32.

Year after year, each teacher chooses to teach the students in their school. This is not necessarily a choice students get to make. They do not get to choose their teacher, or even if they go to a particular school. Teachers, however, chose to study education, chose to teach, and chose from the outset to lay their life down for the students in their care each day. This is the foundation for love that each powerful teacher carries—a posture that says, "I chose you." Think about it—some of you have been teaching so long that you chose to teach your students before they were even born. The choice to love our students on purpose is not based on what they have done before or what they may do in the future. It is not based on whether the student will choose you back. It is based on, "I tell myself what to do, and I do it." Powerful chosen connections.

Powerfulness is understanding, "My students will not ever have to worry about my half of our relationship. While I manage my half of this relationship, we will see how you deal with yours. But I have chosen to stay connected to you. We will find out if you chose to connect to me." Unfortunately, this is not always how we behave in relationship with our students. All relationships do not automatically have that sense of ownership and responsibility moving towards them.

In *Keep Your Love On*, Danny Silk explains that typically one of three dyads are playing out in each relational interaction: two powerless people, a powerless and a powerful person, or two powerful people. What that means is that where there are two or more people, there is always a choice to connect or disconnect. Let us look at how these combinations play out in relationships and in the school environment.

POWERLESS + POWERLESS

Powerlessness is driven by fear and expresses itself as an attempt to control others or the environment. When you have two powerless people in a relationship—perhaps a powerless student and a powerless teacher—each one is blaming the other. They are both saying that the other person is responsible for their happiness, for their day. The teacher is coming into the classroom believing, "This group of middle school students are responsible for my bad day. The way they spoke to me gave me permission to speak disrespectfully back to them. The way they did not complete their task makes them responsible for my anger." The powerless students are saying, "That teacher is always cranky, so I don't have to be nice to them. That teacher is picking on me, so why should I do what I am told? That teacher is being unreasonable, so I am going to just sit here and do nothing." Powerless and powerless—neither person is taking responsibility. Both are expecting the other one to change first and both are trying to control the other toward what will "make" them happy.

Unfortunately, as Danny often says, and I repeat like a parrot, "*There is no remote control.*" Let's face it—anyone who is a teacher would not pick a remote control that says, "Just sit there and do nothing," or "Forget your homework," or "Yell at me." That would be crazy! Our remote buttons would include, "I am your favorite teacher," "You are going to do all your work and ask for extension material," "You are going to listen the first time," "You will wear the correct school uniform," "You are going to hand your draft in early," or my most longed-for button, "Your hat is on your head outside, and off your head inside." There are much better options we could pick if we could control a student.

Likewise, if a student had a remote control, they are not going to pick, "Let us have a cranky teacher today," "Let us have a long, boring lesson in silence," "Please seat me away from my friends," or "Ask me an embarrassing question in front of peers." No way! They are going to be picking options like, "Let us have fun," "Give the teacher a sense of humor," "Let us have a teacher that will break down the task," "Let me sit with friends," "Lower your voice," or, "Explain that again." They would be picking great experiences too.

So really, powerless and powerless does not work because we cannot control each other. All we get from powerless and powerless is a standoff, both people feeling like the victim, blaming a bad guy, no responsibility being taken, and nothing changes. How long can this go on? All year, that's how long!

POWERFUL + POWERLESS

Powerful and powerless is a great setup for codependency, and it can be either the teacher or the student who is powerful or powerless. A teacher may be sunny and shiny because they are going to fix what they perceive as a "broken" student. They believe that although other teachers before them have never been able to do this, "I can, because I have done this before," or "This student does not trust anyone else but me." For example, a teacher comes into a fourth-year class, and a little boy comes along who has been in trouble all the way through his schooling journey because of the mistakes he is making in order to learn. This teacher makes it their goal to "fix him." They are going to come along with all this happiness, energy, and wisdom, they are going to make the day wonderful, and this little boy is saying, "Go for it, give it a go!" And for a while, it works. But eventually, as the year drags on, there is not much change, because this teacher is doing all the work. They are working on their life and the student's life at the same time. The teacher slowly becomes resentful that the student is not appreciative of their hard work and the student neurocepts this as unsafe, going to painful lengths to get away from his teacher who is becoming increasingly unpredictable as their anger builds. We see this play out quite often, particularly in the primary school, where a teacher thinks they can fix the student. But the students are not broken—they are learning through mistake-making.

At other times, we might have a powerless teacher coming into a room, feeling like the whole class is out to get them, and there is a powerful student in the room who believes they can make the most out of the lesson regardless of how the other students or the teacher acts. At first, this appears excellent, and the teacher pours out their favoritism on this student. Eventually, however, that student cannot maintain the pressure of providing the teacher with a sense of worth. When they do make a mistake, or the teacher does not give them the grade they wanted, suddenly each is questioning their internal worth as a reflection of how the other person is responding to them.

POWERFUL + POWERFUL

What we want is to have two powerful people in connection with one another. We want a teacher who is powerful and knows how to manage him or herself, no matter what the student is doing, and we want a student who is also powerful and can manage his or her interactions, no matter what is going on in the classroom or with the teacher (teachers have bad days too, after all). Remember, however, students are not as developed as adults. They have not had years of practice and building context to draw from their smart brains. They are still in training, so really, they are watching closely how we role-model being "powerful" so that they can learn to do this themselves. In the younger grades, they are not going to get this right every time. But they are going to be watching closely to see that we can manage our powerfulness, that we are constantly going to be responsible for our half of the connection, and that we keep choosing to be in connection with them. They are looking to see if we can do who we say we are.

Remember, students do not necessarily choose to come to the school where you are, and they do not get to choose you as their teacher. They may get to choose their subjects in secondary school, but most of the time they have little choice in the situation. You chose to go to university, chose to teach, chose to be at this school. You may not get to choose the classes or students that you are teaching, but you chose to be here. So, you have a lot more freedom already coming in. The goal is to translate that freedom to the students and help them see that they have a choice to connect in this relationship, to be part of the other half of the connection with you. You want to help them see that you are choosing them. Every single day, you turn up to class and choose them, whether they make great choices or whether they are having a day of making poor choices, which might have come from a morning with no breakfast, a rough time with the family fighting, rejection from a peer, or a pet that died. The reasons for their emotions or behavior can be vast and many. It does not mean that you are a bad teacher or that they do not like you. It means that they have a threat detector, and it works.

In Life Academy Kids, Danny and Brittney describe connection like a strong rope held between two people.[8] When both people are in connection, each of them is holding one end of the rope securely. Both people have a choice to hold on or let go. They can choose to stay in connection or they can let go of the rope and disconnect. This effectively leaves a rope dangling from the hand of the one person who is choosing connection. There is nothing you can do to make another person choose connection. All you can do is choose to stay connected yourself. If you let go of the goal of connection, there is nothing a student can do to connect with you. Only you are responsible for your half of the connection.

Many of the students I work with are simultaneously in and out of the educational system and the criminal justice system. Connection is always a deliberate and powerful choice in such a turbulent environment. Charlie was one such student. He would come to talk with me about the challenges in his life and I prioritized connection as Charlie learned about life in front of me. One day, Charlie informed me that he had been charged with a criminal offense and needed to attend court. Charlie was scared and did not know where else to go, so he turned toward our connection. Together, we contacted his parents, arranged a lawyer, and even attended court. The connection was strong.

Soon after, one of his teachers came to learn about Charlie's court hearing and exposed this information to Charlie's peers. Charlie was hurt and embarrassed, as he had not shared this experience outside a small number of people. Looking for a bad guy, Charlie blamed me for letting go of his half of the connection. It did not matter that I had not been involved

---

[8] http://kids.loplifeacademy.com/

in sharing his information. For a long time, I watched on as Charlie completed his parole requirements, holding my end of the connection whilst the rope dangled lifelessly in my hands. Just before graduation, Charlie came to see me and, just like that, picked up his end of the connection. Together, we celebrated his college graduation and parole completion. I can tell you over the time of disconnect there were many moments where I considered letting go of my half of the connection, but I chose Charlie before he even came to be my student. I chose to work with vulnerable students, so I held on whilst Charlie learned to take responsibility for his half of the connection. This meant letting Charlie experience the weight of responsibility for his choices whilst still offering support and guidance to help him manage his responsibility well. Once again, I saw that when you keep your heart turned to your student, they are far more likely to turn their heart back.

What would have happened if I was not there when Charlie decided he was ready to reconnect? What would happen if your student came looking for you to connect but you had decided you did not choose connection with them after all? These students learn that we do not do who we say we are. They learn to mistrust adults and look to their peers for connection rather than powerful people who will walk beside them as they learn about life.

So we are looking for two powerful people. We are looking for a powerful teacher who knows what is involved in being powerful and we are looking for a student who is learning on the journey to becoming powerful him or herself.

POWERFUL VS. POWERLESS LANGUAGE

We can tell the difference between a powerful person and a powerless person by the voice and the language that they use.[9] A powerless person

---

[9] Danny Silk, *Keep Your Love On.*

is going to use language like, "I'll try," "I have to," "I can't." In the class-room we hear:

"I don't know how to do it, Miss."

"I can't read."

"You are making me do this math question."

"I have to go to science."

"Why can't we go to break early?"

Powerless language is assigning blame to others all the time, often passively, which slowly wears our confidence down and gets us sec-ond-guessing ourselves. Listen in your staff room. Do you hear powerless language there as well?

"That class made me lose my temper."

"That student did not do what I told them—they made me act like this. They made me be emotional. They ruined my day."

"I have to go on duty."

"I can't do anything about Johnny's behavior."

"I've tried everything—it's no use."

It is important that we start to catch the language of powerlessness so that we can change it into powerful language.

It is really common in schools to hear teachers encouraging students to say, "I'll try," instead of "I can't," but "I'll try" is simply swapping one powerless term for another equally powerless term. "I'll try" advertises a lack of responsibility. It says that there is no definite intention to follow through. "I didn't say I would do my best work; I said I'll try."

I love the analogy that Danny provides to explain the powerlessness of "I'll try." At any age students only have to hear this once, and they give a half grin as the light bulb moment occurs. I ask, "Have you ever seen a wedding?" Most students have at the very least seen one on television. Then I ask, "What do you think you would do if you were facing the person you love and the celebrant asked, 'Do you take this woman/man to be your wife/husband?' and the person you are marrying shrugged, 'I'll try'?" There are always giggles and acknowledging eyes. Of course, we would not accept that. That is not even a commitment. What we want to hear is "I will" or "I do."

"I will" is the language of powerful teachers.

"I will go to class today."

"I will teach them how to do this math, and I will have fun doing it."

"I will manage my own emotions."

"I will be flexible and adjust to unexpected change."

"I will bring my best to teaching every day."

"I will manage myself in front of you, even if I am tired or sick."

As teachers, we have our lives playing out all the time too. We have health crises. We have family issues. We have sleepless nights. We have unexpected life events. So it is important to be conscious and ask ourselves, "Am I using powerful language or powerless language?" Once you start paying attention to this, you will catch it quickly with other people first. You will hear someone say, "This student did this to me and they ruined my day." You will start to notice this and remind them that what they said does not sound very powerful. Then they will say, "Oh my goodness, you are right! Will you help me to catch this next time?" And you will say, "Yes, I'll try." There comes our own "powerless" coming out of our mouths! We are going to fall into these patterns of powerlessness quite often until we become very conscious of using powerful language. Remember to keep getting it wrong until you get it right. Adults, like students, learn through making mistakes. Do not give up.

TRIANGULATION

In *Keep Your Love On*, Danny provides an excellent summary of "triangulation," also known as the "irresponsibility cycle." Triangulation was first emphasized by Melody Beattie for partners of addicts to help explain how the actions of "caring" can set up a codependent relationship and in fact contribute to continuous relapse.[10] This model can be applied across a myriad of environments, including workplaces, families, school yards, churches, and even governmental systems.

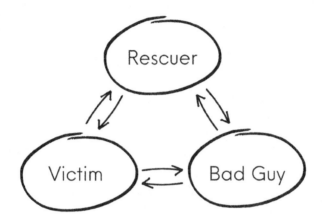

To engage in triangulation, we first need to locate a bad guy. The bad guy is the person who is always doing the wrong thing, ruining your day, every day. Maybe it is Caleb, a student in your class. As soon as you have found the bad guy, then you have also identified the victim—usually you. "The way this five-year-old is acting is making me behave like this. Poor me. I need some time off school because it is not fair that they are acting like this all the time." And so we go to our leadership teams and say, "Hey, Caleb is always making teaching hard. It is terrible. I am now suffering insomnia and back pain because of the stress Caleb is putting me under. I am the victim. You need to give me some time off work and an extra teacher in the classroom." Now the rescuer swoops in and says, "Let me help you. Let me give you all these strategies to work in your classroom with this student." But then, the victim is suddenly thinking, "You think I'm the bad guy because I am not teaching properly. I am going to tell all my colleagues not to trust you." And suddenly the rescuer becomes the bad guy and we are angry at the leadership team: "How dare you not

[10] Melody Beattie, *Codependent No More: How to Stop Controlling Others and Start Caring for Yourself* (USA: Hazelden Information & Educational Services, 1986).

rescue me and do what I demand? You actually want me to grow and develop my skills as a teacher?"

We see this process play out over and over. Think about friendship conflicts. Think about the aggressive parent beating down a path to the principal's office. Where is the original victim? Often they do not even know that all this conflict is happening in the background. We see this in both primary and secondary school where we get involved in other teacher's problems and other people's classes, parents and students, adults and children. It is vital to becoming a powerful person, and thereby a powerful teacher, that we start to catch where we are in this model and take responsibility for short-circuiting triangulation. The bad guy is simply that person who has made a choice that has impacted other people and they are not having a great day. The victim is feeling that the bad guy is out to get them. They are aggressive, believing that the bad guy wants a piece of them and are powerless to protect themselves. The rescuer is just getting involved, often unnecessarily, and often because they perceive that they know better, or because they have decision-making powers and are afraid of broader systemic issues arising. And the cycle goes. Why are you, Mr. Rescuer, getting involved in a problem that is not even yours? Bam! The rescuer is now the new bad guy, and a new victim.

Let us step out of triangulation and become powerful people. Let us not become the victim. Let us not make others the bad guy. Let us not rescue people from their problems, but allow them to carry the weight of responsibility for the choices they have made in their life so as they grow in maturity they learn from it. I am going to get good at inviting my students to take responsibility for their half of the connection. Triangulation is a defense mechanism that breaks connection. Students or adults who have a history of trauma and abuse have lower threshold for defensive behaviors (aggressor and victim) being triggered, and when engaged, these defense mechanisms seek to disrupt connectedness and the ability to co-regulate. We may not be able to control our student's responses, but we are able to catch ourselves when we are being pulled in and stay powerful.

To ensure that we do not step over into powerless behavior, we must hold ourselves to the standard of respectful interactions. This means I require myself to be respectful towards you, and I require you to be respectful towards me. I am not going to let your disrespect turn me into a disrespectful teacher. I am going to show you respect regardless of what you do. I am also going to role-model how you can be respectful towards me, because I am going to set limits. I am going to know what my boundaries are and communicate them really clearly. I am going to know what my needs are, and I am going to let you know what I need out of this connection.

Again, the first step in every situation is always the choice to be powerful and move toward connection, no matter what others are doing. With practice, we will become consistent in using powerful language, managing our emotions, and role-modeling to our students what it looks like to manage yourself and your half of the connection. This is how we break out of disconnection and triangulation and establish a connected culture where each of us is powerful, valuable, and responsible.

7

LOVE IN THE CLASSROOM

ONE OF THE COMPLAINTS I often hear from both students and teachers is, "They don't like me." Typically, what I discover is that both student and teacher are working very hard to show the other person they want to be in connection, but the target in their hearts is not being hit. How can this be?

While there may be many factors affecting our ability to communicate our intentions effectively in any relationship, one important one to consider is that each of us has a different way of "hearing" the message of love and care. Gary Chapman popularized this concept with his book *The 5 Love Languages*, in which he explained that there are five basic modalities or styles to communicating love, and that each of us usually has a dominant "Love Language" in which the message "I love you and care about you" will be heard and received most effectively. The five Love Languages are Gifts, Touch, Acts of Service, Words of Affirmation, and Quality Time.[1]

Understanding the Love Languages of our students gives us a powerful tool to open the door of their hearts and ensure that we are hitting the target when we send the message, "I love teaching you." There are many

---

[1] Gary Chapman, *The 5 Love Languages: The Secret to Love That Lasts*. (Chicago; Moody Press, 2015).

fun resources and activities online you can use in the classroom to learn your student's Love Languages. I encourage you to get creative both in learning about your students and in applying these tools.

I knew one principal who came up with a fun way to use Love Languages to communicate his value for the teaching staff in his school. During the week, he had students and staff write words of encouragement for particular teachers. At the weekly staff meeting, the principal chose one of the teachers and shared the words of affirmation written for them. The staff member could then select from options such as a box of chocolates (gift), a morning sleep-in with their duties covered by the principal (act of service), a beverage delivered to their classroom and a handshake (touch), or morning tea with the principal (quality time). The staff loved the idea and it increased connection with the leadership exponentially.

Let's explore each of the Love Languages and some ways to use them effectively.

GIFTS

A person who receives love through gifts is a person who wants to know that you are thinking about them even when you are not with them. They want to know that they are on your mind, that you like them and that you have thought about them. It is that simple.

I used to frequently work with Ryan, a primary student who was always in the gardens catching lizards, had dirt on his face, and was often distracted in class because he was moving all the time and fiddling with whatever caught his interest. One day, I came across a sticky little yellow toy frog at the bottom of a drawer. It was just an unused sensory tool that didn't cost me a thing. When Ryan next came in to see me, after having been distracted in class and breaking his pencils, I gave him the sticky yellow frog. I suggested that he put it on his desk so that he would have something to put in his hands whenever his body felt busy and he needed to fiddle. I knew I had hit the target because Ryan came and thanked me for that little frog every day for a week. He continued to carry his frog with him even when he moved into secondary school, although by then it wasn't so yellow anymore.

I had another student who was going through some extremely tough times at home, and her stress was coming out in unpleasant ways at school in her reactions to our school culture and her friends and teachers. She was making poor choices that were affecting her health and safety. During one of our discussions, she let me know that her ultimate dream was to be a photographer of landscapes, but then said she was sure she would never be smart enough and was failing all her subjects. We looked together at her academic record and I found she'd been failing ever since she arrived in primary school. Now she was about to start senior school. Remembering her desire for photography, I located an old book of some beautiful landscape photos by Ken Duncan. I told her I believed in her and that I could not wait to see where she was going with this. How exciting it was to see that at the end of the year, before beginning senior school, she passed every one of her assessments for the first time since she was seven years old. It is incredibly important to send the message to the Gifts Love Language students: "I love you. I am thinking about you even when you are not around."

The disconnect for these students happens when we say, "Oops, I forgot. I was going to bring that book to show you, but I forgot. I was going to lend you my special pencil, but I forgot. We were going to have a class pet, but I changed my mind." This sends the message, "I am too busy for you. I'm not actually good at gifts. I'm not thinking about you."

We need to learn to speak their Love Language, even if it is not natural for us and not our Love Language. The gift does not have to cost money! I cannot count the number of times a student has brought me a drawing (primary and secondary) or a flower picked from the school gardens just because they thought of me. These are your Gift Love Language students.

For a time, I worked in alternative education with students who had been expelled from the local public school for truancy, which in itself is ironic—until they came to our program. Time and time again, they told me the number-one punishment their parents would not just threaten but actually do was to "cancel" recognizing their birthday because of their behavior. The message these students received was, "I am not worthy of being born and celebrated."

I took joy in getting to know each student, and on their birthdays I baked them a cake—something really specific to them. For a student who loved going on cruises, I made cupcakes with lolly ships on top. For one student who always wore a specific hat, I carved the cake into the shape of his hat and colored it to match. Soon we started to notice that when a new student entered the program, a hush would come over the room when I asked them when their birthday was. The students would whisper excitedly to the newbie that they were going to get a cake. For the Gift Love Language students, their love bucket was getting filled just knowing that another student was going to get a cake. In addition, the social barrier to welcoming a new student was immediately broken and they were brought into the student group with this hope of their favorite type of cake.

When the day came for my birthday, it just so happened it was in the week that we called "Joy Week"—the week in our program where we focused on the joy found in learning new skills. To give our students an experience of what learning a new skill joyfully would be like, we took them water-skiing and tubing. I noticed a bunch of students with the teacher (I am not their teacher, I am the social worker) huddled in the picnic area. As the skiing fun ensued, students repeatedly went back to check on that area. I learned the boys (keep in mind, these are boys expelled and banned from our local public schools) had organized with the teacher to bring a camp oven and asked the teacher to help them make a cake from scratch for my birthday. They were so excited and so proud to offer up their gift to me. These boys were learning the value of not just receiving love but giving love.

So, make it a priority to keep an eye out to discover what is going to hit the target with your students and help them feel connected. It didn't take long in our alternative school before we experienced 100% attendance. There were many reasons for this, but one key reason was the connection built from looking for the way each student spoke love and feeding into that, so they knew they were valued.

TOUCH

The second Love Language is Touch. A person who needs touch is all about feeling connection through affection. This can seem a little tricky in a school environment, because obviously we need to be following our school policies and careful with our physical boundaries. You can recognize the Touch Love Language students, as they will be the ones sitting at your feet during story time or attempting to hold your hand whilst you are on duty. They will be scratching the backs of their friends, braiding hair as they stand in line, or having to hug everyone before and after every single lesson. We need to get very clever with these students. They will delight in creating a special handshake just between you and them. High fives and fist pumps go a super long way.

One of our prep students wanted a hug every time he saw a new person. This was not sustainable, so we got him a little blanket that we called his "Bear Hug." Every time he wanted a hug, he would go and wrap his Bear Hug around himself and give himself a big squeeze. It was not long before he was doing this in the classroom, and I did not even need to be present for this love tank to be filled.

Similarly, I had a senior boy who solicited long invasive hugs from every staff member he saw daily. This can be a serious breach of policy and cause staff to feel uncomfortable, yet they would continue to engage in full on hugs for fear of rejecting the boy. It's very important to maintain your policies and professionalism in the school context, not only to prevent inappropriate behavior, but also because students thrive with clear boundaries. I explained to this boy that I was not able to participate in a body hug—my general rule is that only Year 3 and under get a side hug—and I asked him if he had any other options for me to greet him each day. His face lit up as he taught me what he called the "hand hug." This is where we do a high five and then wrap our thumb and little finger around the other person's hand in a hug. Other staff began to notice and adjust boundaries appropriately.

Rejection to the Touch student sounds like, "Get off me," "I'm hot," "I don't like to be touched," "Your hands are dirty," or "I'm not allowed to (hug/touch you)." You may not intend to reject them, but that is what they are experiencing. So set your boundaries, but find other ways to connect, like the high five. If you are worried about sticky hands, keep some hand sanitizer on your desk. Many of these students will respond very well to proximity and do not need to be physically touching you. I find that my Touch students feel loved when I invite them into my office, allow them to sit on my chair, stand behind my desk with me, play with one of my stuffed animals, or just pop bubble wrap while we talk. Even without touch, their Love Language is being spoken, allowing them to feel connected, supported, and safe while interacting with me or away from me in the classroom—and no school policy about touch is being breached.

How many students in your classroom are fiddling at any given time? What if we start to recognize that these are our Touch students who are trying to get their love tanks filled?

ACTS OF SERVICE

The next Love Language is Acts of Service. (This is me!) An Acts of Service person just wants your help. It may look like they do not need your help, but it feels so good to them when it happens.

Anyone who has ever lived with or worked with me knows that if I am having a rough day, making me a cup of coffee will instantly fill my love tank. When my colleagues offer to drive to an off-site meeting or my students tidy their own desks and finish their work on time, it brings me a feeling of peace. When I am leading a team, my direct reports learned that it is far more effective to bring me a newsletter article they have finished on time than to bring me chocolate. That is the stuff that fills my love tank! Why? Because they have gotten to know me. We can all do this for our fellow teachers just by doing our jobs well.

Our Acts of Service students will be saying things like, "Can you just do this?" "Can you help me?" or "Will you . . .?" At times, this is frustrating because we know they know how to put their chair up or look in their bag for their lunch, but they keep asking for your help. These are the kids asking for the instructions over again, or asking to borrow one of your pencils even though they have a pencil case in front of them. "Can we change the air conditioning to a different temperature?" "Can I do a job for you (right now in the middle of this maths class)?" "Can you tie my shoelaces (for the tenth time today)?" Our temptation is to think, *Just do it for yourself and grow up!* But we are missing the point. These are often the kids that come and say thank you. They make eye contact and you know you have just hit their target. Both of you feel so good in that moment.

The disconnect happens when we send the message, "What is important to you just is not important to me." Things like, "I won't help you," "I don't have time for you," or "Do it yourself." Not helping feels like invalidation and rejection to these students. So, if we are paying attention and we see a disconnect, we ask something like, "What can I do for you?" "Would you like a glass of water?" "Would you like me to sharpen your pencil?" *Whoosh!* That is their love tank filling up right there.

WORDS OF AFFIRMATION

Words of Affirmation students are nourished by knowing that you do not just like them, but you also get pleasure out of being with them and knowing them. During your interactions with them, you are smiling, laughing, and enjoying them. These students are often our class clowns.

If we do not respond to them, they interpret that we are angry with them, or that we have not noticed them because they are not significant enough. "You didn't see me when you walked by on the footpath." "You didn't notice my work when you walked by my desk." These are students who, when your voice rises and you say something a little firmly, even if it is not to them, they start looking for ways to protect themselves. They are looking for a way to put distance between you and get themselves out of the classroom. They are shutting down. You may not have even been talking to them, or have raised your voice, but they are ready to protect themselves.

"Stop yelling at me!"

"But I wasn't yelling at you. We were just talking."

"You are yelling at me."

If you as the teacher do not understand that their anxiety has risen in response to your raised tone, you will think it is their problem instead of taking responsibility for what is coming out of your mouth. Your behavior is affecting them. You need to fill their love tanks so they know they are not going to be in trouble for surviving you. They need to know that you are enjoying being with them in the present moment, even when their present is not especially fun for you. Very quickly we can rob them of safety by our words and the tone of our voice.

If I need to raise my voice in a room full of students, I will quickly seek out the Words of Affirmation students to reconnect with them in a way that conveys something like, "Hey buddy, thanks for listening while I talked to the class. What do you need from me?" I'm being very deliberate about seeking those students out to ensure that my tone and my voice is not impacting them. I am lowering their anxiety so that they can go on with the task of learning. After all, that is why they are here at school.

As I mentioned earlier, one of the schools I was involved in had a culture in which words of encouragement were sent back and forth between the students and staff throughout the week to acknowledge positive experiences. All ages participated. This gave students an opportunity to tell teachers some of the great things about them and their lesson on a day-to-day basis, and teachers could send affirmations to the students to recognize a specific area of growth or positive choice. The words of encouragement were submitted via an online portal, which created an encouragement card that was printed out and delivered to the staffroom or classroom. Everyone got to send these messages back and forth, so even people who were not very comfortable telling people the good things they liked were able to practice this skill of encouragement. There were innumerable stories of joy brought to teachers, and students love getting them too.

Our senior school boys seem to particularly love giving and receiving words of encouragement. One time, a Year 11 student, James, submitted an encouragement for his math teacher. James came several times to ask if his teacher had received his encouragement card. Impatient, he finally told the teacher he was going to get an encouragement card from him. The teacher got so excited, he too started coming to see if the encouragement card had been created and printed. What joy it was to finally have the encouragement card printed and presented to one very proud math teacher. It was always interesting to observe that it was often the older students and older teachers who responded with the most delight to these words of affirmation and were jointly involved in this back-and-forth communication to send the message, "I love you very much."

I highly recommend that all schools or classrooms find a way to apply a tool such as encouragement cards in their culture to increase the skill for complimenting, encouraging, and affirming one another without the need for reward or punishment. This is a tool for demonstrating unconditional love. Words of affirmation say, "This is what happened in the classroom that I liked . . ." "This is what it was about your assignment that I liked . . ." "When you helped me carry my stuff across the playground, I really appreciated your time and I noticed that you stopped playing the game to help me."

QUALITY TIME

The last Love Language is Quality Time. It is not uncommon for me to hear a complaint from a classroom teacher that there just isn't enough time in a day to connect one-on-one with students. We need to remember that this is not about quantity time—it is about quality. It does not have to take very long to build a heart-to-heart connection with a student. I once heard that if you spend two quality minutes with a student for ten school days, that this is enough time to build a connection.

If you invite a Quality Time student to come and continue a conversation at lunch break, this student will seek you out when you are on duty and walk around with you so they can tell you their story. Perhaps you have noticed that a specific student keeps doing a specific behavior in the classroom because the punishment/reward is quality time with you in their break time. You are frustrated that they just don't care about your time whilst they are reveling in having you all to themselves. Quality Time students want you to engage with them. These are the students who want to download their entire weekend with you first thing on Monday morning, because they feel, "Now we are connected." They want to know they are important to you, and it is a soothing balm to their soul just to spend a moment making eye contact. They may ask you to come and play sport with them or ask to stay back with you in the classroom during lunch. These are the students who will stop and make eye contact with you when you pass in the corridor and ask you about your day. It does not have to be all about them. They want to be interesting to you. They will show you photos of their dog, their motorbike, or their cousin's best friend's baby sister as a way to spend time with you, connect with you, and share themselves with you.

The disconnect for Quality Time students is, "I'm busy," "I don't have time for you," or "I'm distracted, and I can't focus on you right now." When one of these kids comes and sits down with you, it is time to lock your computer screen and turn to make eye contact with them. When they ask for help, even if they only require a one-word answer, pull up a chair and show them, "In this busy moment, I am going to stop and focus on you." It does not have to take long if you make genuine eye contact and smile while you interact with them. The message you are sending is, "I am never too busy for you. I'm going to stop and interact with you because you are important to me." Their anxiety levels will lower if we are good at speaking love their way.

I had a student, Jazhara, stop by my office. I was busy, but took a moment to pause what I was doing to interact with her, yet even then I did not pay a great deal of attention to the significance of this briefest of interactions. Jahzara's mum came to see me the next week and told me how this unremarkable interaction had impacted their home. One night, in the middle of a screaming tantrum, Jahzara suddenly stopped, started taking deep belly breaths, holding them for a count of three, and slowly breathing out of her mouth. After doing this several times, she became calmer and the tantrum stopped. Jahzara's mum asked her what she was doing, and Jahzara explained, "When I was talking to Ms. Godwin the other day, she showed me how my brain worked and taught me how deep breathing would calm my brain down so I don't feel upset." It was important to Jahzara that I took those few moments in my day to stop and focus on what she wanted to know. Jahzara had been looking at my model brain and asked about it. What I said and did in that moment totally hit the target. Man, that is a good feeling! Just taking that time allowed Jahzara to feel loved, and excellent learning was the result.

BEHAVIOR EDUCATION: RESPECT AND RESPONSIBILITY

Another factor that influences the way the message of love and connection is communicated is the way we explain and enforce school behavior policies, which often involves confronting and setting limits around disrespectful or inappropriate behavior. The way we do this speaks volumes about our goal—either to control and punish, or to connect and empower.

Danny often quotes Josh McDowell: "Rules without relationship lead to rebellion." He then adds, "Rules within relationship equals respect and responsibility." This aptly explains the central tension in behavior education policies I see play out over again in classrooms and school environments. Represented as a graph, there are two axes—Rules & Responsibility and Relationship & Connection:

	High Rules Low Relationship = **Rebellion**	High Rules High Relationship = **Respect & Responsibility**
Rules and Responsibility	Low Rules Low Relationship = **Victim**	Low Rules High Relationship = **Chaos**

Relationship and Connection

Where individuals, classrooms, or staff focus on high rules and low relationship, there is usually evidence of rebellion. Individual teachers or students revolt, staffrooms become places of gossip, and parents or staff seek punishment as a right rather than a learning experience. Rules without relationship produce compliance, which might feel good, but they won't produce character. If you're the one in charge, your presence will always be necessary for the rules to be upheld, because you can't trust people to manage themselves without you providing the external threat of punishment to motivate them.

At the other extreme, individuals, classrooms, or staff who focus on low rules and high relationship typically experience chaos in their relationships, classrooms, and internal sense of self. Students run wild with no responsibility required, while staff are worn out from having to be the answer to everything and feeling like no one else is pulling their weight.

What we are looking for is a healthy tension of both high rules/responsibility and high relationship/connection to create a culture full of respect and responsibility. Rules within relationship form character, enabling these students to continue to protect your heart and the relationship long after graduation.

	Bad Guy	Powerful Person
	Victim	Rescuer

Rules and Responsibility (vertical axis)

Relationship and Connection

Another way to look at the character formation aspect of this axis is this. A low rules/low relationship environment trains people to be victims. Victims will be tempted to gravitate either toward high rules *or* high relationship to cope and protect themselves, which ultimately encourages them to be bad guys or rescuers, both of which are expressions of fear and powerlessness. Students do this, parents do this, and even staff do this. But in moving away from fear, powerlessness, and control of others toward love, freedom, and self-control, we are developing the character that thrives in the tension of rules and relationship. We are learning to be powerful people so that we can role-model this to our students as they work toward this in their own lives. High responsibility and rules combined with high relationship and connection will result in classrooms full of students who are happy to take responsibility for their mistakes because their goal is to protect their connection with you.

We are after teaching our students the value and power of relationship and love, not about compliance or obedience. Those things happen, but they don't happen as the ultimate, but as the fruit of a heart-to-heart connection. As powerful teachers, we have the ability to lead our students with love as they develop character that will inform the choices they make whether we are there or not, every second of every day.

In the various schools where I have worked, it is common for students to come speak with me when they have been asked to leave the classroom or even suspended from attending school because they have been disruptive, unsafe, or disrespectful. The teacher or leader responded to the student's behavior by setting a clear boundary to ensure that they can go on with educating the other students in the room in a safe, respectful environment. It is great when teachers are empowered to respectfully set limits by applying the school's behavior education process. The gift of these processes is that it shifts the weight of responsibility onto the right person and then offers a process for coaching the student through how to manage their responsibility well and make responsible choices in their future. There is an important distinction between responsibility and fault. Responsibility occurs in the present and is applied to current minute-to-minute choices, whilst fault reflects the past choices that have already made a mess that needs to be cleaned up.

There are many behavior models available that can assist schools in keeping a healthy balance and tension between rules and relationship. Currently, the most common models I observe in the schools I work with are restorative justice, positive psychology, and responsible thinking. Ultimately, a good behavior education process should be clear, ensuring that each student knows how to apply the school rules and values. There is also the expectation that these are embedded into the various classrooms and playgrounds consistently. Another key factor to quality behavior education is that students are participants in the process. Students should be given clear choices to adjust and stay connected in the classroom, prior to requiring additional support as well as when receiving support. Students should be clearly informed about what will happen if they choose to ignore the school's code of behavior and continue the behavior. As a result, both teachers and students have a clear blueprint to orient themselves each day in connection with one another. In this way, students and teachers participate in a predictable sequence of behavior education that removes "offense" and instead puts the situation in front of each person to reflect on and adjust.

Consider again the Safety Stool. Students are more likely to thrive in a safe, enriched environment—the foundation on which the Stool rests—and much of safety and enrichment comes directly from the presence of consistent, clear rules combined with loving, safe connection. In a safe, enriched environment, students are more likely to approach quality connections and attachments, pursue pleasure in their learning, and be able to easily orientate themselves in their environment because they have control over the choices they are making. Subsequently, these students develop a strong sense of self as they participate in their schooling environment by approaching new skills and developing higher order cognitive and social structures.

Where the schooling environment is compromised and experienced as unsafe, however—again, largely due to an insufficient presence and balance of rules and relationship—students are less likely to approach new learning and instead apply avoidance behavior strategies to survive the experience they are having. Compromised school cultures may have characteristics such as conflict in leadership, unpredictable behavior approaches, high staff turnover, and mistrust between students and teachers or leaders. The general experience is that the worst is expected rather than seeing students and teachers as inherently good and wanting them to succeed. Where students or teachers are unable to orient themselves to a predictable sequence of events, it often leads to a breakdown of connection and relationships. Uncertain of when the punishment will be applied or the context in which a behavior is considered unacceptable, the student or teacher begin to avoid pain by hiding themselves or bracing themselves for a fight to get their needs met. Mistrust then develops due to unpredictability and this further corrodes attachments and connections, resulting in a culture of fear and avoidance.

Quality behavior education allows students the freedom to choose to be connected in class or not. Does that mean when the student finds the teacher's limit, they are happy? No, not usually. Does it mean the student will sometimes choose to leave the classroom or stay disconnected? Absolutely. In fact, every student referred to me has at some point chosen to disconnect from their teacher in some way and the student is often not happy with the weight of responsibility they are experiencing from their choice. You know what? That is okay. This moment is when everyone can work together to learn something valuable about one another. So straight away, quality behavior education does not mean everyone is happy all the time. Conflict is never fun. But in every relationship there are times of conflict, and the sooner we accept that conflict and disconnection are not fun, the sooner we can move on to resolving the problem rather than focusing all our energy in trying to make the other person fun whilst the conflict plays out.

The day I learned this lesson was a light bulb moment. I was sitting with my fiancé (now husband), Jayden, and we were having a "talk." Each of us was frustrated that the other person was not being fun to talk to and we each wanted to ask the other person to be more gracious whilst we were experiencing big feelings during conflict. Suddenly, I remembered an action Jayden had used in a previous discussion when we spoke about moving a problem from between us and instead looking out at the problem in front of us together so that we stay connected. I used my hands to pick up the imaginary problem that was between us and placed it on the picnic table in front of us so that we were now positioned side by side, looking at the problem together.

"Our problem is that we each want the other person to be fun whilst we are in conflict, but this is the conflict here," I said, pointing to the imaginary problem on the table in front of us, "Conflict is not meant to be fun."

Both of us paused, let those words sink in, and released a deep breath, letting go of all tension. The whole conflict was over, and we now had a shared understanding. We did not even have a conflict—we were just trying to control the other person's expression of their unfun feelings. We both cleaned up our mess and went for a walk hand in hand through the forest.

In schools, these disconnected, unfun students stomp into my office stating that they do not want to talk to anyone, then slump down onto the couch as if they cannot hold themselves up one second longer. If they are not ready, that's okay. I will help them notice by saying, "It does not seem like you are ready to talk. How about you chill out for a bit and let me know when you are ready?" I may add if they start speaking rudely, "I am going to talk to you nicely. I will know you are ready to talk when you can talk to me nicely." With students in primary school, sometimes they need extra coaching about what "ready" looks like. I will ask them, "What are your eyes doing? What are your ears doing? What is your voice doing? What is your body doing?"

And they start to take notice. "My eyes are angry. My mouth is clenched, my hands are in fists, my foot is stomping."

"That sounds right. So when you are speaking like me and using a gentle, calm voice, nice calm eyes, and your hands are relaxed, then we are going to talk together. I cannot wait to help you fix it, because hey, I'm like Bob the Builder. I will help you fix it, when we are speaking nicely together."

Then I walk away or turn back to working at my desk. I will wait until they are ready to talk, checking in every so often, but letting them take as long as they need to self-soothe and become ready. What am I waiting for? I am waiting for them to perceive that they are safe, and move the blood flow away from the threat detector and toward the prefrontal cortex where effective empathy and problem solving are developed. Whilst waiting, I am increasing their experience of control by offering choices. "Would you like some tap water or fridge water? Would you like the orange cup or the blue cup? Would you like the weighted blanket or the sensory cushion?" I am helping restore their sense of control and I am staying alert, because as soon as they are ready, that is the little life I want to speak into.

It works similarly with high school students. I might say to them, "It does not sound like you are speaking respectfully to me. I want to listen to you, so you let me know when you are ready to speak respectfully so I can hear what you are saying. I will stop whatever I am doing to talk to you, come and find me at my desk." Then I walk away.

When they are ready, they come and approach me and say, "Miss, I am ready to talk."

"Awesome. I am so looking forward to this chat. Would you like to talk in my office or go for a walk?" Remember, offer choices!

I am showing them with my words and actions that I am going to be powerful no matter what they do. If they come into my room angry, I am not going to respond by getting equally angry. Imagine what would happen if the school behavior educator reflects the emotions of each escalated student who walks into their room. The student has been sent to see me because they are angry, but because the student is angry, now I am angry. It's an endless cycle. Yet, it is not uncommon for teachers to expect the person intervening in the behavior to carry their experience of anger within them. No, you are not the same person. Your role is to be neutral whilst two powerful people take responsibility for their half of the relationship. In this situation, you are here to guide the student in their self-responsibility journey, not ensure that the teacher's will is done.

Having both of us angry is not going to get us anywhere. I am calm and role-modeling what I want to see from them, waiting for them to co-regulate with me so that we can move forward together. I have seen this play out many times, and it works. It can be time consuming, and it does require repetition and a whole lot of trust and patience with the process. Central to building trust is, once again, the development of connection. It does not mean that the next day that student is just going to get it. It may take many, many repetitions before they walk in and say, "I am not ready to talk. I will let you know when I am ready." When you get to that moment, there is real cause for celebration, and it is exciting to see students recognizing when they are emotionally escalated and taking powerful steps to self-soothe and calm down. Occasionally, I have needed to share with a student, "I do not feel calm right now. I am going to have a break and come back when I am ready to talk calmly." It is important that we acknowledge our own internal experience and role-model what it looks like to act responsibly when we are experiencing frustration or anger. We are not teaching our students to never have negative feelings—we are teaching them how to manage their strong feelings.

A powerful teacher has learned to recognize and name their emotions. They know what they need and how to communicate this need, and no matter what happens in the classroom, they are not going to be afraid of their students. They are daily sending the message, "I will manage me while you manage you." The powerful teacher takes responsibility for their side of the connection and no more. Most importantly, they understand that there is a line where their life stops and another person's life starts.

FIXING A DISCONNECT–CLEANING UP MESSES

This leads to the obvious question: what happens when we experience disconnection?

First it is important to consider the disconnect in proportion to the incident and the relationship. A disconnect, whilst unpleasant, does not require a catastrophized reaction in which we completely withdraw ourselves into a position of self-preservation. Yet, this is often what happens.

I often use the metaphor of building a Lego castle. Everyone knows what Legos are, so as a school-wide metaphor it works well—even the parents get it. Put simply, imagine that your day is a Lego castle. Every day we are building this castle by selecting the pieces to go together with the purpose and intention to build something beautiful. Sometimes we choose a Lego piece that just does not fit into our castle design very well. It is in these moments that we need to decide whether to keep on trying to make that piece fit or to throw it out and find a better piece that will be more suitable for the creation of our beautiful castle. However, what happens to the Lego piece that we throw away? Well, if we leave it on the floor, someone is likely to stand on it, and we all know that Legos hurt! We need to clean up our mess and put that piece away so that we can continue making something beautiful without anyone getting hurt. This is why it is important that we talk about cleaning up our messes.

Sometimes, we metaphorically see a student or parent who is intent on holding tightly to the one piece of Lego that did not fit while his whole castle ends up in the bin. For example, there may be an incident in class when the student was talking out of turn, and the whole day becomes defined by that five minutes of disconnection. The beautiful day they had been building, the good choices they had made in all their other lessons, are all forgotten as everything becomes focused on the one poor choice. Parents or teachers can become consumed with embarrassment or frustration that this child made them look bad for those few minutes, often missing the amazing positive learning going on within the student.

What we want to help students, teachers, and parents learn is that we need to value all the intrinsic learning going on whilst the student learns from mistakes. The beautiful castle the student has been building with their life and their day needs to be our focus. A poor choice is just that—a poor choice. When students learn how to clean up their poor choices to ensure that nobody gets hurt by it, they are developing complex life skills that will set them up for resilience and success as an adult. They learn that they are not a mistake, but they make mistakes. They learn that they can keep building something beautiful, despite their mistakes. Some students even discover that because of what they learned through making a mistake, their life creations are enhanced, daring, and strengthened. Let us not throw out all the good choices because of one poor choice that gets far too much focus.

So we need to get good at recognizing when a disconnect has occurred, manage our half of the relationship, and clean up any mess so that we can restore the connection. We need to get good at cleaning up our own messes and get alongside students to coach them on how to clean up their own messes. We all need to practice how to apologize, how to take responsibility, and how to be powerful and not act the victim.

Many systems, programs, and people are satisfied with confession as the only thing required to clean up a mess. If someone is wronged, the simple act of admitting the behavior is enough. This fits with our legal system, which seeks a confession and then applies punishment accordingly. I want to challenge you to consider that in a connected classroom, we should pursue a greater goal than confession and punishment. Whilst admitting the truth is a part of the process, we want our students to own the truth, learn from the truth, and ultimately change their behavior at the cognitive and neural level—to actually take joyful responsibility for their own choices and cleaning up their messes.

The Greek word for this kind of mind and behavior transformation is *metanoia*, often translated "repentance." In *Unpunishable*, Danny illustrates repentance with the story of Simba in *The Lion King*.[2] Simba, broken by shame and unworthiness, flees the lion pride because of his fear of punishment. He self-protects by living in isolation and ignoring his responsibility as king of the pride. (Shame-based identities so often become our narratives during childhood that lead us to operate within a punishment paradigm.) Through visits from Nala, who calls out of him his worth and character, and Rafiki, who reminds him who he is and what

---

[2] Danny Silk, *Unpunishable*.

he was meant to do, Simba shifts his fundamental identity out of shame and toward his value and position as king—much like my own experience of learning that I am worthy to be beloved, chosen, and cherished. Immediately after shifting his identity, Simba's behavior shifts from avoidance to approach as he courageously seeks reconnection with the pride, takes his true position as king, and cleans up the mess created in his absence.

Danny Silk has walked alongside many executives and global leaders as they have taken steps toward true repentance. I have also had the pleasure of working with hundreds of students who have learned to surpass simple confessions and walk out a genuine change in their thinking and behavior as they clean up a mess. Both Danny and I agree that this is not a quick process. The timeline for confronting someone and helping them transform their thinking and behavior is rarely the work of a moment, a day, or a week. For this process of learning to occur in the internal hearts and minds of our students, we must consistently offer them a place to repent whilst applying appropriate boundaries as they learn and grow. Boundaries are not walls. Walls are designed to keep others out and self-protect; they communicate fear and rejection, and are a form of punishment. Boundaries, however, are designed to protect something of value. A boundary applied to a student who is devaluing their relationship through irresponsibility and disrespect says, "I require high levels of respect and responsibility in my relational connections. I need you to adjust and clean up your mess so we can restore the connection. If you refuse to do that, you are demonstrating that you are not safe to be at school or in this classroom or with the responsibility you have been given." Boundaries communicate that there is hope for reconciliation.

Unfortunately, what I observe often in schools are repetitive experiences of confession and punishment, which over time become "cultural" to the point where specific behaviors are dealt with repeatedly with little-to-no change. Leadership, teachers, and parents become exacerbated and frustrated as the student improves their avoidance and survival techniques. The problem with punishment-based environments, according to

Danny, is that we either do not provide a place for people to repent, or if they do repent, we insist that they still be punished. This is especially common in school systems where offense has entered the relationship and the teacher has responded with disconnection. The student may have had a powerfully reflective experience when considering how their behavior impacted others, but the teacher, blinded by their offense, remains unhappy unless a punishment is provided. Not only does this reinforce that the teacher's love is conditional, the student also learns that internal self-growth that informs their foundational identity, and which can be hard, vulnerable work, is going to be punished anyway, so why bother? It is always easier for a student to confess, complete the punishment, and go on with their day with no change required. It is much harder to go on a journey of self-discovery that requires responsibility, repentance, and transformed behavior.

Danny implores us to resist the temptation to be satisfied with confession and apologies. Admitting all the gory details of your poor choice is not repentance—it is just a way for other people to feel better about applying a punishment. "Sorry" is not repentance—it's just a request to do it again. Neither confession nor apologies lead to change, because they never get to the problem. If we want our students to actually change their minds and behavior, then they must identify the root problem in their thinking and beliefs and address it, and helping them do that through confrontation, good questions, and healthy boundaries should be our goal.

Genuine transformation of the mind—our core beliefs and identity narrative—always results in visible behavior change. Specifically, when a student shifts from a shame-based identity to a love-based identity, the greatest display of fruit will be the shift from fear to love, avoiding to approaching, surviving to thriving, and disconnection to connection. They don't just stop the negative behavior—they start to build a new life of loving, healthy, safe, truth-filled connections with themselves and others.

Changed behavior is what leads to the restoration of connection—to reconciliation. Reconciliation is not an automatic restoration to full trust, but a rebuilding of trust that should require visible change. From a punishment perspective, people never really change. This is why what typically happens in schools is that the student who made the mess confesses and apologizes, pays the penance for their behavior or jumps through whatever hoops required, and then the fate of their relationship is decided for them, whether they return to the classroom or school, or not. Either the teacher or leadership decides to cut them off from the relationship or take them back and sweep their mess under the carpet. Typically, this reinstated relationship is fuelled with shame, anxiety and control, which makes future messes not only possible, but inevitable.

Restoration and reconciliation require the combination of genuine forgiveness and repentance. Together these produce transformation. It requires the two people to build a new relational connection. We have the privilege to forgive and support our students as they become freed from their past and who they thought they were, empowered to develop a new internal identity, forgive themselves, transform their thinking, and restore their relationships by choosing connection as their goal. Meanwhile, we are inviting them toward this goal every step of the way because connection is our goal too.

We do this by sending the message: "I love you very much. Throughout a disconnect, a mess, a set limit, or whatever you are learning right now in front of me, my goal is going to stay the same—to manage me and my half of this relationship, and stay connected to you no matter what. I am excited to see what you do on the other side of this consequence or learning experience. Let me stand here beside you while you clean up your mess. I am Bob the Builder—I will help you fix it. I am cheering you on. I want to see you step into your optimal learning zones and thrive academically. I want to see you wanting to learn, because you want to be a part of this relationship. I want to see you bringing your half of the connection, so I am going to be role-modeling to you how to do this by learning your language of love and communicating that to you every single day. Most of all, I want to see you developing your internal character and a secure identity in which you know that you are worthy to be loved, chosen, and cherished."

8

TOOLS FOR MANAGING
YOURSELF AND SETTING LIMITS

ALONG WITH LEARNING TO speak love in the way your students hear it, one of the most effective tools you can use as a powerful, connected teacher is empowering language. In this chapter, I'm going to introduce you to the empowering language tools I use, which I learned from the "Love and Logic" program by Foster Cline and Jim Fay[1] and *Loving our Kids on Purpose* by Danny Silk.[2]

Whenever I go into schools or talk to teachers, there are two things I always notice. The first is that teaching is by far one of the most difficult and time-intensive careers there is. Teachers deserve their holidays! The second is that all teachers, like parents, want to eradicate the same set of behaviors in their classrooms and school environments—disrespect, disorganization, disengagement, talking and calling out, back chatting and arguing, friendship conflicts, technology issues and low self-esteem. Again, these are age-appropriate behaviors that present throughout the child's developmental journey while they are learning and making mistakes, and the challenge for us is how to reduce our anxiety produced by

---

[1] Foster Cline and Jim Fay, *Parenting with Love & Logic* (Colorado Springs, NavPress, 2005).
[2] Danny Silk, producer and director, *Loving Our Kids on Purpose*. [DVD]. (Redding, California: Loving on Purpose, 2013).

LOVING OUR *Students* ON PURPOSE

these behaviors. We need tools to manage ourselves in those moments where we are thinking, *I can't believe you did that, right in front of me!*

This makes me think of a phone call I received many years ago from a Year 1 teacher. She was very distressed when she called and told me that Susie had just poked her tongue out at her. My initial thought was, *So . . . did you poke your tongue out back at her?* But that was clearly not an appropriate response. It was an excellent example, though, of a teacher feeling powerless in front of a six-year-old who was doing something quite age-appropriate, yet disrespectful. We have this type of complaint all the time between students: "He poked his tongue out at me!" Here was a teacher complaining in the same way. I also see so many parents use "poking their tongue out" as a communication tool with their children, simply because they are having fun together, so we can't always be sure the child is intentionally being disrespectful when they copy the same behavior or just experimenting with it. If we do not find a way to manage ourselves in the presence of this behavior, we will misread it and respond inappropriately to it—in which case, we are the ones in this situation with the problem.

Let's take a moment to reflect on our own behavior. How many of us have called out to a student across the room? When have we exacerbated a situation, made a joke, got the class carried away, and then had to pull back and felt angry when the students did not calm down immediately? Have we ever arrived late to a staff meeting, checked Facebook, emailed, or texted during a meeting? Have we called out, argued a point, or even been disrespectful? Have we ever pushed our own agenda, spoken over the top of someone, or made a joke and got a meeting off track? I am sure I am not the only one who has talked to the person next to me whilst I am listening along. And if I need the bathroom, I just walk out of the room—without permission.

We are not that different from our students. We want the same free-doms they do. We are just further along in learning how to manage those freedoms without violating the rights of others in the process (most of the time). We are all in the process of learning new strategies and skills to get our needs met. It is a good thing that we can learn new tricks!

This new language will mean that you never have to argue with a student again. How amazing would that be? In fact, the only time I get into an argument with a student is when I stop managing myself and give my control away. I believe I never need to argue with a student. Every interaction we have is going to be a respectful exchange because I am going to role-model how to do this daily. Yes, I make mistakes, but my goal is to always work on my half of the connection and ensure that I am always having an interactive, respectful, connected exchange every step of the way.

POWERFUL TEACHERS SAY LESS: ONE-LINERS

A little while ago, an upper primary teacher Mr. Fox came to me frustrated that his students, who are all little lawyers at this point in their development, argued with him about every little detail, pulling apart his instructions and facetiously questioning his implied meanings. They would argue, he would argue, they would argue, and he would argue. These exchanges were going back and forth and becoming disrespectful. By the end of the first term, Mr Fox was completely frustrated. He saw there was a problem, and he was ready to ask for help. "I don't know what to do!"

Here is a heart that I want to work with! That day I shared with him the Love & Logic one-liners and invited to complete the Loving your Kids on Purpose program. I also gave him a little cheat card listing the one-liners for him to practice. The one-liners are five memorable phrases:

"I know."

"Probably so."

"That may be."

"I don't know."

"Nice try."[3]

After reading this list, Mr. Fox looked at me blankly and said, "That's not going to work."

"Probably so," I said.

"The kids will just keep arguing."

"That may be."

"Do you even want to help me?"

"Nice try, Paul."

"You are not even arguing your point?"

"I know."

"Oh," he said. "You are doing it to me right now aren't you?"

"Probably so."

Well, he took those one-liners back to his classroom and completed Loving our Kids on Purpose via Life Academy. By the end of second term, Mr Fox's classroom was revolutionized and he had made some incredibly strong connections with some tough students.

The one-liners are my way of staying sane while you argue with yourself. Whether you are a parent, a teacher, or even a student, I am not going to let my blood pressure go up. Rather, I am going to sit back while yours does. This is how I stay powerful in the school environment without ever having to argue with a student of any age again (or staff member or spouse).

"What time is lunch, miss?"

"I don't know."

"Yes, you do!"

"Probably so."

"Can we go out early?"

"Nice try!" (I'm smiling.)

"You never let us go early."

"That could be."

---

[3] Cline and Fay, *Parenting with Love & Logic*.

"It's not fair!"

"I know."

"Nice try" is an excellent one-liner when students bring work or something to show you that is not up to the standard for the task to be completed. It communicates that the student needs to do more without sending the message "not good enough." You just look at the work and say, "Nice try. Keep going." The student instantly knows to go away, fix it up a little bit, and bring it back. I love using the phrase "Nice try" because it gives the student an opportunity to make an adjustment without me saying too much, and especially without saying anything negative that will cut them down. What a useful tool!

It is also a great tool when a student is stretching the truth. For example, a student may come to me and say, "Mr. Jones said I could work in the study hall during sport." I know that we have very clear expectations and that any teacher would prearrange such a plan with me because we are a united team, so I say, "Nice try, buddy."

Next comes a whingy, "But miss, it's so hot today."

"I know," I reply, and I am genuinely empathetic, but I am still holding the same consistent standard for all students at our school. My goal is to make Mr. Jones look like a genius and support the student to make good decisions about his life. I am not getting drawn into a potential power play.

POWERFUL TEACHERS HAVE A PLAN

So how do you implement this? You need to have a plan. You need to know what your response is going to be when their behavior catches you off guard. Because guess what? Your beloved students are going to talk in your class again, day after day, and if you do not have a plan you will start finding your frustration building. Those Year 7s, 8s, and 9s are going to be unprepared for class. The senior students are going to not want to do work sometimes, leave school without permission, or order Uber Eats (seriously!). Those primary kids are going to walk like a pack of unruly ducklings between music and art lessons rather than march in perfect military formation. And they are going to run everywhere they go, whether it is grass or concrete. These humans you are teaching are going to want freedom to control their own lives. So, what are you going to do in these situations?

I am committed to never assault my connection with an argument. Sometimes, however, I get it wrong and make a mess to clean up. One time I had an angry teacher march a group of Year 8 boys into my office after a lunchtime playground incident. They were escalated, loud, and defending their innocence. They were talking rapidly over the top of one another and me and were not listening, and when James touched my lunch, my yellow truck burst forth.

"Get out!" I said aggressively, pointing to the door. I did not speak respectfully. I was not fun. Wide-eyed, James left my office, holding back tears, and I immediately saw the mess I had made. I took a moment to breathe and calm down whilst the other boys sat silently waiting for my next response. I apologized to them, explaining that I needed a respectful exchange. We talked through the incident and they all left with a resolution to their problem that they owned, our connection restored.

Then I went out and invited a nervous looking James into my office. He came in and sat down silently. I could see in his eyes that he was still fearful. I had created an obstacle to my own goal—to provide a safe environment for students to learn from their mistakes. These students had never seen me angry, so on the one hand I had a lot of relational credit built up, but on the other, I had now broken consistency and become unpredictable. I explained to James how I experienced the interaction and what I needed when we were participating in a respectful exchange.

"I feel disrespected when you touch my belongings," I explained. "I need to know that my office is my safe place and that my belongings are safe. In the same way, if I was invited into your bedroom you would want to know that your things were safe and that I would not touch them because they belong to you. I am sorry for losing my temper."

James smiled at the idea of me touching his things. He accepted my apology and apologized back for touching my belongings. Then we worked through what was happening earlier with his peers.

Since that conversation, James and I have had a super-strong connection. Wherever I see him, whether it is in our behavior room or walking around the school, if his behavior is sending a disrespectful message, I can simply ask, "Hey James, is this fun for both of us?" and he will instantly respond and recalibrate his behavior and words.

I remember one occasion where I spotted James carrying a Minion™ toy from the primary school through the bushes on a stealth mission to impress his friends. I called out through the bushes, "Hey James," and I heard through the leaves, "I will go put it back, Miss." The toy was never taken from the primary school again.

This is an example of the kind of amazing positive connections built from our own moments of weakness—an adult making a mistake in front of a student, cleaning up their mess, and role-modeling how to do it whilst the student gets to experience the feeling of unconditional love and respect. We all need to get good at role-modeling how to be a powerful person, not a perfect person. One of the values I want to instill in students is *excellence*. Excellence is not about academic success, compliance, or impeccable manners. Excellence is bravely going on the learning journey of making mistakes and cleaning up our messes well. My goal is to live out this value in my own life so that students learn a new way—not to please from a place of performance and perfection, but to grow and learn whilst developing their character and internal control system from within. Our students are watching and learning every step of the way.

In addition to the one-liners, there are a few more phrases that will be pivotal to helping you remain in control of yourself whilst giving the student the freedom to clean up their own mess. These phrases help us to stay calm and not trigger our own "yellow truck" fear response. As always, we are seeking to manage ourselves whilst we protect the connection—we are not trying to control how the student thinks or behaves.

These phrases will equip you to manage your responses so that your blood pressure is not going to go up whilst the person in front of you loses control.

"OH NO!"

The time to introduce this little phrase is when I want to communicate, "I am really sad for you right now. The lessons coming your way are like a freight train. There are a whole lot of consequences on board that probably won't be fun, but I love you and I'm here beside you while you go through this."

We had a group of Year 7s playing what they considered was a fun game in which they were running in and out of a set of doors. However, the doors were glass and brand new. The game was simple. One of the students held the door shut, and another ran straight into it to overpower the strength of the student holding the door closed. Eventually—you guessed it—the glass cracked. The two boys reported themselves to me, knowing that breaking a brand-new glass door would be a pretty big deal, especially to the brand-new sports center that had only just been opened to students.

Looking suitably chastised, the boys shared what happened and I listened quietly. After a little silence, I repeated, "Oh no!" and sighed deeply, leaning back against my chair. The students sat there, not knowing what to do. But it was time to slide the power into their twelve-year-old hands. I knew they could do something about this, and I was there to help them, not to take their problem away from them. So I used the next phrase in my LoKoP arsenal and pulled out the power question, "What are you going to do?"

They stared back at me.

"What do you mean, what are we going to do? We don't know how to fix it. The glass is broken!"

"Oh no! So, what are you going to do?"

"I don't know." They look at each other desperately.

"Do you need my help?"

"Yes, we want help."

This was the opening of the doors to their heart, allowing me to throw in my pearls of wisdom. First, they needed to acknowledge they had a problem and needed some help. Someone who does not have a problem does not want my help.

"I have some ideas if you need some."

"What are your ideas?"

"Well, we need to fix the door. Do you know how much that might cost?"

"I don't know. How could we find out?"

"I think the groundsman will have to call someone and get a quote. Would you like to go and find the groundsman, or shall I ask him to come up here?"

"Can you ask him to come here?"

"Sure."

"Once we get a quote, how are you going to pay for the damage?"

"I don't know . . ."

One student shared that his parents would "kill" him. The other reflected that they do not make enough money.

"What are you going to do?"

"Do you have any ideas?"

I smiled. These students were geniuses and learning fast. "Well, you could work off the cost, or you could ask your parents if they would give you a loan, or you could pay for the door out of your own money."

"I don't have any money," they said in unison.

"Okay, so what are you going to do?"

"Maybe we could work off the cost?"

"Great idea. Would you like to do this at school during your own time or at home with your parents?"

"I would like to work it off during break time."

"All right. How much per hour do you think you are worth?"

"Hmm . . . maybe about $10."

"Okay, well with the maturity you are both demonstrating, I think you would do a very responsible job. I suggest you are worth about $15 an hour if you concentrate."

Then we worked out how many hours it would take them to work it off the cost based on the quote.

"Would you like to do this during morning tea breaks or during lunch breaks?"

"Can I do it at morning tea?"

"Absolutely. Would you like to do it in the Tech Shed or in the playground?"

"I'd like to do it in the Tech Shed."

"Would you like to do Mondays or Thursdays?"

"I'd like to do it on Mondays."

"Would you like to tell your parents, or would you like me to tell your parents?"

"I will tell Mum, and then you could follow it up with a phone call this afternoon."

"Sure, no worries."

Through lots and lots of questions, we give students the chance to solve the problem they have created in their own lives. We are offering love by offering freedom and choices. We are not angry or blaming, and we are not saying that this is the worst thing they have ever done. We are saying, "Hey, look at this mess. Would you like some help to fix it? Would you like some help to put together a plan so that you can manage your own life and the mistakes you have made?"

We see students making incredible decisions and outcomes using this strategy. Every day students are learning lessons about the consequences of their choices right in front of us. I am here to walk beside them while they are learning to clean up their mess. And the best part of it is that I am not upset. I am not losing sleep over a broken window that is going to cost a lot of money, and neither are they. Yet these students are experiencing the weight of the choices they have made.

"NO PROBLEM."

Sometimes, however, we run into a student or a situation where there is a power struggle. They are not budging. There are those students who have learned the power of "No." They can be some of the most difficult students to work with. This is where another great and simple phrase is useful: "No problem."

What "No problem" means is, "No problem for me, but possibly a problem coming up for you." This could play out, for example, when a student has been sent to someone in our behavior team because the student refused to complete work. They come into our room, push their books on the floor, sit down, and say, "I'm not doing it."

"No problem."

Then I just walk away. I go and work with another student or go back to what I was doing. The student will be wondering what is going to happen. Since nothing seems to be happening, they may decide that it is okay to put their head down and do no work. They don't know that a possible problem is coming their way, and that I already have a plan and know the limits.

After a while, I return to the student and ask, "How's the work going?"

"I'm not doing it."

"Oh. So, would you like to do it at lunch break, or would you like to do it after school?"

"Huh?"

"Would you like to talk to me about this, or would you like to talk to a Head of School?"

Again, lots of choices. The message they are receiving is, "How are you going to solve your problem? Because right now this work needs to happen."

"Would you like me to call your parents and organize for you to stay after school, or would you like to go home and finish your school work with them for the rest of the day?"

Usually this scenario only happens once with any given student. The second time they come in stating, "I'm not doing it," it is usually enough for me to say, "No problem, Buddy. What are you going to do?"

They will respond with something like, "I'm going to sit over there and do the work." Off they stomp. Makes me grin inside every time.

"Great idea," I'll say. "Can you show me the work when it is done?"

"Yeah, no worries."

Sometimes students just need some time to calm down. They may need a place to sit, to be offered a drink of water, or an opportunity to have some music on. They may respond differently if I offer to read the question to them again. Most of the time our students have all the solutions already built into them. Our role is to draw out what they need to enable them to move forward with their problem and not get stuck where they are.

So, "No problem" means, "No problem for me—possible problem coming up for you." It means I am not afraid of the choices you make. I am not afraid of your non-compliance. I am not going to let my blood pressure go up and get angry. Occasionally it may need a few repetitions, but our kids are geniuses. They learn super fast!

"FUN TO BE WITH."

Another phrase I find myself using frequently is "fun to be with." "Fun to be with" is what I require of you to be in my presence. I need you to be fun to be with. I am not going to be working harder on your life than you are, and I am not going to be in a disrespectful exchange. So, if you want help with this problem, you are going to need to be fun.

When a student, perhaps a prep student or a Year 7 student, comes in having a tantrum, yelling, maybe swearing, stomping, throwing things, moving furniture, and punching walls, I say, "No problem. Head into the chill-out room and let me know when you are fun to be with." I wait until it sounds calm. and then I pop my head in. "Are you ready to be fun?" I ask. The student may say "No," in which case I leave them for a little longer. Or they may say, "Yes I am," which means we can start to talk about it.

I might have to explain to students what "fun" looks like. "Fun means we are talking nicely to each other, we are sitting together on the couch, we are looking after the property of the school. This right now"—as I point to a broken pencil or some other evidence of their disrespectful behavior—"this is not fun for me. I will come back when you are ready to be fun." And yes, I have had students voluntarily replace a pencil out of their own savings. Responsibility is catchy once they start to get good at it.

The four and five-year-olds catch on to this very fast. I will explain that fun looks like a smile, happy eyes, and safe hands. Then I point out that what is going on right now is not fun.

Sometimes they will try to smile and try to look happy. "That's a really great effort," I affirm. "I love seeing you being fun. Let's get on with this task."

Other times they will tell me, "I'm not fun. I need to go into the chill-out room."

"No worries. You let me know when you are ready to be fun."

In a little while they'll come out and say, "I'm ready to be fun now."

We can use this all the way into upper primary and even into high school. To be completely honest, I use this on myself. Many times I have put myself in my office to regulate my emotions so I can be fun again. Our students simply need to be educated about how to recognize and understand their emotions and how these lead to behaviors which can cause disconnection with others. It is so important that we are role-modeling our humanity whilst we are around these developing adults.

A Year 7 student who has had his iPad confiscated may be furiously angry at the perceived injustice. How dare the teacher try to control him! He is throwing things and venting.

"Hey, Lachlan, that is not fun for me right now," I tell him. "I really want to help you solve this problem. It does not look like it's fun for you either. Let's do this together." And we work towards calming down.

This is also a useful strategy for the playground. It's not uncommon to see children getting into little conflicts over a game that they are playing. Sometimes it is simply because one is getting carried away and almost being too much fun—perhaps their "happy" is too loud. So, you say, "Boys, is this fun?"

"Yes, I'm having fun!"

Of course they are—they are being silly, getting everyone upset, and pushing all the buttons they can find. So, the follow-up question is, "Is this everyone's kind of fun?" This student will usually stop and admit that no, this is not everyone's kind of fun.

"Alright. What will happen if this keeps on?"

"I'll have to sit down."

"Would you like to sit down, or would you like to choose a new game?"

"New game."

"Great choice."

POWERFUL TEACHERS ASK GOOD QUESTIONS

The behavior education program I utilize most frequently is the responsible thinking process (RTP) pioneered by Ed Ford.[4] RTP, like many other behavior programs, often gets a bad rap when it is applied incorrectly as a behavior management and punishment tool. From the perspective of behavior education, however, RTP is an excellent tool to grow students' self-responsibility and prefrontal cortex skills such as problem-solving, developing context, and empathy through repetition and boundaries. RTP applies perceptual control theory to help students to determine

---

[4] Ed Ford, *Discipline for Home and School, Fundamentals* (3rd Ed). (Scottsdale, Arizona: Brandt Publishing, 2003).

what they need and how to get their needs met without violating the rights of other people in their school community. It requires the teachers to use a predetermined series of questions as a tool to guide the student to make their own choices about their behavior and the outcome of their behavior.

The process begins in the classroom when a teacher needs support with a student who is choosing to make a mess in front of them. Hopefully until this point the teacher has managed him or herself well and offered adjustments. So, it is not that the teacher cannot respond to the student, but they have a competing responsibility to a full class of students they need to continue teaching. RTP is a process that is best applied across a school system, although it can be used in individual classrooms as well. As a school-wide approach, consistency in language and expectations results in predictability, which increases student's engagement in the process. These children are geniuses—they are checking to see if we mean what we say and will be consistent.

So how do we apply responsible thinking? Let's take Noah who, energized after break, is talking and calling out in his math class. I have italicized the sequence of RTP questions the teacher will ask Noah to invite him to take responsibility for his choices and adjust his behavior:

"Noah, what are you doing?"

"Talking."

"What should you be doing?"

"I should be doing my work."

"What happens if you keep talking?"

"I'll need to go to the responsible thinking room."

"Is that what you want?"

"Not really."

"So, what are you going to do?"

"I'm going to do my work."

"Great choice, buddy."

It is a quick, friendly exchange in which the teacher guides the student through what their choices are if they continue to choose this specific behavior that is disrupting or compromising safety in the class. There are consequences and very clear predetermined boundaries that are predictable to the student, and it is the teacher who gets to protect these boundaries. The teacher is sending the message, "I am letting you know my limits, but you still have the freedom to make your own choices."

It may be that a little while later Noah is out of his seat again, talking to his mate. The teacher reengages the RTP questions and is prepared to reinforce the consequences Noah just described himself for continued talking.

"Hey Noah, *what are you doing?*"

"Asking Lance for some help."

"*What should you be doing?*"

"I should be doing my work."

"*What did you say you would do next time you were talking instead of working?*"

"I said I would go to the responsible thinking room."

"Great idea, Noah. How about you do that, and we will talk when you get back."

The responsible thinking room is where the responsible thinking facilitators get involved. Trained in guiding students to experience the weight of responsibility, they are ready to support Noah when he arrives, greeting him warmly with more RTP questions:

"*Hi Noah, what were you doing?*"

"I was talking in class."

"*What should you have been doing?*"

"My math work."

"*What is our school rule?*"

"I can respect the right of others to learn."

"That's right. We need to come up with a plan. *Would you like my help?*"

"No, I've got it."

"Excellent, pop your hand up when you are ready for me to come and negotiate your plan with you."

Noah goes and gets a responsible thinking plan worksheet to complete independently. On this plan, the student is going to start working through specific aspects of the situation: What was their perspective? What was the teacher's perspective? These are very rarely the same, because they are the perspectives of two totally different people with completely different goals in the environment and interaction. Noah's perspective may be that he was waiting for the teacher to help him, and was talking to a friend to see if he could help him. The teacher's perspective may be that Noah was interrupting the friend and preventing him from doing his work. Both are right, but from very different perspectives. The RTP facilitator may need to assist the student to consider the teacher's perspective as they develop their context and empathic skills.

The plan also asks Noah to consider, "What can I control?" He will remember that he can control himself, where he sits, who he speaks to, and the amount of work he completes.

Then he will consider, "What can't I control?" In this situation, Noah could not control the subject, the teacher, or the instruction at the start of the lesson for silent work. He can, however, control what happens next time.

Now the RTP facilitator starts to help Noah reflect on his past behavior choices and their efficacy and consequences: "What have you tried? What worked for you last time in a similar situation? Did you put your hand up? Did you ask your teacher for help? How did these work out for you?"

The purpose of this reflection process is not to affix blame, shame, or punishment, but purely to help Noah learn and build a plan to adjust his behavior next time, because there will be a next time. Unlike a punishment, this plan is not something imposed on him—he is building it and we are coming alongside him to offer help and guidance, quietly waiting for or inviting him to ask us for help with ideas so he can build a plan that will be successful. To make any plan successful, the goals need to be achievable, visible so success can be measured, and realistic (think SMART goals).

Again, when the RTP facilitator does offer help, it is in the form of questions that encourage thinking. "What are you going to do next time? If I walked past the window in the next lesson, what would I see you doing? I cannot see you think and I cannot see you remember. I need to see you doing tangible things."

So Noah might say, "Next lesson I'm going to be focusing on my work, and I'll know I've been focusing because it will be finished by the end of the session and my mouth is closed."

"Great idea. What might stop you focusing on your work?"

"Well, my friends are in my class. We had a fun conversation at lunchtime, and I wanted to finish it off. We didn't have time, so I was talking to him about the ending to the movie he saw on the weekend."

"All right, talking to our friends and showing interest in their lives is a great way to build connection with them. When is an appropriate time to do that?"

"I will talk to my friend in the next lunch break."

"Great idea. What else are you going to do, Noah?"

The aim is to come up with a few options. "Well, actually, I was struggling to focus, so next time I'm going to ask the teacher if I can go and get a drink of water. It was hot at break time."

"Another great idea. What are you going to do if the teacher says no?"

"Well, maybe I could bring a drink bottle into the classroom."

"Noah, you are a genius."

Finally, we ask, "What are you going to do about this situation if your idea does not work in helping you to meet your goal?" We are helping them plan and replan, think about what they are going to do and what might disrupt them from achieving that goal.

After talking through his plan with an RTP facilitator, Noah is going to start to feel good about himself, because he has made a plan that will help him meet his goals. He leaves encouraged and we cheer him on as he heads back to the classroom with his plan in hand, fully written so that he can show the teacher what he is going to do next time. This is the golden moment—the moment of reconnection, when the teacher gets alongside Noah and asks him to share his experience of the situation.

"Noah, what was your perspective on what happened? What do you think my perspective was? What do you think you could do next time to manage this differently, so you do not end up losing your focus and missing class time again?"

Now Noah can participate in the conversation with his teacher with confidence. As Noah repeats this process of making and cleaning up mistakes, he develops higher thinking skills, including problem solving, context, and empathy. The first time students participate in the process, their reflection is not going to be very refined. In fact, they will probably not like it. It is so much easier to be yelled at and accept a punishment than to take responsibility and think critically about one's thinking, motives, behavior, and consequences. Developing problem solving, context, and repetition—skills innate to the prefrontal cortex—requires lots of repetitions. Some say thousands of repetitions.[5]

On the other hand, the fear responses may only require one experience.[6] One scary interaction with a teacher can result in a student becoming silent in class forever, never pushing themselves to develop new skills in communication or creativity in their work. Is that going to enhance the optimal learning zone? Are there students sitting in our classrooms who are afraid to put their hand up or to get something wrong for fear of being laughed at, yelled at, or rejected? We want students to be comfortable with making mistakes and to take risks, because as they grow up these will enable them to go on to do amazing things and thrive.

You need to have skills, strategies, and a plan for what you are going to do when a student is simply being an age-appropriate developing child in front of you. If you have no plan, your anxiety is going to go through

---

[5] P. J. Rossouw, *Neuropsychotherapy: Theoretical Underpinnings and Clinical.* (USA: Mediros, 2014).
[6] Stephen W. Porges and Deb Dana, *Clinical Applications of the Polyvagal Theory: The Emergence of Polyvagal-Informed Therapies.* (New York, NY: Norton, 2018).

the roof. You are going to try to control them and get into a tussle. Someone is going to get hurt, there is going to be a disconnect, and you will be left trying to figure out why the students do not want your pearls of wisdom. In fact, it is not that they do not want your wisdom—it is that they do not want to be controlled and they will fight for their freedom. Students will fight for their lives if they feel they are being controlled or if they are unsafe. We do the same thing ourselves.

Most of us have the idea that it is the teacher's job to control the students and control the class, but it's not. It's our job to teach the students how to control themselves. We do this by learning how to control us while things are happening right in front of us. We are not going to be afraid or intimidated by our students or allow them to be in control of us. We are going to manage ourselves and lovingly invite them to do the same.

9

EMPOWERMENT MODEL FOR PROBLEM-SOLVING (THE 5 Es)

SCHOOLS ATTRACT PEOPLE OF all backgrounds, ages, and socio-economic status. They are complex systems focused on providing students an education whilst acting as the child's caregiver, character builder, and boundaries coach. Where so many humans are gathered, differences of opinion, response style, and even morals become apparent. Judgment can quickly enter the environment and impose expectations on how each family or child should behave. What is important, however, is to meet each family or child where they are, allowing them the freedom to make decisions about how they want to live and interact with the environment. For example, one family may attend every school event because one parent doesn't work, whilst another family may be unable to attend events due to both parents needing to work. Neither is wrong. Both families have good motives. But if we were to compare and set expectations based on our personal opinions or circumstance, it is possible that one family may be isolated or shamed.

With a backdrop of acceptance and non-judgment, it is still common for schools to find themselves drawn into family, social, lifestyle, or significant behavior messes. Generally speaking, these are "moral messes," as opposed to legal messes, such as domestic violence, sexual or physical abuse, distribution of child images, or provision of illegal substances, which require education facilities to follow legal processes for reporting to the relevant authorities. Legal authorities are the ones with the jurisdiction to determine consequences and how things will proceed in those cases. That said, there may be some supports made available via the school such as school counselling, parenting courses, and safety planning. These are never exclusive or to supersede legal responsibilities.

Moral messes in a school context may include concerns such as a student's ongoing disruptive behavior, damage to school or other's property, inappropriate use of technology, continuous disrespect toward others, truancy, plagiarism or cheating, significant breaches of school rules and policy, mental heath concerns such as self-harming or suicide attempts, differentiation development for students with disabilities, substance misuse, and so much more. There are many times when there will be disagreement over whether the mess occurring is actually a mess. For example, the school may consider it their moral duty to confront a student's behavior that indicates a possible disability and is impacting the student's learning or social engagement.

It is at the heart of schools to set students up to win academically and this is always more successful when working with the family to develop a more effective process to support the child's educational journey. On the other hand, the parent may not want to consider a diagnosis or discuss the student's behavior, but instead will argue for the school to adjust their boundaries to suit their personal expectations. It is also not uncommon to come across conflicting moral perspectives. A common example is where parents may be themselves engaging in substance use or inappropriate use of technology such as sexting and providing these opportunities to students at home, whilst not identifying that the student engaging in similar behaviors may be breaking the law, requiring mandatory reporting or other intervention to mitigate the broader impact on a school community. Schools are in a unique position to support students in the development of their moral compass, but there is a fine line to walk between supporting a family and unwelcome intervention.

Keep in mind that teachers are often parents too. They also may be managing complex family dynamics or dealing with divorce, depression, anxiety, grief and loss, substance misuse, family illness, and other stresses that impact their own sense of self and well-being. Sometimes it is appropriate to walk alongside a staff member as they work through a mess or complex situation in their own life. Sometimes these are exposed at school in some way. Sometimes it is their children, who are attending the school, who are the ones exposing what is happening at home.

The tools for engaging in confronting conversations over these moral messes are for everyone. You may even wish to consider including them into your performance review processes. Again, before pursuing a confronting conversation, it is necessary to first determine if the problem is a moral one or a legal one. Sometimes it might be a combination, in that legal reporting is required whilst the moral impact can be worked through at a school level. For example, if a student discloses domestic violence in the home, a report may be mandatory to meet legal obligations for ensuring the child's safety, yet the school may also offer support to help the child increase their social and emotional skills expressed at school. On a smaller scale, a teacher may consider a student's unkempt uniform or lunchbox selection as a concern against their own moral expectations as a parent, but not necessarily a breach of the law.

So when is it appropriate to facilitate a confronting conversation? Danny suggests that confrontation occurs when an unacceptable level of anxiety has entered the relationship, usually through some kind of disrespect or irresponsibility, and it's damaging the connection. Again, it all comes back to connection. This is the point where something in the relationship will change, either because you have a successful conversation and there is an adjustment to restore respect and responsibility that restores the connection, or because you avoid or fumble the confrontation, and choose distance to protect yourselves from each other.

The reason a mess is occurring in the first place is that someone has entered into self-preservation mode, and driven by shame and the fear of punishment has chosen distance as their goal. In the process, they begin to punish themselves through distance and disconnection. It is important to recognize that the only way a confrontation is going to be successful is if I can convince the person I am confronting that I pose zero threat. Danny uses the example of patting a scared deer to describe this careful approach. It is imperative to reduce anxiety by sending the message, "I do not need to control you. I am not afraid of you or your mess. I am not here to punish you, shame you, or try to protect other people from you. I am just here to help you get out of this hole."

Clearly, the ability to confront successfully is directly related to your ability to build trust and manage your half of the connection. Consider a deputy principal sitting across the table from two distressed parents who are afraid their ten-year-old boy is going to be excluded from the school because of ongoing behavior issues. Fear and anxiety are flooding the room. Before a successful conversation can happen, that fear must be lowered. When working with vulnerable students and families, I am sending the message that I am in this for the long haul. If they have further trouble, I want them to know they can be honest and speak with me. If they agree to walk this out together, they can be sure that I will walk with them.

Since trust is foundational to any successful confrontation, that is always where I begin. Sometimes I have already established a relationship from being involved in a school for a long time. Other times, however, especially as a consultant social worker called in when big messes happen, I need to "borrow" trust by bringing in a trusted leader, teacher, or peer into the discussion. For example, often when I complete intake with a new student at a school, a chaplain or principal may sit in the first session to assist in the development of rapport. Alternatively, if I am at the specific school for a while, I may ask a peer to attend a session together to start the connection. Regarding serious breaches of misconduct that reach an enrollment review stage, ensuring that parents and students participate is important, so if they have a good connection with a teacher, teacher aide, or well-being staff member, it may be beneficial to include these people in the initial meeting. For many school leaders, they may not come into the intervention until after multiple conversations and interventions have already occurred, and at that point the teacher, social worker, or chaplain play an important role in helping the student and/or parents transfer trust to the leader who has decision-making responsibility.

Ultimately, in a confrontation we are inviting the student or parent into a relational exchange that will function like a partnership. We will share information transparently as we take collective responsibility to find the problem and go to work building an effective solution. Silk encourages us that when we emerge from this dark and scary place, we will have a new level of trust for each other. I have experienced this truth many times. The trust I build walking alongside students following an enrollment review due to substance use, inappropriate use of technology, a physical altercation, or even a legal proceeding is so strong that they bring their peers or even their parents to see me when future messes occur.

I remember working with one student, Robert, through multiple behavior incidents such as punching walls, breaking school property, and disrespectful exchanges with teachers. Through engaging with him and his family, we were able to identify what the problem was and apply appropriate solutions. In one specific instance, we identified that the way staff were providing information to Robert resulted in an escalated reaction. Through consultation with his pediatrician, Robert was diagnosed with autism. This resulted in staff making appropriate adjustments to his work, the way they communicated with him, and the support provided. So too, the well-being team supported Robert to develop his social and emotional skills, providing him with the necessary tools to self-regulate his emotions. A while later, Robert stopped by to report himself for requesting a nude image from a peer. Despite initially making a mess, he remembered he had someone he trusted to help him clean up the mess, which he had been unable to do on his own. Through previous interactions with his parents, Robert also trusted that they would participate in the solution, knowing they would be informed and knowing there was a legal reporting requirement.

Walking a student or family through a mess is akin to a doctor walking through a pregnancy and delivery with a woman. It is impossible to experience such a deep place of vulnerability and trust without forming a bond of connection. The students who bring me the most excitement by their daily successes are those with whom I have walked through the deepest valleys. The incredible fruit of confrontation supersedes the fear of stepping into a mess with someone, because it fills me with confidence that there will be transformation through the process. I am honored to walk this journey with them.

In schools when big messes happen it can be scary. It can be tempting to respond to a big mess with a big punishment. Much like a cartoon where the first character hits the head of the second character with a little hammer and then the other character pulls out an even bigger hammer and squashes the first character—"That will teach them." What if there were options available to the school, leadership, and teachers that can be implemented long before an expulsion is considered?

One of the greatest tools I have come across for supporting anyone who is working through a problem and cleaning up a mess is the Empowerment Model for Problem Solving. This technique is expanded on in Danny's series People Helping People and his book *Unpunishable*. As we go through this model, you may notice that some overlap with the Responsible Thinking Process introduced in the chapter. Like RTP, the Empowerment Model uses powerful questions to help someone build a successful plan to solve the problems that are causing damage to their lives and relationships. It starts with asking the question, "Whose problem is it?"

WHOSE PROBLEM IS IT?

Have you noticed that some people do not want your help? You walk up to certain students at their desks and they do not actually want you to help them with the problems they are working on. As a teacher, this can feel incredibly frustrating. You know the answer and you desire to help. I am not just talking about academic problems, but also about a range of everyday problems children and young people are dealing with, from complex family dynamics to friendship conflicts, cyber safety, social skills, self-esteem, and identity. Regardless of our good intentions and exceptional insight, we cannot actually help people who do not want to change, and it can be really frustrating trying to help someone who does not want help.

It is the same when you are trying to help a parent or a teacher who does not seem to have a problem. *You* can see the problem, but they do not. You have noticed that their child is displaying symptoms of anxiety and difficulty with concentration, their attendance is poor, and their lunchbox is full of sugary snacks, yet despite your well-intentioned help, the parent or student continues to resist change. Why? Because some people do not have a problem and they do not want to change. So we need to start with asking the question, "Are you working on your own problem, or am I working on your problem?"

You see, when I am working on your problem or your life harder than you are, then I am probably going to start feeling frustrated pretty quickly. So, the more I become a powerful teacher, the more I am going to focus on managing me, because I do not want to feel frustrated. I am going to work on my problems and I am going to let you, the student, parent, or colleague, work on your problems. I am going to remain powerful, even though some onlookers judge me as harsh or uncaring and pressure me with emotive language to take on the rescuer role. It is not uncommon for a teacher to exclaim, "What do you mean you are not going to do anything about it?" I mean just that. No action is action. There are many circumstances where no action is required. I am not going to be making everyone else's problem my problem.

Take, for example, the very familiar scenario where a child refuses to bring their lunch to school or eat what is packed. You may have a moral issue with the parent not providing what the child prefers, but that parent may be making lunches with a limited budget, reinforcing healthy food choices that the child does not like, or following medical instructions. After ruling out any concerns related to neglect, I am un-likely to get involved in a parent-child dispute over lunch. If the child is interested, I may work with them to increase their awareness of healthy eating or how to communicate with a parent about their preferences more successfully so they are equipped to solve their own problem. Yet it is incredible how often lunches become a place of tension and judgment in schools. The child is not being mistreated. They are provided lunch every day, they just don't like it.

Remember, we are not looking for opportunities to take the role of rescuer in a child's or parent's life. We will be invited to take this role daily, so we need to get good at recognizing the appeal (especially be-cause it can feel good to be "needed") and responding with gentleness that reinforces our boundaries. I am sure each one of us at some point has spoken to a student who is in the throes of an angry outburst and said, "What were you thinking? Why did you throw that iPad? Why would you swear at the deputy? You should . . . (fill in the blank)." It doesn't take long before that student turns their anger on you, saying things like, "Stop judging me," "You always take their side," "You don't control me," or "You cannot make me." Or they simply walk away. This cycle only leads to us being both the bad guy in their story and the victim in our own story, and only distracts them from seeing their own problem. Staying out of the triangulation cycle requires us to be proactive, rather than reactively responding to pressure to rescue another person. The rescuer request can come from any direction. It might be the leadership wanting to be res-cued from bad PR— "Quick, change this procedure now. Someone is angry at me"—a student—"I am failing because they are a bad teacher"—or a parent—"This school needs stricter punishment. You made my child this way." Victims soliciting a rescuer rarely see the problem. So this is where we need to start. You can see the problem, but do they see the problem?

DO THEY SEE THE PROBLEM?

I weekly observe this question playing out at home. We have a five-year-old who loves to "do it himself." It is not uncommon to find him ready to leave with his hat, water bottle, sunglasses, and flip-flops on the wrong feet. Does he see the problem? Or do only I see the problem? I have quickly learned that I can point out the problem—his toes hanging off the side of his flip-flops as they curve in the wrong direction—but he does not see this as a problem. He is more than happy to wear his flip-flops that way and is proud of his accomplishment putting them on himself. Any suggestion on my part is met with, "I like them like this." He simply does not have a problem.

Now, I know that our five-year-old is incredibly smart and is not going to grow up to be an adult who insists on wearing his shoes on the wrong feet to make a point. He simply does not see the problem at this stage in his life. So I chose to trust him as he walked out the learning process, literally. Just the other day, he came and asked me to help him to learn which foot each flip-flop goes on. His heart was ready for my wisdom. Why? Because I did not react to his lack of compliance when I confronted him with a problem I saw in his life. Rather, I kept our connection strong and built trust so that when he was ready, he knew he could ask for help.

So often, we try to give away our wisdom to people who don't have a problem. We see their problem and we are driving ourselves crazy trying to "make them" fix it. We are even losing sleep, developing burnout, and compromising our own mental health. This is very important to remember when working with students. It may be true that you bring wisdom to every student interaction, but not everybody wants your wisdom and that can hurt. Not every student thinks they have a problem, so you need to be careful who you are giving your pearls of wisdom to.

Step one starts by asking really great questions. We need to find out if the person actually sees what the problem is, and we do this by helping draw out from the inside what they see going on and whether they are open to a solution and working on it. I want to send the message, "I know you and I know you already have the answers to this problem you are having inside you. Let us talk it out together." So often we are told that our role is to "invest" into students. "It's my wisdom in them that will make them great." I want to challenge this perspective and suggest our role is to "draw out" the wisdom that is already inside of them, showing them that they can and will manage the freedom in their daily lives. So often, we come alongside a student and say, "Let me tell you the answer to your problem, the answer to your life. Better yet, let me fix it for you." In the Empowerment Model, we are saying, "Let me help you to draw the answers from within you. Talk with me as I walk beside you."

When I met Mark, he was angry, dismissive, and barely willing to stay in the room. I was providing a consultant support session, so I had no connection to draw on. The greatest tool in my toolbelt was honesty. Mark started the session by informing me that he would not listen to any of my ideas or do what I told him, and the session was a waste of time. I responded, "Good, because I wasn't going to tell you what to do anyway."

There was a pause as Mark sized me up and slowly sat down. "What do you mean?"

"I don't want to control you," I continued, pausing for those words to sink in. "As far as I see it, you have been making all of the decisions about your life up until now, which means you are in control of you."

Mark stayed quiet, nodding at me to go on.

"So, I believe you already have all of the answers to your problems inside of you. What if I simply listen to you share your perspective, and if I hear a technique or tool you have used to solve your problem, I can name it and put it on the table in front of us to reflect on?"

"So you will only say things that I say?" Mark queried dubiously.

"Exactly. I will only talk about things that are already your thoughts and what you are already doing. I will not tell you what to do. I may have some ideas along the way, though, if you would like to hear them."

Thus started a fun connection and process of guiding Mark to see the strengths he brought to his own life and that he was already equipped to manage his freedom. It was not long before his teachers reported back the change they experienced in his classroom behavior.

How often do we think as a teacher, coach, leader, or parent that it is our job to tell you what to do so that everything will turn out alright? How often do our students or parents expect teachers to spoon-feed and rescue them from responsibility? Sounds familiar, right? We get so quickly pulled into thinking and having answers for others, but that is not how we grow powerful people. Instead, we get to empower them to draw out the answers that are already within them. By doing this, we are not only showing them we believe in them and how to discover the amazing solutions to their problems. We are also equipping them with the skills to be powerful in their own future adult lives.

Every single day in the connected classroom, we are going to come alongside students and ask them questions to see if they see the problem, if they know who is affected, if they see the solution, and what they are going to do about it. It starts with us figuring out whether they see the problem, and when they do, asking, "How can I help you? How can I help you come up with a solution or a plan for you to put in place for the problem in your life? You see, I am not going to be working harder on the solution for your life than you are." And this is going be the template for how we help everyone we are connected with. We start with, "Do you see the problem?" and from there we begin to find a solution and develop a plan.

EMPOWERMENT MODEL FOR PROBLEM SOLVING

Danny Silk refers to this process as The Five Es Confrontation Model. These Five Es are designed to help you walk alongside someone else, whether it is a student, colleague, parent, or friend, to identify choices so they can thrive as they figure out what they are going to do with the problem in their life. Remember, it is not your problem. This is their journey, and you are a part of that in the way you offer tools and show them how to use those tools, but not by doing it for them. This is not a method to rescue and control others.

These are the Five Es (with a bonus Sixth E, that I have added) that allow us to see those around us step into being a powerful person too:

1. EMPATHY: Lay the foundation for trust (rapport, vulnerability, responsibility)
2. EMPOWER: Introduce powerful questions to help the person take ownership of their mess and start searching for its root cause.
3. EXPLORE: Discover the root problem that led to the mess and who has been affected by it.
4. EDUCATE: Help the person build a plan for cleaning up their mess.
5. EXPECT: Create a target with goals and dates for when the mess will be cleaned up.

The Sixth E

6. ENCOURAGE: Stand back and cheer the person on as they work toward implementing their plan.

1. EMPATHY:
"I feel sad for you."

The big question: "Oh no, WHAT happened?"

When our students start to notice, "Hey this is my part of the problem," my first response is to give them empathy. I come alongside them with, "I am really sad for you. That sounds difficult. That sounds scary. I can see that you might be afraid to approach your friend about that problem. It sounds like you might feel rejected." I am genuinely asking how I can connect with the student so he or she feels safe to share with me how they are feeling about the problem going on in their life.

2. EMPOWER:
"You have the answers to solve your problem inside of you."

The big question: "WHAT is the problem and WHAT are you going to do about it?"

After that, I am going to slide power across to the student, because I know the student has the solution to their problem within them. I do this by asking the power-shifting question, "What are you going to do?" "What are you going to do?" reinforces to a student, teacher, or parent that I believe in them, that I know they can do this, and that they have the solution within them. I am letting them know that I am here while they process the situation.

3. EXPLORE:
"What steps have you already taken to clean up this mess?"

The big question: "WHO is affected by this problem?"

Sometimes you ask the question, "What are you going to do?" and the person looks back at you with a blank stare. "Well . . ." they say, "I do not know what I am going to do with this problem in my life." This is a really good time to start exploring what they have already tried. It is very rare when a problem comes up that someone has not already tried to solve. They most likely have made attempts on a number of occasions. In the classroom, students will have tried lots of solutions, such as putting their hands up to ask a question, calling out, talking to a friend, taking an unapproved break, etc. Of course, these types of solutions may have resulted in them getting in trouble in class for interrupting or being disruptive or non-compliant. We might find that a student is cold sitting under the blast of the air conditioner, so they moved without permission to an empty seat at the back, which the teacher deemed to be non-compliance with their seating arrangement. We might find that the parent we are talking to has already taken their child to see a pediatrician because they noticed some concerning behaviors at home, but after trying to change diet or sleep routines, they gave up because being consistent was really hard in a single-parent home. So we are asking lots and lots of questions to find out, "What have you already tried? What has worked for you in the past? What did not work for you? Who is being affected by this mess?"

It is amazing to find how many strategies students, parents, and teachers put into place to solve the problems in their lives every day. We each make adjustments all the time to solve the problems in our lives and we do not even notice we are doing it. This is exactly the same when I meet with teachers and ask about their classroom environments. So many teachers are already making useful adjustments to work alongside the different student needs and dynamics in their classrooms. Many of these incredible teachers do not even know the adjustments they are making are not simply "normal classroom teaching," and they are not always aware of how much these adjustments are actually helping the class and the students learn. This is why it is so great to be able to ask good questions to draw out of the teacher, student, or parent you are working with in that given moment, "What strategies are you already using? What are the amazing adjustments, skills, and tools you have already applied? How did these work? What did not work?" Let us pull out some of the gold that they have got buried inside, and learn from each other tools we are already applying in our classroom and school environments.

4. EDUCATE:
"I have some ideas if you want to hear them."

The big question: "WHAT are you willing to do to clean up this mess?"

I started with empathy—"I'm feeling sad for you"—introduced the power question—"What are you going to do?"—and then asked, "What have you tried?" At this point, I get to hand over some new ideas they might not have tried before. This is the moment I have been waiting for, the moment where I get to say, "I have some ideas if you'd like to hear them." I have been continuously building connection and trust with the student, parents, or teacher, and now their hearts are finally open and willing to hear the pearls of wisdom I have to offer. I have waited for them to be ready, because I do not want those pearls bouncing off a closed heart that is not ready to listen. I am wanting to build an emotionally secure connection with that person so they feel safe to hear what I have to say. I want students, teachers, and parents to know the wisdom I am offering them, and that it is their choice what they do with it.

So how am I going to do this? I am going to continue asking great questions. I am not going to come in saying, "You need to do this list of things that I suggest for you." No, I am going to actually ask lots of questions. "Have you been to see a psychologist? Have you had an occupational capacity assessment for how you learn best? Have you asked your friend how they feel about that situation? Have you approached the teacher about that technique you saw them use?"

When I am talking to teachers I will be asking, "Have you listened to this podcast about Love Languages? What do you think of the recent research on the neuroscience of brain development and learning? Have you enrolled in Loving our Kids on Purpose? What effect did the strategies have in your classroom?"

To the students I am asking things like, "Have you tried getting to know your teacher? What type of things do they enjoy doing? Do they have a pet? What is their favourite color? What worked for you last year when you had a new teacher—how did you get to know them? How long does it take to get to know your new teacher? How will you know you are successful in getting to know them? How do you know when this specific teacher signals you to be quiet?"

By asking great questions, I can draw out of the student, the teacher, and the parent all the things they have already tried that might have been really successful. At the same time, I am planting seeds of ideas of things that they can go and try—listening to a podcast, reading a book, speaking to so-and-so. I am offering suggestions and ideas that may be valuable resources for them to go and look into themselves.

As I speak with them and ask these questions, I am educating them on where they could learn more information about the problem they are having. Many schools have a library available with a range of resources from development to communication, resilience, managing ourselves well, and more. If not, we all have local libraries we can access. Does the school offer allied health resources like occupational therapy and speech pathology and psychology? If not, we have a list of external service contacts like child and youth mental health services, pediatricians, or community counseling. I am using this opportunity to guide the other person to consider where they could get more information about the problem in their life, where they might find answers to help them move toward a solution to their problem.

5. EXPECT:
"You have all of the information now to make a great plan to resolve this problem."

The big question: "WHO will be helping you through this process and WHEN will I be convinced that this mess is cleaned up?"

So it is more questions, questions, questions. "Have you tried? Have you watched? Have you seen? Have you read? Are you interested in this research?" Lots and lots of questions. And after we have dropped all these great ideas, we offer another power question: "What are you going to do now?" Once we have given them all of our great ideas, we let them choose what they are going do with those great ideas. How are they going to take the strategies we have given them and make their own choices as they put them into practice? What is your plan? What do you need to implement this plan? When will you have that done by? How will you know you were successful?

6. ENCOURAGE:
"I am cheering you on as you work on your problem."

The big question: "WHAT do you need?"

It is true, I do not have the ability to take away problems. I do not have the solution for everybody, but I can help coach others toward thriving, provide them with good information, and allow them to move toward their own solution because I did not take away the problem. Rather, I am here cheering you on as you work on your problem.

It is really important that we do not actively control and try to take away the problem. We need to let the person, whether it is the student, parent, or teacher, experience the weight of their problem. We are coming alongside them and looking out with them toward the problem. We are working toward, "I see the problem—do you see the problem? Are we standing side by side, looking out at the same problem?" The parent of the child is also not the problem. I am not looking at them saying, "You are the problem. This is what you must do." No, I'm standing alongside them.

And then I am asking, "What would you like to do about that problem? What have you tried to do about that problem? Would you like some help? I have some ideas if you would like to hear them." Then together we are working towards a plan. I am drawing out of them, using great questions, the wisdom and answers already deep within them. And then I am cheering them on as they go to work applying the strategies they have come up with to solve the problem in their life. My role is, through safety and connection, to provide confidence and courage to face their problem. In that process, I am strengthening them with my empathy and compassion, through the power question, "What are you going to do?" I am constantly sending the message, "I believe in you. I know you can do this, and I am here cheering you on." More than that, I am going home each night knowing that I am not staying up late working on solutions for someone else's problems. In fact, I am sleeping soundly because I am not even thinking about the other person. I am that confident they can and will take responsibility for their own life.

Sometimes, no matter what you do, some people do not want your help. There are people who do not want your wisdom and they will choose to go on their way and refuse to look at their problem at all. Sometimes, as we are standing alongside someone, we can see the problem but they cannot or will not see it. This can be really frustrating, especially if we have a particular student regularly in our classroom who does not see the problem and does not want to work on the problem. It can be very painful. This is when it is important for us to continually strengthen our relationship and build trust with them, because one day they are going to see the problem. On that day, they are going to turn around and need to ask somebody for some help, and who is going to be the person there waiting for them?

It may take a long time. Some students do not always see the problem until they are in senior school, or even post school, so it can be a long and difficult process for each teacher to stand by and say, "We can see the problem. Do you see the problem?" And the student says, "No," over and over again. But when we create an environment and culture within a classroom that allows the student to one day turn around and say, "I think I do see the problem," they are going to remember that you were always standing beside them, ready for the moment they wanted to hear your wisdom. The student is going to remember that you did not force your way in, yell, or lecture at them, but offered them solutions if they wanted to hear them, and you allowed them to make mistakes because you were not afraid of their mistakes. In that process, that student is going to remember that you kept your love on toward them even when they were not showing you the best version of themselves.

Eli was a student we supported through the Loving our Students in Purpose and Responsible Thinking Process for four years. Despite supporting him to see the problem each day, he was at the time unable to understand that he had a choice and control over his own life. Eventually he made a series of choices which meant he was required to leave the school. Here is Eli's reflection of his experience years later:

> I was a student at my first high school from 2012 to 2015 and during my time there I spent a lot of time with the LoSoP team. At a young age I was diagnosed with ADHD and struggled frequently with disruptive classroom behavior and motivation. When I was a student, I failed to see the value of responsibility. I had completed countless plans about what I was intending to do, yet I was never able to find the motivation to follow the plans I had written. When I was sent to speak with the LoSoP team from the classroom, it often felt more like a hassle than a punishment. Even though I was in there almost every day, the team never once gave up working with me. I always felt comfortable talking to them in a safe space.
>
> Unfortunately, I had given the school a bit too much grief and as a result I was required to leave the school. I got a big wakeup call after

moving to a local public school. This school used a detention system for students that misbehave, and after being sent once I immediately noticed the big difference between Loving on Purpose and detention. I saw that detention treats students like prisoners—if you did something wrong, you had to do time for it. I began to realize the value of personal responsibility and the responsible thinking process. I saw the value of sitting down next to a student, helping them realize what needs to change and encouraging the student to build better habits.

In my final year of high school, I asked my old school if I could return for a week of work experience in the LoSoP team, as I wanted to be a youth worker, a goal which I have now achieved. Thankfully, I was accepted, and I was able to go back and really see the difference Loving our Students on Purpose makes. Being able to help young people learn to self-reflect and encouraging them to control their own behavior themselves rather than just being told to change. Even as an adult today I still mentally use the Loving on Purpose and responsibility tools when I am faced with new challenges.

So be encouraged to practice these strategies: Whose problem is it? Do they see the problem, or is it just me who sees it? If they see the problem, how am I going to come alongside them to enable them to find a solution, make a plan and put it into practice, so that every day is a powerful day for that person?

What we are looking for is a student who wants to work alongside us and parents who want to participate in our school culture, both demonstrating willingness to clean up each mess with the goal of not repeating it in the future. Messes will be repeated, of course—again, these children are professional mistake-makers. They are probably going to repeat the mistakes a few times or more, and we need to be ready for that. Each time, we must be consistent in our approach of coming alongside them whilst they look at their own problems, yet refusing to work harder on their life, academics, or relationships than they are. Each mess is one more opportunity to improve our skill of asking really good questions that will guide the student, parent, or even teacher to explore what they are thinking about their own lives.

You may have noticed that not one of the questions I have proposed are "Why" questions. When we ask "Why," we are immediately asking the other person to explain themselves and prove to us that there is a right or a wrong that we may or may not accept. A "Why" question is a challenge. It does not allow for depth of reflection; rather, it is a fruitless demand which typically drives up anxiety, resulting in the amygdala firing off and slowing down complex reasoning and thinking. (This is different to a discovery "Why" question where we explore the workings of science and the mechanics of something.) It can be very difficult for students to understand the subtlety of the question, so changing the question to "How" or "What" provides a softer landing for thought processing, rather than the feeling of an inquisition.

Another technique I apply when developing plans is to remove the word "not." Whilst guiding any student, parent, or teacher to the answers they have within themselves, we are looking for what is there, rather than what is missing. I often ask the person to rephrase any "not" answer to something they can achieve. For example, if a student says, "I will not squirt yogurt on someone," I work with the student until they can re-phrase this as, "I will respect other people's property." Or with a teacher who says, "I will not tolerate Martha's behavior in my classroom," I invite them to rephrase it positively as, "I will use the behavior education pro-cess consistently when speaking with Martha." I want the last thought in their "I will" statement to be something they can enact. "I will be quiet in class," rather than, "I will not talk." "I will be safe," rather than, "I will not hit." "I will listen to the teacher," rather than, "I will not ignore the teacher." "I will eat my lunch," rather than, "I will not throw food." It is an incredible life skill to remove the Whys and the Nots from our language in communication with others. It not only builds connection—it also empowers us to own our own "I will" decisions.

10

TOUGH CASES

THE EMPOWERMENT MODEL CAN be applied across every scenario you can think of in a school sector. Issues may arise in relation to disability, discipline, trauma, friendship, and well-being. This model can also be used for parent engagement, disability discussions/planning meetings, or for staff appraisals, redirection, and self-reflection. Do not limit the application to these examples.

Keeping our love on consistently is going to be key in offering a location for students, teachers, and families to connect and engage; however, it is a choice and not everyone will choose to connect. There will be times where the person you are talking to will not want the solution to their problem. They may not even see that they have a problem. It hurts when someone chooses to disconnect, but they have the freedom to choose what they are going to do with the problems in their life.

During any of these discussions, we want our parents and students to hear that we love them, that we want them in our school, and that we can handle their mistakes. This is not a "three strikes and you're out" policy. Your mistakes do not change how much we value you, even if it means you need to attend a different school. Finally, we are showing our parents and students that we are learning equally from them whilst they are learning from us and that we are co-teachers in this experience. Through applying the Empowerment model, you will learn some amazing strategies that may benefit other students or even impact whole school initiatives. Many of the most successful strategies I have seen implemented over the years have been suggested by students as we have navigated this process together.

For example, years ago, I noticed that students were coming to see me consistently for "talking," yet when I spoke with the students, they explained, "I was answering my friend." It is always the second student who is heard speaking by the teacher (because the first student drew the teacher's attention), and they are indignant that they were doing the right thing.

There is an interesting phenomenon that happens in schools in which we try to break students of home strategies. What do I mean? Well at home if you ask a child a question, parents expect an answer. If a parent calls out from another room, the child must respond or even come find the parent immediately. At the dinner table, it is rare for a child to put their hand up—instead, they will honor the unspoken family rule of jumping in when there is a gap of conversation. Many of my students were finding themselves in trouble for "doing as their parents taught them—manners." We used the Empowerment Model to find out what they had tried, determine what had worked and what hadn't worked, and come up with new ideas. Soon these students had developed a range of hand signals to communicate with teachers and peers without making noise. This concept was taken on as a whole school approach and reduced the number of students "talking back to a peer" significantly. Signs included, "Ask the teacher," "I want to hear what you have to say later," "I need the bathroom," "Please don't talk to me," "I am concentrating," and more.

We are going to have a look at how to apply the empowerment model to various cases. Again please don't limit your imagination. You can follow these steps when a colleague comes to complain to you for the umpteenth time, when a parent wants to badmouth another parent, or when friendship conflicts happen in the playground. The empowerment model is designed to help the other person walk toward a powerful outcome for the problem in their life as you cheer them on.

DISABILITY CASES

Andy was ten years old when I met her. She was also hearing impaired and had been diagnosed with Asperger's. Andy was so used to her previous school isolating her from peers that she did not know that having friends was even a possibility, let alone that she could want friends. Due to Andy's behavioral responses, her schooling history was characterized by staff protecting the other students from her. When Andy started working with us, she had already established that isolation was her only option, so when other students came near her, she felt unsafe and would react physically to ensure they moved away. Here was a girl with highly developed tools to create distance and survive rejection.

Upon meeting Andy, it was immediately evident that she was a high risk of harm toward other students. After all, this was her learned behavioral response when her survival brain was triggered and it had kept Andy safe all these years. This meant there was likely to be a long and difficult road to navigate with parents and teachers who may not know how to support Andy as she learned new ways to respond to the perception of danger. Inevitably, she would fall into previously established behaviors during the learning process. With my eyes securely on the goal—Andy's development of new interpersonal skills and experience of acceptance into the school community, specifically making a friend—we engaged a team approach to plan for success.

The first few months were extremely difficult. We observed Andy having many tantrums and physical reactions toward other students. When I attempted to walk Andy through the process of taking responsibility, she would simply take out her hearing aid and refuse to talk to anyone. Going back to basics, we started by reinforcing empathy and love over and over again, sending messages like, "You matter to us. We want to hear your side. Help us understand. We love having you at our school. Oh, that was a boundary. I am sorry that this is not fun for you." It took a significant time to build trust and connection through these consistent messages of love, acceptance, and empathy, but slowly we edged our way toward bringing the powerful question into the discussion: "What are you going to do?" I know from working with many students who have Asperger's or autism that repetition and predictability are essential. I trusted that in time Andy would come to expect the same response to her behavior, which would create safe boundaries for her to predict outcomes and thereby make informed choices. In addition, we could see, and we were waiting for her to see, that being removed from peers every day was not a solution, so we started supporting Andy through the use of social stories to plan how she would respond to small common issues that would come up in the classroom and the playground. We spent many conversations asking, "What have you tried? How did that work out? I have ideas—would you like to hear them?"

Through revisiting the Empowerment Model frequently, Andy began creating a toolkit to draw on in future situations. Andy learned about the warning signs she displayed when she was starting to escalate and how to recover after an eruption. Her parents also sought professional psychology to assist Andy's development of self-awareness. As a school, we engaged the whole cohort in education about hearing impairment, specifically helping students to be conscious about the misinterpretation of speaking fast or soft or approaching Andy from behind, which could startle her triggering a physical reaction. We spent a long time working with Andy to understand each person's contribution in a conflict and how to reflect on what was her part and what was the other person's part. Over time, we found that despite Andy's justice-driven nature, she started to see the value in focusing on and owning her part of the interaction.

One day, after a year of working almost daily with Andy on small and large issues that arose, she came to me with a big smile and said, "I just hit Brodie, but it's okay because I've written an apology note and I've given it to him, and he's forgiven me. Now I am here to plan what to do next time so Brodie doesn't get hurt." Boom, what a moment of celebration. Andy had walked herself through the entire Empowerment Model and was developing her own powerful person plan.

Please hear this: apologizing or admitting a mistake does not mean that the original issue does not need to be explored. There was still a conflict, and there may be a mess to be cleaned up. However, it is always a sweet moment when a student starts taking responsibility and makes a genuine effort to clean up his or her mess. It is a sure sign that you as the teacher have been building safety and trust when your students know it is okay to make mistakes, admit mistakes, and even at times make mistakes as they clean up their own messes. They are risking, learning, and coming back to you to coach them as they grow in confidence to apply their own internal solutions to the problems in their own lives.

Andy is now in secondary school and learning to navigate new hormones. The new students in secondary are not familiar with her hearing impairment or Asperger's traits, and as a result, some of the behaviors we saw in the early days have re-emerged. But because of the relationship and connection we have built over the years, Andy's positive responses and desire to stay connected in her school community are strong, and now she knows how to clean up messes and take ownership. What is more, Andy has a whole group of friends who accept and love her unconditionally. Inclusive education has made significant strides in accommodating students with a variety of disability needs in the classroom. Working with students with disabilities does not need to be daunting; rather, it can be incredibly rewarding for students to learn acceptance and positive regard toward those different to themselves.

DISCIPLINE CASES

One question I get asked by every school I consult with is, "What do you do when the student, parent, teacher, or even the principal does not change or accept your help? In other words, what do you do when someone in your culture is not acting powerfully or says, 'No'? When can we have permission to ask that student to leave our school?"

The Empowerment Model can be used when meeting with parents and students as a response to a significant behavior mess or a big, non-compliant "No." These are the scary messes that can potentially impact a large number of people in your community, and often have legal ramifications, as I mentioned in the last chapter. I am referring to drugs or alcohol on-site, inappropriate physical touch between students, cyber-safety, bullying, violence, willful damage to property, theft, defamation of the school on social media, serious truancy, and repetitive levels of disrespect. When we encounter "big messes," our immediate reaction is to reach for the "expel them" option. Why? These are the messes that scare people, which puts added pressure and scrutiny on leaders to deal with the mess in an appropriately decisive, and usually punishing, way.

What if there was another option than simply removing the offender? What if you had a tool to walk alongside both the perpetrator and the victims in the most difficult situations that will come up in your school? What if your school culture and identity were secure and not tossed back and forth by the waves of opinion, but instead supported a hurting student or family as they regained stability? Using the empowerment model for enrollment reviews will help you to navigate these scary situations successfully. It won't stop you being criticized, but it will help you to focus on your goal—connection.

Enrollment reviews or stakeholder meetings typically occur following a serious breach of conduct. When a student has behaved in a way that has impacted the school culture, whether their classroom, cohort, or even just a few people who know what has happened, those impacted and responsible need to sit down to determine what is to be done. A team, including senior leadership, parents, and the student, meet to consider what has been happening in the classroom and/or school campus that has caused at least one member of that team to feel like there is a problem.

The first step is to ask, "Do we all see the problem? Are we looking at the same problem?" Once we are on the same page, we initiate the Empowerment Model and offer empathy. "This is not a fun situation to be in.

I am sorry you are hurting. How about you share what is going on for you right now?' We want to find out what is going on in this young person's life at home, at school, between them and their teacher, or between them and their friends that preceded the conflict or poor choice. We also want to find out, "How are you feeling about this? Are you feeling disconnected? Are you feeling rejected? Are you feeling hurt? Are you feeling scared? Are you feeling worthless?" Understanding what the student is feeling lays the foundation for emotional connection, trust, and rapport during this confrontation. We want the parents to hear a similar message: "We love your child and we want to have them in our school if they want to participate in protecting the connection. How are they experiencing their schooling career right now? Is it working for them? Is it working for you as the parent?"

After acknowledging the experience our student and parents are having, we then slide across the table the power question: "*What are you going to do?*" We can do this no matter the student's age. Even the little preppies understand when we ask, "What are you going to do with this problem in your life?"

Often the student will stare back with no answer to this question, so this is the moment where we get to start asking great questions like, "*What have you already tried?*" "What have you tried with your teacher? What have you tried with your friends? What have you tried with your parents?" We also ask the parents, "What works for you at home? What strategies have you been using? What cognitive or medical assessments have you done? What external help have you engaged?" This is usually the time in the conversation we also get an insight into what is happening at home. This is where we find out about parents recently separating, children who have had early childhood trauma, medical interventions that have happened prior to school attendance, blended family dynamics, and parenting techniques and styles that are quite different to what we are using at the school, particularly those reinforcing behavior with the reward or punishment.

As we move through the process of questions, questions, questions, we eventually get to that part of the conversation when a student and parent say, "We need your help," or "Is there anything we have not thought of?" This is the moment where we offer, "*I have some ideas if you would like to hear them,*" and now we are collectively putting together a plan of action. We have wisdom we are willing to share, but we need to be sharing it with somebody who is open and wants to hear it for any momentum to occur. When we have a parent asking, "What else can we do?" "How come the student is listening to you at school?" or "We have spoken to other families and they said to ask you for ideas," this is the moment where we get to offer our pearls.

There are many ideas in the toolkit you can consider and write down prior to this meeting that would be both applicable and simple to implement because they are actually part of your school culture. Ideas may include being able to drop a subject, getting extra support with the learning enrichment team, using a monitor card to track success, participating in allied health support services on site, referrals to external services you hear good reports about, working with a staff mentor, participating in programs such as grief and loss programs, resiliency-building programs, social skills programs, engaging in medical reviews, participating in the parenting Loving our Kids on Purpose program, accessing resources in the library for parents or students, and the list goes on and on and on. As we offer lots of choices and options, we want the parent to know we are standing alongside them as they develop their own plan of action for their student to continue to be enrolled.

After empathy, empowerment, exploration, and education, we return to the power question: "*What are you going to do now?*" This is the opportunity for the student or parent to agree on their action plan for what they are going to do next to manage the problem in their life. In the process we also ask, "*What do you need from us?*" The parent and student may be feeling a little overwhelmed, so we don't want to send them away with a list of tasks they are unlikely to even remember. We want them to feel that we are cheering them on and helping them build a plan that will be successful. Typically, I am the one during the meeting who has been managing my emotions well, keeping the discussion on track, and taking notes, so it's most expedient for me to write the plan down, set dates for when appointments will be attended or a follow-up meeting will be scheduled, and then send a summary email outlining what we discussed and committed to.

When the big messes come up that automatically initiate the enrolment review process, it is common to get questions about what we will do with a parent or student who does not see the problem. This is a real possibility and something we plan for leading up to the review meeting. As a team, we consider what ideas may be suitable for this situation, what expectations we would need to see met to feel confident keeping the student enrolled, what adjustments may we need to consider making for the student, and what behavior choices may result in the need to cancel an enrollment. A lot hinges on whether the parent or student can see the problem. Perhaps the problem is that we cannot have our students at risk of accessing prohibited substances at school. Perhaps we do not want to expose the school culture to a parent or family who encourages their child to use physical violence as a reaction rather than honoring non-violent communication. Perhaps a parent is unable to recognize that their child's actions were illegal or grossly inappropriate. Perhaps the mental health of a teacher is at risk due to ongoing aggressive or inappropriate behavior by a student or their parents. What do you do then?

Remember, this only works if we are sitting side by side looking out at the problem. It will not work if I am looking at them saying, "You are the problem and this is what you need to do." Neither does it work if the parent is saying, "The school is the problem and this is what needs to change." It is not uncommon that you will have a parent request that you change your whole school behavior process and policy to be punishment-oriented rather than responsibility-oriented. It is easy to feel swayed by an angry parent who wants vindication for their child. It is even easier to be swayed by tears. You must be prepared for this. Other people's emotional behavior does not control your decision. You can and should have empathy while keeping your boundaries. There are many things that can be adjusted and changed, and sometimes this is very appropriate. But your core values and culture as a school must stand strong. These are what attract your families in the first place and build trust.

From the school's perspective, the leadership needs to ensure collective safety of students and staff, rebuild trust, and protect culture. They may be asking the student, "How are you going to make us look like a genius for keeping you enrolled?" A parent refusing to take steps to support the school culture or recognize that the problem is hindering the ongoing enrolment of their child may be asked directly, "Is this the right school environment for them? Do they actually want to support the values that the school is maintaining? Do they want to participate in the culture of the school? Or is this the right environment for them and their family's needs?" For a student they may be asking similar questions: "Do you want to attend this school? Do you want to uphold the values of the school? Do you want to participate in the culture that the school is offering?"

There are many great schools. Perhaps some families need the opportunity to choose one that best fits their family's or student's values. If a student does not want to wear a uniform, their parents do not support the uniform policy, and this is a constant point of conflict at school, perhaps a school with a less stringent uniform policy is required. If a parent wants to endorse physical violence as a means of conflict resolution, perhaps they need to select a school that does not require non-violent communication. Remember, there are many different types of schools. As you reflect with the family, it is okay to consider that this one might not be the right fit for this specific student. Sometimes the student just does not want to attend. Ideally, this should be determined at the very first enrollment meeting when a family arrives at a school. However, sometimes this comes to light as the year progresses. So again, we are sitting side by side looking out at the problem, and as we work toward a solution, one of those solutions may be changing schools.

There are times where one of the parties does not want to work towards a solution. Elyse was one of these students. Elyse was an unhappy fourteen-year-old whose behavior presented as grossly disrespectful toward her teachers. She did not complete work and argued excessively. When we entered a parent meeting with Elyse and her mother, it was not surprising when her mother spoke equally disrespectfully toward the leadership and teachers. We could see the problem, but they could not see the problem. We needed to set clear expectations about what a respectful conversation would look like if we were to continue the meeting. We offered to pause the meeting and wait until they could both speak appropriately (no different to how we interact with students daily). The duo reined in their emotions, but Elyse assured us that she did not want to be a part of our school culture. Her mother attempted to coax her to consider listening to our ideas, but she would not. In the end, Elyse left the meeting and went down the road to the public school and enrolled.

The very next afternoon, we got a phone call from Elyse requesting another meeting. What had happened at the school across the road? What had changed this girl's heart? Curious, we met with Elyse and her mother again. Elyse was now taking responsibility and participating in the discussion. She shared that she had not expected to feel so lost and alone at her new school, and quickly realized that the culture of love and connection we were offering every day was where she wanted to be. She acknowledged how hard her teachers worked to support her and their patience at her frequent outbursts and disrespect. She then apologized for her behavior and for taking for granted the care and support she had been given for years. Elyse did not know how she was going to make us look like geniuses for re-enrolling her, but she was now willing and open to hear our ideas. We gladly took the risk, set our expectations, offered ideas, made a plan, and re-enrolled her.

Elyse blossomed into a young woman, completed her final years, and transitioned successfully into further study and the workplace. In those final years, she still struggled with being reactive to authority, with identity and feelings of worthlessness, and with getting her work done on time, but there was a huge change. Elyse started to notice when she became disrespectful and learned to walk away, calm down, and even return to the teacher and apologize. Elyse also began noticing that her work ethic needed to improve to get the results she wanted in her subject areas. She began seeking support to process communication conflicts and develop social skills so that she could improve her friendships and connections, not only at school but also at home with her parents. This young woman was set up for success not because anyone was telling her what to do, but because she continuously sought the answers to the problems in her own life. We let her know that we loved her, wanted her in our school, had solutions and strategies she might want to hear about, and that she knows how to find us. We also let her know what our boundaries were and what her choices would be if she continued to break trust with us. Elyse chose to protect our connection and stay enrolled.

It is an incredible moment when you walk the long road with a family or student and get to the point of an expulsion. When the parent or student looks into your eyes, acknowledges that you have done all you can and they have made their choice, usually by their behavior, and shakes your hand as they say, "Thank you" before leaving, I genuinely wish them well. I remember that in almost every situation, these are the students who come back to visit and let me know how they are doing. Often they ask to re-enroll a year later or even return to do work experience.

TRAUMA AND WELL-BEING CASES

Many of the students who need our love are those who have experienced trauma in their lives. Negative behavior should not simply be justified as "bad," "defiant," "manipulative," or "oppositional." Quite often, these students' behaviors reflect some very strong internal emotions resulting from scary and traumatic interactions in their environments, usually with significant adults in their lives. Sometimes, these behaviors are an expression of a damaged sense of worth and well-being. Frequently, it is both.

Whenever a behavior occurs, I aim to consider the bigger picture and the history that led to the behavior. Understanding a student's history increases our capacity for empathy and compassion as we confront them being frustrating and defiant to our face. There are many times where I don't know a student's history, but their behavior clearly suggests their sense of safety has been compromised. I choose to proceed each time with empathy. A student's life experiences never excuse disrespectful behavior, but they help us understand why they are behaving in a fight, flight, or freeze sequence, which in turn informs my response and boundary.

Take Layla, for example. She is loud and disruptive when she is in class, yet she is also frequently missing from class, wandering around the school and even walking into other classrooms and causing confusion and disruption. In addition to these behaviors, Layla has complex mental health concerns, which are expressed in frequent self-harm through cutting or taking medication that she finds.

Layla's mental health declined significantly after her older brother Tom committed suicide. From Layla's perspective as a ten-year-old, Tom had been sent home early from school again. Maybe he was sick, maybe he was in trouble—to Layla this wasn't unusual, so she did not think much of it at the time. As she was walking home later that day, Layla stopped by the corner store to purchase lollies. When she returned home a little later than usual, she was the one to discover Tom dead. She screamed for help, but it was too late. Complex grief ensued with little family support or education about suicide postvention or grief and loss. Layla internalized that her brother's death was her fault—if she had not stopped for lollies, she could have gotten home in time to save Tom. At fifteen, the same age her brother was when he died, Layla continues to blame herself and now is experiencing guilt that she has outlived him.

On the one hand, a student like Layla poses a safety risk to the school because she requires constant supervision. She is also a distraction to other students and a resource-intense student who draws on the support of multiple staff to assist in self-regulating. On the other hand, she is also a safety risk to herself. Amid fears of self-harming on campus and the impact this would have on other students, we must manage additional concerns for her psychological health and well-being.

Criticism that students like Layla get too much attention, require too many resources, and are forgiven too often is not uncommon in a school environment where compassion and boundaries are filtered differently by other people's perspectives. Yet most significant behavior problems at schools are undergirded by trauma and complexity which are protected by privacy policies. It is a balance between boundaries and grace. Would we ask a student to leave the school for having low self-worth or a traumatic life-event? Of course not! Would we consider asking a student to leave if they are frequently missing from class, or causing panic or frequent disruption that impacts the right of others to learn? Certainly there may be a place for this after repeated unsuccessful interventions.

Inviting Layla's parents to engage in a meeting to discuss her behaviors was important, yet too often her parents' emotional states are also heightened, as they are fearful of Layla being expelled. We start every meeting with *empathy*: "I am concerned for your safety, Layla. I know this has been a difficult time for you. We love having you at our school. However, right now it is not working for us. How is it working for you?" We are looking for whether Layla and her parents can see the problem. We may ask directly, "Layla, do you see the problem?"

The problem is not that Layla has mental health concerns. We are prepared with ideas for how to support her and her family through this for as long as she chooses to stay enrolled. The problem is that Layla is experiencing unresolved complex grief, which is presenting as behaviors that are compromising the safety of our school environment for herself and for others. The boundary Layla and her parents are about to experience is that Layla needs to be safe to remain at our school, and to do this she needs to engage in professional support. She is going to have some choices that she is being guided through in this conversation.

Once we have established that Layla understands the severity of self-harming on campus, exposing students to this, frequently missing class, and the impact this has on others as well as her own grades, we then offer her the power question, "What are you going to do?"

Layla thinks about it for a while, but has no ideas. She looks to her parents, but they are worn out and have no new ideas either. This is the cue for us to ask the parents to start exploring what they have tried before. Layla had been to a grief and loss children's program when she was much younger, but as she did not "appear" to be impacted by her brother's suicide at the time, they let her drop out. In addition, she had been asked to see a psychologist by her previous school and they almost considered it, but then it was expensive and complicated, so they decided to change schools instead. Layla seemed to enjoy her new school initially, and they surmised she had forgotten about Tom because she was young at the time and never mentioned him.

As they shared these historical steps, we could tell that Layla's parents were reconsidering these types of interventions and freshly recognizing the problem. After a thorough exploration of previous actions taken, we could now offer our ideas. This was the perfect time to educate Layla and her parents on psychologists that have a good reputation, referring Layla to the GP for a mental health assessment, and putting in a referral to a child and youth mental health service or mental health social worker. Layla could also benefit, we said, from working with the school guidance officer on some memory-making activities to help her incorporate Tom's memory into her life appropriately. We also suggested to Layla's parents that they might need help understanding the process of engaging with allied health support and education related to the myths of a mental health label, as well as their own grief support. Perhaps they could benefit from a course about mental health and teenagers, such as a youth mental health first aid course, so that they learn how to support her confidently and effectively. We also let Layla know that she had alternative options to attending this school.

During this whole conversation, we did not ignore the impact Layla's behavior was having on other students. As we entered the Expect step of the process, we ensured that Layla's well-being and behaviors were being planned for and educated Layla and her parents on the school expectation for safety and appropriate classroom engagement. We developed a safety plan that outlined where Layla could go prior to self-harming to get support, what areas of the school were out of bounds to her, who her safe people were to talk to, and how the school will respond if she chooses to self-harm on site, such as phoning an ambulance or calling the police. Her parents identified what steps they would take to get Layla suitable support through doctors and psychology services. Further, we identified what triggers were causing Layla to escalate in the classroom and either leave or become a disruption, and decided how to plan for those. As Layla and the team developed this plan collaboratively, there was an inherent commitment that when the meeting ended, all persons agreed to uphold their part of the plan. It was written down, everyone got a copy, and we all committed to it.

Then we entered the Encourage stage. "I am here cheering you on. What do you need from me? Would you benefit from a weekly check-in for a while? Let me know as soon as you have booked that appointment. Come and show me your attendance monitor card so we can celebrate that you are staying in class."

If the behavior continues, then the plan may need a review or another meeting to consider if everyone understood their agreement. At some point, we may also need to step back and consider the impact Layla's behavior is having on the school as a whole. In most situations, however, trauma and well-being support plans can be activated and reviewed in a way that supports everyone to stay connected and engaged.

FRIENDSHIP CASES

One of the common problems we see each day on the playground is students bickering and fighting with each other. Friendship conflicts are actually important. Proverbs even says, "As iron sharpens iron, so a friendship sharpens a friend."[1] But watching it play out can be painful. It can be especially painful for parents to watch their young one experiencing rejection and sadness as they learn about social skills. So, it is important to help our families and students to learn what healthy friendship conflicts are and what they are not. We need to know when to step in and help, and when to step back and let your child persevere in the development of their social skills, boundary negotiation, and resilience.

Duty teachers typically spend the entire break opening tricky snack packs, telling students to walk on the concrete, and listening to students tell on their peers. "They did this! They touched this! They said this!" This can be really exhausting. The empowerment model works really well in these situations as well. When little Johnny comes to you and says, "Sally stood on my yogurt," the first thing that comes out of your mouth is empathy. "Oh no, that does not sound fun. That sounds like it hurt. How are you feeling about that?" Johnny may be angry, crying, or indifferent, but listening to him gives him the start of a foundation on which to build his solution.

Next, the power question: "What are you going to do?" Typically in this type of situation, Johnny already knows what he is going to do and may have actually already done it. When I asked this question to a student who had reported that their sibling squirted their yogurt on them (yes, it is all too frequently yogurt) she informed me that her friends had already gone to get her some paper towel to help clean it up. What a great solution to the problem in her life! "Well done! What great friends you have."

---

[1] Proverbs 27:17

After offering empathy, asking the power question, and discovering the actions they have taken, we may still need to work toward a solution. We have a golden opportunity to coach these young people through everyday situations to learn how to resolve conflict successfully. That is where we can have some really great questions ready to explore what happened and what they want to do about it. "What was happening before the incident? Did you speak with the other student? What did you say? Do you think it may have been accidental? Do you know what an accident is? (Always ask this question—a lot of students do not know the difference between an accident and deliberate action.) Do you need to speak to them?"

Sometimes the student still feels hurt and angry. What we do not want to do is to swoop in and rescue them from the opportunity to resolve the conflict. Instead, we can offer, "I have some suggestions if you'd like to hear them." In some situations, students will let us know that they want to go and speak to the other person first, but they will come back if that does not work. Sometimes we find they bring their friend back with them and ask us to help them together. In Johnny's case, he asked for our ideas. "Well Johnny," I told him, "you could go and speak to Sally and let her know that you are upset." After Johnny thinks about this for a little while, I ask, "How would that work out for you?"

"Well, Sally is my friend. She might listen to me."

"Okay well how about you give it a go and let me know how it works out?"

Off he runs to talk to Sally.

Ultimately, I am coaching Johnny to discover how to stay connected with Sally. What is he going to do to meet that goal? What might happen if he is unsuccessful? This is really important. For example, when Johnny says sorry to Sally for the name he called her when she stood on his yogurt, he may expect her to say sorry back. But what if she does not? This is an invaluable teaching moment where we get to explore with Johnny the idea that he can be sorry and take ownership of his part, but that he does not control Sally's reaction, and that can hurt. What is important is that he cleans up his side of the dispute.

Sally, meanwhile, might need some more intense support with an adult to work through what happened separately. She might be feeling very angry and need help to emotionally regulate before she is ready to take ownership for her part. It is always important to remember that there are two people involved in any interaction. Both people need to work through their part of the problem and move toward their solution to the problem. However, each person is only responsible for their part. These kids are learning that they cannot demand justice or restitution from another person. What they can do is seek connection, own their part, express what they need, and let the other person work through what they are going to do with the problem in their young life.

We are starting to teach students at a young age how to be powerful, how to notice when they have made a mess, and how to clean up that mess. We want our students to work toward being powerful so that when they graduate and have jobs or families of their own, they will be able to speak up effectively. We want them to be gracious employers, loving partners, and patient parents who are able to guide their own children towards being powerful people. So we are looking for opportunities every day as we observe and interact with our young people to practice the strategies. "Do you see the problem? What solutions have you already tried? I have some ideas if you would like to hear them? What are you going to do now? How's that going to work out for you? Let me know how it goes!"

Asking good questions as they solve the small everyday problems is what sets them up for success when they encounter the big scary problems of adult life, and it helps build resilience and the wisdom to solve their own problems from the inside. We have the great joy of instilling in our students confidence in who they are created to be and that they can manage their own lives effectively. We are sending the message, "We believe in you and your success."

Again, some people do not want help and it does not matter what we do—they still do not want our help. Sometimes one of the greatest gifts we can offer to help a student or parent is to do nothing. No action is always one of the options. No action is a choice you can make every single day. So too, saying "no" is also an option. As Danny reminds us, whatever we say yes to means we are saying no to something else, and whatever we say no to means we are saying yes to something else. My hope is for you to come away with the confidence to set limits, be confident in your yes and no, have strategies to coach students and parents toward thriving, and know when to step back and do nothing whilst they are empowered to work harder on their lives than you are.

As you are probably noticing, this is a repetitious process. I often get asked, "How long? How many repetitions? When will they learn?" The answer is simple. Teachers are there from day one when students enroll in prep or kindergarten and onward for the thirteen years they will journey through school before transitioning to teachers in their workplaces, universities, or trade centers. There is no shortcut to learning about life. There is no shortcut to learning the skill of being powerful. We find that some students learn the skills of being powerful and take ownership for themselves quickly, while other students use the full thirteen years. With others, we may not ever see the fruit until well after graduation. And there are some who choose never to take responsibility for their lives. Remember that every student develops differently during their schooling journey. Every student comes with a different parenting template and family culture that impact the decisions they make. Every student has their own unique personality and gifts that are being sharpened in the school environment, which is full of social and emotional pressures. Each student is going to grow and develop differently, whilst looking to that powerful adult at school or in their sporting community, youth group, or family who believes in them during their poor choices and shows them that they have the answers to their own life's problems already inside of them.

11

WORKING WITH PARENTS AND ADMINISTRATION

TWO DECADES HAVE PASSED since my first experience with "behavior education," responding powerlessly as I tried to control Rebecca. Rebecca is now a mother and qualified school social worker herself. I had the pleasure of speaking with Mrs. Roberts, who to this day thanks me for not giving up on her daughter. It was a long journey for both Rebecca and Mrs Roberts. I was only there for a moment in time, but it made a small difference.

So often we don't get to see the difference we make in a single moment, but it is there. We are not responsible for walking beside our students through their lifetime——we are setting them on a path of success and cheering them on as they continue the adventure without us. One of my mentors, Aaron Salisbury, often reminds me, "The coach doesn't play on game day." This is a good reminder that there is a time for skill-building and practice, and a time to let the student demonstrate their skills and take responsibility for their life.

With that said, it is important to ensure students stay connected to a parent or significant caregiver, as their life journey is going to take them places where we cannot go. Schools are full of parents and caregivers. Every student who comes to school has an adult looking after them. Some of these adults are powerful and responsible, whilst others are earnestly learning these skills, and others yet are sadly the source of trauma in a child's life. What has been consistently true in my schooling experiences is that when we start loving our students on purpose and teaching them responsibility, parents notice. Here is just one testimony from a parent who experienced the support of a school that loved her children on purpose:

> We have five kids that have attended the same school. Our daughter is our eldest. She worked hard at school and out of school. She was studious and we never once had to ask her to do her homework. She got great results and was one of a handful of students who were rewarded with a special afternoon tea by the principal for demonstrating responsible thinking throughout her entire schooling journey.
>
> The other four of our kids are boys. Some of them thought the Living Room was a core subject in the curriculum. I just did a search in my emails for "Behaviour Notification" and found literally hundreds of emails from the Living Room who kept us well-informed letting me know that one of the boys had made use of their services. Two of my boys were eventually expelled, one returned to complete Year 12.
>
> When I think back over the darkness and trauma of those years, my times spent with Bernii and the principals were some of the brightest places of hope and grace I experienced. I never felt judged. They never tried to lay blame. They were always calm and considered. They included and empowered us as parents in the process. They stuck to the facts and clearly articulated the standards and consequences. They were solution-oriented but student-empowering. They walked at the pace of the student's ability to own their behaviour and consequences, and create a plan to make better choices in the future. For all the grief, darkness, and chaos we were living through as parents, they were life and light.

> *When I ask the boys (now tradesmen in their twenties) about how they were treated by the school during their "Great Rebellion," they express appreciation for the way Bernii "never gave up on me even when I never really treated her the way she deserved. I'm thankful for that." She kept her love on. There were many things they questioned during those years, about school and life and faith and family, but Bernii's love was never in question. It was joyful and stern, gentle and strong, peaceful and kind. It never dishonoured them or sought its own ends. It was never brought to anger and didn't keep a record of wrongs. It took no delight in evil but rejoiced with them in truth. It protected, trusted, hoped, and persevered. It did not fail.*

Parents may notice that their child keeps bumping up against boundaries, resulting in support meetings and discussions, or they may notice that their child is changing in their confidence, independence, and increased schooling success. Some parents may respond with aggression, anger, and powerlessness themselves, and others with curiosity. Regardless of the manner in which parents seek to understand your connection with their child, it is a great place to start a conversation. Don't allow yourself to be taken by surprise by an angry parent who does not like the boundary you set. Be ready to explain why you are seeking connection, what this looks like in a connected classroom culture, and how they can help create a seamless connection between home and school. Encourage parents to learn more about what loving our students on purpose looks like by referring them to this book in your parent resource library. You may even start a parenting revolution in your students' homes as parents learn how to turn their hearts toward their children and keep their love turned on.

Parenting is often one of the core obstacles our students are facing. We support many students who have learned how to navigate their parent's negative reactions, which can be a huge distraction to them living in freedom as they learn and grow. It is incredibly common that a student afraid of their parent's negative consequences will react with a fear response—crying, yelling, negotiating, pleading, lying, or even shutting down and not communicating at all. Schools do well to remember that when it comes to consequences, students have to consider their options—upsetting their parents, their peers, or the school. For example, a parent may train their child to "hit back," while the school usually has a policy about being safe; thus, the student has to decide whether to please their parent or their school.

Anticipating a parent's negative reaction can keep a student from focusing on their day. Arnold is an excellent example. Since prep, Arnold was a talker, muttering to himself as he processed aloud, making unusual noises, being dirty, and refusing to work. Arnold would experience a meltdown when his teachers attempted to confront these minor issues, often resulting in him needing to go home, as he was unable to settle enough to safely return to school. Prior to going home, Arnold would have escalated to hitting the teacher, breaking furniture, locking himself in rooms, and swearing uncontrollably. Through his verbal rants, we learned that when Arnold went home, his parents would require him to sit in an empty bathtub for the remainder of the day as a punishment. Once we learned this was happening, we were able to have a conversation with his parents. Parents are not always going to support a culture of love over fear and punishment, however, and Arnold's parents refused to change their technique. In lieu of his parents not wanting to engage, our next option was to support Arnold to first survive the experience he was having with his parents, then work backward to learn how to respond appropriately to his teacher, and then finally learn how to manage his noise level in class—a much longer process.

You may be wondering why we did not simply teach Arnold how to manage his noise level in class. Arnold's threat detector was so acutely responsive that it would instantaneously react fearfully—this was his most developed response. We first had to show him how to manage his emotional responses and feel safe and connected at school before we could teach him new skills in the classroom requiring him to engage his less developed smart brain. Managing his fear of his parents' reaction, and then his teacher's reaction, became preludes for learning great classroom skills. We did this by teaching Arnold activities he could do by using his imagination to pass the time. Arnold loved reading, and even without access to books he would imagine the most wonderful adventures whilst sitting in the bathtub. In addition, his teachers worked with us to adjust their own reactions. They started to allow Arnold to use a stand-up desk, keep a fiddle tool and an oral sensory tool, such as a piece of straw to suck on, which distracted his mouth from making noises whilst activating deep breathing. He was permitted to read work questions aloud, and his teacher ignored the dirt smears that were a positive sign he had had great fun connecting with peers playing cars in the dirt tracks.

Getting to know Arnold took time. As a five-year-old, he did not have sufficient words to explain his feelings, and when he acted them out, it was often loud and distracting for the whole class. Even though Arnold could not explain his fear, we recognized his reactions as typical signs of punishments or bribes (some people call these "rewards") occurring at home.

Over the years, Arnold learned how to manage his internal response and his parents became curious about the change. Arnold's teacher was ready with ideas the moment his parents asked the question. They were starting to see the problem because his behaviors at home continued whilst he was improving at school. Arnold's teacher informed them about Loving our Kids on Purpose, and they attended a course facilitated at the school. The family experienced significant improvement as connection became their goal.

One day, Arnold was sitting in the reflection room coming up with a plan for the next time he felt the urge to call out in his excitement to share the answer to the class question, when a younger student came into the room crying uncontrollably. Arnold went over, put his hand on the child's back and out of his mouth came empathy. "It's okay. Your parents might be mad for a little while, but you are not in trouble here. You don't need to be sad because you are going to learn how to make good choices for yourself. What can you do next time?" Just like that, the little one calmed down and Arnold initiated the Empowerment Model. Arnold had just become a role model and leader among his peers.

TEACHING LoKoP TO PARENTS

The very first time I was involved in offering Loving our Kids on Purpose to a group of school families, we invited a small group of about ten parents whose children had been involved in behavior education repeatedly and were already curious about how we were engaging with their kids. They were eager with questions, and we were eager to share the one-liners and power statements taught through Danny's humorous stories of "Spooky on the bus" and "Brittney and the chicken coop." We reminded them that we did not wield a remote control; rather, we had some tools we were willing to share with anyone who was interested. They were interested!

In our first group of parents was a dad whose son Bart regularly ended up requiring support from the behavior education team. He and his wife were frustrated enough to enroll in the LoKoP program. Every week before we got into the material, we would offer a time of testimony for parents to share what had worked, what had backfired, and what they were experimenting with. Some of my favorite testimonies came from parents who took a tool, thought outside the box, and offered us new ideas in future classes. Our parents are geniuses! One of my most impacting moments however, was the testimony given by this young dad from our first course. On the last night, he tentatively raised his hand and offered to share. Bart was in lower primary at this stage, and with tears unashamedly flowing, his dad shared the joy of passing Bart in the hallway at home, saying he no longer flinched or turned his back to the wall in fear of being smacked as his dad passed him. This young dad described having a new tool kit that replaced the old tools of punishing and shaming, which meant that now Bart came to him for help and genuinely hugged him without shrinking back. Their relationship and trust were being restored.

Engaging parents in a school community can be difficult, especially if it is not already normal. I speak with many schools frustrated that they put on big events and only a few people turn up—usually the ones who didn't need to turn up. My advice to schools is to start small. Identify exactly which five-to-ten families you would like to engage with and invite them to an intimate special event. Adding a small cost can also increase the professionalism and commitment levels. Then focus on this small group, invest and reflect together, offer access to resources, and guide them through strategy application. Ask them for testimonies and encourage them to share what they are learning with others. The next term, do the same, keeping the groups small and starting a waiting list if required. In one school, over a period of five years they hosted fifteen small LoKoP courses with ten-to-twenty parents. This equated to thirty percent of their school families (one in three families) who completed the course onsite. Many more hired the books and DVDs out of the parent library offered by the school. The broader impact was that every single teacher chose to complete LoKoP because they started to see the positive impact in their students and parent relationships. It was a creep, not a leap, but the impact was that this school's language became one of love and consistency. With the majority of staff and parents becoming powerful and managing themselves well, the students started to mirror this behavior and the school community thrived.

In this school it became normal for students to tell their teachers what is going on in their lives and their peers' lives because they trusted them not to react but to love them into restoration in their own identity and with their parents. Initially, it actually looked like there was a sudden surge in serious life, behavior, and well-being events, but in truth, it was simply becoming safe to share concerns and ask for help. I have observed several schools go on this journey, first with their staff and then with their parents as they recalibrate to connected classroom cultures.

In this environment, students thrive. When teachers say they love their students, they mean it and there is no place they can hide from this love.

This is especially true when supporting the most serious misconduct cases. When parents get alongside the school and work together, the outcomes are invariably positive for the child and for the family. Like Bart's dad, when parents show up and turn their hearts toward love and away from fear, lives are changed. In schools we have a platform not only to educate parents, but also to role-model this relational dynamic in how we interact with students each day.

Many of the schools I consult with provide a special evening or event to introduce and orientate new families to their culture. New students also benefit from a school induction process which demystifies their behavior and well-being processes. For new students who have not grown up in a culture that endorses discipline over punishment, they may initially stand out as they learn how to live in a loving, transparent culture. It can be quite overwhelming to new students and parents, and hard for a student to accept that one is loved and accepted for who they are—imperfect mistake makers. When new families come in, it is important to educate parents on your culture of love and the process of behavior education that their child will be participating in. As Brené Brown reminds us, "Clear is kind," and this reduces any fear the parent may have of being found inadequate in light of their child's behavior.

THE STORY OF BRIAN

Recently, I was hosting an information evening with new families in a secondary school where I was working. Coming in a little later than the other parents and standing to the side was a familiar dad. He was familiar because his son Brian had previously attended our school. I remember, because I made sure I was in the audience the day Brian crossed over the stage and got his certificate. I let out a huge breath of relief as I cheered along with the crowd. Brian had graduated!

Brian came to me in his senior year. He was a quiet student who completed minimal work but knew how to stay under the radar. A few weeks before graduating his senior year, I started hearing concerns about his academic levels and that he may not graduate. I had no history with this young man, so I connected with a peer who had done the heart journey with me in years previously (so many stories) and she encouraged him to come and meet me. To my surprise, the next lunch break he was asking for me. When we met, he was clearly not interested in talking to me. His mood appeared low and his presentation concerning, so I used the opportunity to speak about depression and how to access support. I completed a mental health assessment and I offered my services, which he politely declined.

A week passed and I was informed that Brian was intoxicated at school. When I found him, Brian had indeed brought alcohol to school and consumed it. He was angry, he was scared, and most of all he was in way over his head. Prior to this, Brian's parents and I had not met each other. They had only been at the school for less than twelve months and it was two weeks until graduation day. Brian's future was in serious jeopardy. Together with his parents, we worked through a process of taking responsibility. Brian was permitted back to school, but he refused to come to school. I completed a home visit, where he shared what was happening outside of school, demonstrating an unusual level of secure attachment and blatant honesty, given our newly developed connection. He still refused to come to school and now I was on alert for suicidal ideation as well—our discussion had felt all too much like a confession. At this point, Brian refused all further interactions, but Brian's dad in his distress accepted support. Hourly over the next few days, I coached him using the LoKoP tools, educated him on the signs of suicidal behavior, and provided information on drug awareness. Brian's dad listened, taking a position of trust and ultimately keeping his connection with Brian.

A few days later, Brian ran away from home. My confidence began to waver, but Brian's dad was looking to me for direction and hope. It was a tense few hours waiting to hear if Brian would be located and the condition he would be in. Apparently, Brian had gotten involved in serious drug use and was seeking a fix. To my amazement, I received a phone call from Brian's dad asking if Brian could come immediately and speak to me as they were driving past the school. Brian entered my room, sat on my couch, and poured out the story of his run-in with the authorities, being taken to his dad's work, and his unexpected dad's loving response. "It's like he is reading a script," Brian said, his tone accusatory.

I held his eye contact and agreed. "Yes, it was like he was reading a script. Would he like to see our text messages?"

I learned a long time ago with young people that honesty and transparency are a truth serum. I held up my phone so he could see our discussions. Brian went on and divulged all that was going on, his suicidal thoughts, his fear of being targeted by the drug dealers, and his pain at disappointing his family, which was driving him to live as far from them as possible so they didn't see who he really was. Brian did not want to change his behavior, but he did want help to take control of his life back. His driving desire was to live independently—a great goal. How could we get there without hurting anyone in the process?

Brian began to strategize. He discovered he needed to complete his assessments, to graduate, to get a job, to earn money, and to move out. Okay, now we had a plan. Brian not only finished his assessment, but also passed and went on to graduate. After all that, Brian chose to continue living at home and work for his dad, because in the process of putting his plan into effect, they had restored connection and Brian was no longer trying to hide who he was. He left the drug life to protect the connection with his dad.

So why was Brian's dad standing to the side of my new parent orientation? It turned out Brian had a brother and they had decided to transfer him to our school so we could love on him too. Brian's story is one of many where I have watched parents trust in the message of love over fear as we navigate difficult periods of growth in their child's lives. I can confidently say every single time a parent has kept their heart turned toward their child, their child has turned their heart back toward them. Not always straight away, and the pain of waiting can feel unbearable, but what a wonder when it does.

So often, it is actually the student who turns their heart toward their parent first and role-models to their parent how to keep their love on. Those students are my heroes. I have one particular middle school boy who frequently comes and asks me how to keep his love on toward his parents when things feel hard. He never blames them or gets angry, he just recognizes his pain and asks for advice. This is a young man who took it upon himself to learn about Love Languages and then he went home and sat with his parents whilst they did the test so he could learn how to communicate love with them more effectively. I have no doubt before graduation day I am going to see his parents turn their hearts of love and tenderness toward him, but even if they don't, he is already set up to be an excellent role model of a loving father for his own children one day.

Implementing a culture of love not only impacts the students you work with—it will impact your team members too. I have a colleague who recently experienced the feeling of his heart suddenly turning toward his father. After his mother died many years ago, he disconnected from his father and family. In that time, he had a son of his own and his anger toward his dad kept him from ever seeing or communicating with him. Just before the birth of his second son, my friend contacted me and shared how he realized his dad was simply grieving and had never intended to hurt him. He described a sudden longing to know his father again and forgiveness broke through. A week later they were reunited and his father was able to learn about and meet his grandsons for the first time. These stories just keep on happening to our students, our parents, and our staff.

ADMINISTRATION ENGAGEMENT WITH EDUCATIONAL SYSTEMS, BOARDS, AND PRINCIPALS

Developing a culture of love in your school is a task that any individual can press into and strive toward. If we accept the premise that culture is "how people behave regardless of whether they are being observed," this is certainly an achievable characteristic of students and teachers. Moreover, it is broadly accepted that culture is the collective implementation of a set of unwritten rules for how things really work. These rules reflect the underlying mindset of an organization's leaders working silently in the background to direct how the cultural participants think, make decisions, and actually behave. So whilst as individuals we are valuable participants in our school cultures, we should also take responsibility for learning exactly how the culture is being defined, implemented, and assessed. School administrators and boards are responsible for setting the vision, strategy, culture, and ethics of their organization in which the staff and community participate.[1]

School slogans and billboards notoriously have aspirational vision and mission statements promising their unique interpretation of what successful graduates will look like. This raises an interesting set of questions. Are school boards solely responsible as the cultural custodians? Are school boards effectively measuring the promises they make? And how are they keeping the school community engaged and informed? If the school board are the cultural custodians, then the principal is the keeper of culture at an operations level. It is therefore imperative that the board and principal work collaboratively. What has become observable in many schools is that without clear governance, their cultural intentions are weakened and even polluted.

The board, along with the principal, needs to communicate that at this school we will not tolerate certain things. We don't just have val-

---

[1] H. Coyer, "School Culture, Success and Sustainability," *Independent School Briefing* Vol 21, 8, 1-4 (2017).

ues—we live our values as a lifestyle in all of our interactions. There are non-negotiables that we will not compromise. It is not unusual, especially for those in school leadership, to hear criticism that a decision is both too harsh whilst equally demanding that they "protect" students with behavior concerns. The truth is there will always be criticism because there are so many people involved in the life of a school and each family group and teacher and leader has their own set of "Cider House rules." Also a movie, *The Cider House Rules* is a metaphor for the unspoken rules of society—the "rules" are posted for the migrant workers of an orchard to follow and be held accountable to, but the migrant workers can't read, so they must rely on other people to explain or interpret the rules for them. Similarly, each of us has a list of "rules" we expect from every family, classroom, or school because they are our perceived normal. We put this standard on one another, criticizing or punishing others when they do not meet the unspoken, mysterious expectations.

The most common "Cider House rule" in the classroom is the teacher's expectation for silence. One teacher expects their students to know when they stand in the middle of the classroom they want silence. Another wants their students to know that when they hold their hand up they want silence. Yet another expects that when they move to the back of the classroom they want silence. Teachers do a great job stirring engagement and discussions, but we often fail to inform students of our signals and then we get upset when they don't do as we expect. I have had so many sessions educating students on how to learn each of their different teacher's "Cider House rules" that half my job would be obsolete if teachers just took time to find out what our personal internal "rules" are, decide if they are important, and then educate our students explicitly on how to successfully meet these expectations or needs.

Boards are answerable to the school they serve and are therefore responsible for maintaining the "trust" ledger within the school community. When boards can clearly describe the unwritten rules that undergird their values, definition of success, development of evaluative tools, community communication, and member selection of diverse members to help achieve their goals, the likelihood of cultural pollution decreases. To do this well, Helen Coyer, deputy executive director for Independent Schools Queensland purports that board members must embed the intended culture first into their own personal beliefs and lifestyles before permeating the school.[2] Greer, et al, further elaborates that if school board members fail to live up to the espoused culture, it has little chance of fostering or protecting such a culture.[3] Culture and the success of the school are intrinsically linked.

It is easy to feel frustrated when you are working in a school environment that does not ascribe to a culture of love over fear and punishment at the board level. We wonder, "Who am I to make this change?" and all too frequently join the band of complainers making noise without progress. I hear your frustration, but don't give up and become a victim to the educational system. Choose to be powerful. What are you going to do?

PUSHING OFF FROM THE BOTTOM

The question that comes to mind whenever I am talking to a teacher or school looking to implement Loving our Students on Purpose into their culture is, "Is it bad enough yet?" Things generally have to become bad enough before any solution, change, or progress can be made. Until it is bad enough, it is easy to complain, blame, and come up with a ton of excuses why every idea will not work. Until it is bad enough, often the person you are talking to does not have a problem and they definitely do not want your solution. Schools have been chugging along for centuries, churning out students with satisfactory results and maintaining relative calm in their teaching teams and classrooms. Happiness is often far from their agenda, and they accept, "You can't keep everyone happy."

---

[2] Helen Coyer, "School Culture, Success and Sustainability."

[3] P. Greer, C.Horst, A. Haggard, *Mission Drift: The Unspoken Crisis Facing Leaders, Charities, and Churches* (Australia: Baker Publishing Group, 2014).

For many, this type of "no frills" homeostasis is success. This is true in any business, system, family, counseling room, or conversation. The truth is that sometimes the best thing that can happen to you or to them is hitting rock bottom. Sadly, I have watched on as so many schools ache internally—teachers burned-out and exhausting themselves needlessly fighting the "systemic" and "leadership" bad guys whilst simultaneously trying to motivate rescuers to save them. Their leaders are hurting from the lack of "buy-in" from staff over the latest program change and feel disillusioned with the idea that joyful responsibility is possible for adults, let alone students.

As a school leader, have you ever found yourself wasting your precious time monitoring staff car parking because of adult defiance, staying back late turning off lights and checking general tidiness, mediating squabbles between teaching partners, or saying "Because I said so" in response to a whiny "Why do I have to attend staff meeting?"—all whilst being chastised that you are not present enough walking around the school? Trust me, it is bad enough. Schools cannot afford to not consider moving from weary to powerful, from punishment and disconnection to trust and connected classroom cultures.

Last summer, I took my nine-year-old friend Jaz for a swim. I knew Jaz had not been to lessons in a while and I was watching closely to see how confident she would be. With my heart in my mouth, I watched her sink down to the bottom of the deep end of the pool. I waited and watched, poised ready to dive in to help her, and then suddenly she pushed to the surface kicking furiously, took a huge breath looking around to see where she was, and then sank down again. This continued as she slowly jumped her way to where she wanted to be and held on to the edge of the pool. I asked Jaz what she was doing. She explained that she was taught in her swimming lessons how to push off the bottom and get your bearings so you don't worry about being in the deep end and can get to safety.

What a life lesson. In that moment, I realized what an incredible life-giving gift it could be when your feet hit the bottom. My young friend showed me that when you hit the bottom, you can push off toward the surface and get your bearings. Not only this but when things get bad enough, when you hit the bottom and exhaustion kicks in, this is the greatest opportunity for change. You see, after a while Jaz came over to where I was and asked if I could help her improve her swimming. Absolutely! We spent the afternoon learning how to float on top of the water.

This is the place where most of my clients come to me. Teachers and school leaders who are tired of seeing the same problems cycling and hoping there is another way. Teachers frustrated with feeling like their administration does not listen, won't change, and won't do things their way. Teachers who have incredible skills in teaching but have become victims of the education system. They have stopped taking responsibility for themselves and their protests are against the oscillating rescuer-bad guy leaders who can and will never be able to please everyone. Despondent and disillusioned are two consistent descriptors for the teachers and school leaders I meet with. Weary and close to giving up, they are willing to risk one more time and make one last-ditch push off the bottom to talk to me.

As I have already stated, school boards and leaders simply cannot afford to ignore the cries of teachers, and teachers cannot afford to settle for complaining and inaction. It is time to strike out toward becoming powerful. Why? Because positive student success is linked to strong staff well-being, and strong staff well-being is linked to a supportive principal, a supportive principal is one who excels at managing their own well-being, and principal's well-being is directly linked to a positive relationship with a supportive board.[4]

---

[4] J. Wise, "Well-Being and Educational Leadership," *Independent School Briefing* Vol 21, 8, 6-11 (2017).

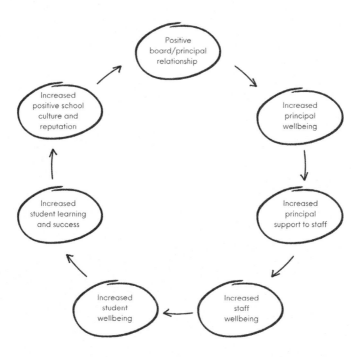

Preservice teacher and emerging principal training programs have historically exempted their graduates from vigorous strategies for managing stress and burnout—prevalent experiences in industries such as psychology and social work where high emotive interactions occur. In these industries, quality professional support, supervision, and debriefing are standard and expected procedures. Unnecessarily, this lack of professional supervision has resulted in lower and declining well-being scores for school leaders than the average citizen.[5] According to Winthorp Professor Donna Cross, teachers in Australia, UK, and USA are united in reporting the highest levels of daily occupational stress compared with other professions, with 40-50% of teachers and principals reporting daily

---

[5] P. Riley, *The Australian Principal Occupational Health, Safety and Well-Being Survey.* Institute of Positive Psychology and Education, Australian Catholic University: Melbourne, Australia.(2020).

stress impacting their physical and mental health.[6] Gardner identifies that the impact of stress is far-reaching and includes burnout, physical and emotional distress, reduced self-confidence and self-esteem, and damaged personal relationships.[7] Further, Cross reports that 81% of teachers who responded to the National Union of Teachers in the United Kingdom acknowledged experiencing workplace stress, depression, and anxiety. Howard and Johnson say it bluntly—stress is forcing teachers to leave the profession, resulting in significant loss of experience, skills, absenteeism (and presenteeism), all of which are having a hefty financial cost and impacting availability of teachers into the future.[8]

In seeking to determine why some teachers thrive and others survive or simply leave the profession, Schwarzer and Hallum report that self-efficacy was a key ingredient.[9] They found that attrition reflected one's ability to engage positively with personal coping resources—the ability to be powerful. Whilst burnout was indicated by a number of negative personality characteristics, including low levels of self-efficacy—staying powerless. Extrapolating from this data, Cross recommends that an immediate increase in skills that promote boundaries in work/life balance, self-reflecting and determining, student behavior education, parent and conflict management, and increased connection and communication with administration are urgent.

POWERFUL PEOPLE INFILTRATE CULTURES

Whilst on the one hand, the board and principal are integral to sustaining good staff well-being, it is equally true that every individual is

[6] D. Cross, "Teacher Well-Being and its Impact on Student Learning" [Powerpoint slides]. University of Western Australia, 2014). https://www.research.uwa.edu.au/__data/assets/pdf_file/0010/2633590/teacher-wellbeing-and-student.pdf

[7] S. Gardner, "Stress Among Prospective Teachers: A Review of the Literature." *Australian Journal of Teacher Education*, 35 (8), 2 (2010).

[8] S. Howard & B. Johnson, "Resilient Teachers: Resisting Stress and Burnout," *Social Psychology of Education*, 7, 399-420.(2014).

[9] R. Schwarzer, and S. Hallum, *Perceived Teacher Self-Efficacy as a Predictor of Job Stress and Burnout: Mediation Analyses*. Applied Psychology, 57, 152-171 (2008).

responsible for their own well-being.[10] Learning to work with your administration has a lot less to do with their behavior (since you do not have a remote control for this) and a whole lot to do with you becoming a powerful teacher and influencer in your school community. Remember, as a powerful teacher you require respectful relationships, you know how to set limits, and you manage yourself no matter what is happening in front of you. This is as true for your students as it is for your leaders and board members. You get to do your half of you.

You have a choice. You may decide to leave your school because the culture is not a powerful loving one, but it is unlikely that you will find many schools that have already established the culture you are seeking. So what is the alternative? What are you going to do? You could choose to be the agent for change in your life, which will flow over into your classroom, your school, and even your whole school district—your impact is only bound by your imagination. Instead of throwing a victim pity party, frustrated that no one responded to your foot-stomping or inspiring speech, get up and decide to be the solution you want to see, and then recruit others to join you. Let's cheer one another on and begin the start of a world-wide education recalibration.

It starts with just one person in a school community. Ruth was, by all accounts, unremarkable. She was an indulgent mother and diligent school office worker who grew tired from workplace conflict and family demands and became somewhat surly as she went about her duties each day. She worked a few days a week assisting the front desk at one of the schools where I attended to support student behavior and well-being. Ruth would sit back eyeing me suspiciously, observing my comings and goings, asking questions (which sounded like statements being snapped), and even belittling my role as she prophesied the students' pending failure. Yet, every day she was there, watching me like a hawk whilst I patiently answered her questions and provided education. One day she

---

[10] J. Wise, "Well-Being and Educational Leadership," *Independent School Briefing* Vol 21, 8, 6-11.(2017).

called me over. I steeled myself for another, "You are wasting your time—they should just bring back the cane," comment.

Instead, she whispered so the other ladies in the office did not hear, "Bernii, why do the students you work with listen to you? I have been watching you. They don't listen to their teachers. Some of them don't even listen to their parents. But when you speak with them, they tell you the truth and they take responsibility. What are you doing?"

I almost fell over backwards. Instead, I whispered back, "Would you like to borrow the training I did on DVD?"

"Yes, please."

The next time I saw Ruth, I silently handed her a copy of the LoKoP DVDs (lest one of the other office ladies see that she was interested in me and damage her reputation). She watched the DVD series and could not stop talking about them. She started coming down to my office to ask me questions in her break time and after school, then started using the one-liners and strategies in her own family. She started to tell other parents and other staff, and some of the other office staff started to ostracize her for being "different." But Ruth did not care—she was experiencing connection in her relationships and it felt good. Every opportunity she got she shared what she was learning. Most importantly, she changed the way she engaged with the students and parents who came to the office. Becoming a safe person resulted in parents and even teachers asking her about the change in her presentation, her newfound smile, joy, and the way she interacted with students who were no longer afraid of going to the office. Ruth asked permission to facilitate LoKoP for a small group of parents advocating directly to the principal. She told everyone who would listen. When she had no one left to tell at her school, Ruth applied to be a chaplain at the local state school and started to share these strategies there too. Ruth is a great example of one powerful person who can make a huge difference to a school and district.

You do not need the whole school system on board before you start to be powerful. You just get started on your journey toward being powerful.

You also don't need to reject your school policy and procedures to be powerful. There are many wonderful behavior and well-being programs already operating in schools. What would it look like if you were to support those staff who are working tirelessly to uphold character values and life skill lessons? What would it look like if instead of responding to a behavior program as a victim—"I have to do it"—you instead were powerful—"I am supporting the development of my students as they learn to take responsibility for their behavior using (insert program here)."

A POWERFUL TEACHER

Mrs. Beech was a placement student when I first observed her teaching. In that final year of university, she was deciding which tools she would keep and her supervising teacher was a powerful, love-filled coach. Mrs. Beech chose the way of loving her students on purpose. She honored her school behavior policy and used it consistently, applying love in the way she worded the process and guiding her students to take responsibility. Mrs. Beech spoke well of her leaders, and always spoke well of her students, even on difficult days. She was not afraid of her students making mistakes in front of her, and could be heard cheering them on—"Oh no! What are you going to do?" "I can't wait to see what your ideas are for next time."

Mrs. Beech shared with me about one particular chatty group of girls in her class. When seated together, these girls were struggling to make good choices in their learning. Mrs. Beech needed to set some limits and adjusted the class seating plan. The year continued and Mrs. Beech had many classroom discussions about how to be a powerful student who joyfully took responsibility for your own choices without violating the right of other students to learn. Returning from lunch one day, Mrs. Beech found a note on her desk that said, "Dear Mrs. Beech, please could Becky and I sit together for the remainder of the term? We will do our work quietly and talk together in our break times. If you let us sit together we will make you look like a genius."

Mrs. Beech allowed the girls to sit together and they finished off the term demonstrating that they had learned how to be responsible not only in their own relationship, but also because they actively pursued their connection with their teacher. I bet anything that the girls' teacher the following year benefited greatly from the powerful boundaries Mrs. Beech set with these students.

A POWERFUL PRINCIPAL

Alister is a principal whom I have had the pleasure of working alongside. Alister shared vulnerably that he came from a strict upbringing where children were to obey, any faults were to be punished, and perfection was the goal. After a significant incident in his own life, Alister's belief relating to control and punishment was challenged, and he started to ask himself questions about love, grace, self-responsibility, and connection.

As an employee, he had ignored me for many months, but having heard about Loving on Purpose, Alister came unashamedly armed with his questions. Alister's heart moved toward becoming a powerful person and not surprisingly, a powerful principal. First, he changed the way he led the staff body. He got to know every one of his teachers by name and learned details of their personal lives. He shared his vulnerable journey of growth in staff meetings, showed value for the roles traditionally ignored such as tuck shop and cleaners, and implemented a Love Language-based recognition program to acknowledge the hard work of staff in all areas of the school. Alister also began showing an interest in the students who made the messiest mistakes in schools. He shared with their parents what he was learning and applying in his own family about living a life of respect and limits whilst allowing children to grow and make mistakes.

When I first met Alister, he was a principal that was feared. Being called to see him triggered anyone's anxiety. His heart change transformed him into a principal who was awed. Staff and students were honored to be invited to his office, and he regularly was seen connecting with others as he walked throughout the school. From a place of significant influence, Alister impacted his school community to be one of love.

Whenever I am asked what I see as the most influential aspect of setting and maintaining a culture, I answer, "Its top leader." In schools one may think this is the principal, but research agrees that it is higher than this. I have come to learn that the culture is significantly influenced and guided by the principal, but it is set by the board and by governmental systems that guide decisions and policy long before they are put into practice. Yet, I strongly believe that regardless of the system or principal, culture is within each individual person, like Ruth, Mrs. Beech, and Alister. It is a way of living that oozes out and impacts those in our sphere of influence. Therefore, it is incredibly important for governing bodies and school leaders to select the right staff to bring into their environment. Just one staff member refusing to recalibrate to the culture of love can cause distress in the environment.

Mind you, the opposite is also true. I started out as one disgruntled teacher aide, doing everything I could to get out of working in traditional school systems. Then I caught on to the foundational vision of love and held on, championing the principal, the school board, and the vision, and I discovered that one person can make a huge impact. No one creates a culture alone. It takes each person in the organization making the choice to commit to the power of uniting together towards a singular vision and set of rules.

So, culture is led both from the top and from the staff. Culture also already exists in the families. Schools are one of the few services that impact almost every family in the world. If the school culture is being driven by families with strong punitive requirements, it will be an uphill struggle to implement a culture of love. From experience, it is likely that this is the place where every school will start. If you are new to the journey of culture change in your school, the place you will need to begin is with your teachers and parents who will usually push back against the change. It took a lot of perseverance in the early days of implementing

Loving our Students on Purpose, but eventually my leadership heard the success stories from parents, then the teachers saw the changes in the students. Your students are the easy ones—they will simply mirror the adults around them. They will recalibrate to whatever the culture is around them as long as it is clear, confident, and consistent enough to infiltrate their peer culture. And it is possible!

ONE PERSON CAN MAKE A DIFFERENCE!

A champion of behavior education, Meagan has worked for many years in her school to lead the culture away from irresponsibility and toward responsibility. Her singular goal was to replace fear and punishment with love and discipline in all of her individual interactions with students. Heading up the behavior education unit, Meagan took many blows from powerless staff who were frustrated with a program that does not "teach that child a lesson." In their experience, the bad day they are having is the student's fault. Meagan's school was historically characterized by victim—bad guy—rescuer cycles, but with the hard work of a team of staff who banded together, is now moving toward being powerful.

Meagan has a choice daily to listen to the few frustrated angry staff members or parents blaming her for the child's behavior, or to focus on the child who is learning about life in front of her through their mistakes. Behavior education is a thankless job. Someone is always angry at you, and it is difficult to please the trifecta of student, teacher, and parent (not to mention the leadership and board). But Meagan is a powerful person. When she arrives at school, she knows that each student referred to speak with her has made a mistake, and whilst she is not responsible for it, she has the honor of guiding them toward taking responsibility and learning how to apply new self-control skills through offering safety, repetition, and connection. She is not in control of the swirl of angry responses from victims which threaten to engulf her. Daily, she repeats the importance of self-control, taking responsibility, not violating the rights of others, and setting limits.

To encourage Meagan, I set the task of writing a weekly reflection about what she observed, who her frequent flyers were, and what the main issues were. I then encouraged Meagan to visit her school deputy and principal once a week, starting with the goal of establishing connection but eventually creating a dialogue in which she could share some of her observations and data. Meagan started to notice the patterns evident in each term and semester, the peaks or troughs of behavior and well-being issues, and the waves of new students learning new skills whilst previous frequent behavior students moved into the background, having learned what they needed. Patterns are worth capturing, so Meagan started to develop a way to collect data she could use to communicate back to her behavior team in staff meetings and report to principals or boards. Refusing to be a victim, Meagan used the data to anticipate trends such as increased number of well-being cases after the long summer holidays or increased inappropriate use of technology during study week. She could share this data with her leaders, send out well-timed tips of the week to teachers, and write newsletter articles to raise parent and staff awareness. Meagan's principal started to expect her unscheduled visits, and even sought her out for information and started to hypothesize with her.

Meagan's behavior education team used the data to move from offensive, reactive responses to proactive planning. Instead of leaders coming to blame her or the team for the student's behaviors, they began to come and ask for help to understand what was driving the particular surge in a specific issue or trend. I remember on one occasion Meagan sharing the sudden increase in students hitting one another with their lunchboxes in Year 1. A quick survey of the younger students identified that the students were role-playing "lightsaber" games after the release of a new Star Wars cartoon. Another time it was "doctor" games when a new kids operation show began gaining popularity in the lower grades. What was important was that instead of looking for a bad guy, the school teams were working together to find out what was going on behind the behavior and with that understanding could go about responding without needing to blame anyone.

SETTING THE CULTURE–THEORY OF CARE

In your school environment, increasing safety by preserving your connection with your students should be a priority. Our goal is to drive a culture of love by creating an environment where safety and security are primary. It is essential, therefore, that we are able to set and maintain the thermostat of the culture rather than using a thermometer. A thermostat sets the culture and is not governed by situational ethics. Situational ethics, as the term indicates, allow the situation to determine ethics and therefore the reaction to the situation. A strong culture, in contrast, will set the ethical standard and maintain it regardless of how a situation threatens to impact the environment. Culture is not something you switch on and off when it is convenient. It is not something we change to please an upset parent. A culture is first who we are, then what we do, and it is consistent.

Through accurate data collection, schools are able to regularly check that each cohort is being allocated resources effectively, and adjust once the need is no longer there. We want to be sure that the majority of our students are assimilating and thriving in our culture simply through our consistent classroom programs, and to make sure that those who need the most intensive help are being identified and given what they need. We do this by collecting data that reflects a consistency in our cultural thermostat. This is what I refer to as *theory of care*.

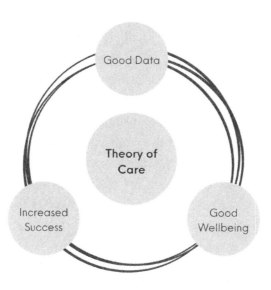

Through the data schools collect you can keep track of where each student, each cohort, and each year level is, as well as whole school data. Good data provides very useful information about the specific areas where you need to focus, whether for an individual student, a group, or even the whole school sector, such as the secondary or primary schools. Good data helps us to move towards good outcomes and ultimately generate high levels of well-being and educational success. If we have good data, we can recognize when a student needs specific support and put it in place for them. When this is done effectively, their sense of self and well-being improves. The better the student's sense of well-being, the more likely they are to engage with learning in the classroom and engage relationally with teachers and fellow students. They are enabled to thrive, experience success, and develop a further increase in well-being—a beautiful upward spiral. Good data collection will let us know that this is happening.

Meagan applied the theory of care to her school community. With the support of administration, she collected a range of useful data across the school. It was a massive undertaking. However, immediately it highlighted a significant concern—the number of students in Meagan's secondary school who were failing assessment items was far too high. This was not new information to Meagan, who had sat with many distraught students who had failed and even more students who were making poor choices to be "kicked out of class" to get away from certain teachers, thus missing out on learning and affecting their grades.

Meagan sought concrete data to emphasize what anecdotal data was not. Having recognized the large number of students who were being impacted by their "failures," the school leadership put a system in place that enabled teachers to communicate feedback with parents for each individual assessment item, including draft submissions, final submissions, and exams. Very soon, the "failed" grades began to decrease. Reduced fail grades meant rising pass grades, and the more students were passing their assessments, the more they began to engage with teachers and peers, enjoy their learning, and find their school experience fulfilling. The school leaders also decided to review the assessment items, found that some were not appropriate, and instituted changes to make the tasks more achievable and applicable to students. Another win. The outcomes and success of the changes that came through collecting data were very encouraging. From 2013 when Meagan started to collect failed grade data to 2019 there was a 68% decrease in failed grades; however, Meagan noted that the school had increased in student numbers by 25%. This reflected an increase in passing results along with an increase in student numbers, suggesting an increase in positive school reputation. The board loved that!

Data can change student's lives. David was a teacher at a small alternative school for students expelled from public school. Most of the students were frequently absent from their previous school due to truancy, violence, disengagement, and substance use. After a few months in David's classroom, these students would often be ready to return to mainstream school. The problem was that David could not convince the students that they could, let alone should, return. Applying the theory of care, David started to track student's attendance on a visible chart for them to follow along. And he was right, their attendance was impressive. On one occasion, an incident occurred in which David needed to send one of the students home early. Through tears, the boy sobbed that he would no longer have the 100% attendance record he was so proud of.

In order to care effectively, it is essential to collect data about how students are behaving, how many support sessions they are seeking out, what interaction we are having with parents, and how students are progressing in individual subjects and with their different teachers. Data collection will help you and your leaders to make informed decisions about which programs to implement, which teachers to place in various grades, where to allocate resources and so on. By consistent collection and use of data in your school, you will be informed about when you need to intervene so that you are enabled to plan for and care for your students effectively.

I'm from Africa. When I was there on holidays a few years ago, my grandma took me on a safari drive. She paid a lot of money, it seemed, to sit in a car and learn about trees. For over an hour, our guide showed us different trees and plants, near and far. I was thinking about the cost—all that money Grandma had paid to see aloe trees! About an hour into the trip, when negativity was starting to seep in and I was getting distracted, the guide turned to us and whispered, "Now, I want you to look at that aloe tree, then follow the line of sight to that acacia tree in the distance. Now . . . look between the acacia and the baobab tree. Do you see the giraffe and her baby?" Suddenly I realized that he had given the entire group language that enabled us to see that the bush was teeming with life. He gave us strategies to be able to communicate more effectively so that we could find what he was pointing to in unknown territory. This is very similar to what data does for us. It gives us eyes and it gives us language.

Data shows us what is going on in our school environment so we can communicate to our leaders and community what we are seeing and what we need. Great data enables great vision. To be successful as educators, we need to learn to truly see and to better understand. It is our responsibility to collect the right information, to be aware and attentive to what is going on in our schoolyard, and to deliberately set the thermostat so that angry parents, politics, and external pressures do not cause us to "adjust" our values and core cultural DNA. Our aim is to set the thermostat—to insert love and safety, to document well, to make change in accordance to our school culture, and to see student breakthrough and success. Our interventions, supported by carefully gathered and analyzed data, will work for our students' benefit. Every step of the way we manage ourselves and test ourselves to grow in our capacity to be powerful people.

I encourage you to take time to get to know your school culture through data collection and develop your understanding about what is going on in all these areas. If there is no data being collected, perhaps you can start this process like Meagan did in her school. Discover what is being done well, what is amazing and working beautifully, and where there are holes that need filling or areas that need recalibrating. In the nitty gritty of your classroom, ask yourself again if there are strategies you have forgotten that worked well in the past, that you can use again. Practice self-management. First and foremost, it is you and I who must learn to walk in connection with others and our leadership team, ask great questions, and learn to speak the languages of love to people around me.

Whatever is needed, I encourage you to begin to have discussions with leaders and colleagues, using powerful language, and making changes, first in your own classroom or sphere and then on a broader scale. Perhaps your own family will find reconnection, love, and safety increasing too.

As you speak up, you will find a longing to find another way besides punishment and detentions, yelling and telling, control and management, and burned-out weary teachers from yet another behavior system to set up and manage. It isn't working, it hasn't been working for a long time. Together, we are embarking on the journey of Loving Our Students on Purpose. These little people are our future employers, business owners, country leaders, pastors, teachers, breadwinners, homemakers, and parents. We have the opportunity on a huge scale, to embed the tools of love, responsibility, grace, work ethic, and forgiveness into our next generation.

THE FINAL CHARGE

The heart of each person is where the real journey to apply the principles of love over fear begins. Taking the vision of love and putting it into the hands of staff who value fear and punishment is not likely to have positive results. Loving Our Students on Purpose is about preparing your individual heart or the hearts of your teaching teams who are already committed to a culture of love.

Again, it is not always possible to find whole school communities who have recalibrated away from traditional punishment and control techniques, but it is possible for you to be the catalyst for change. I challenge you to find one or two colleagues in your school who are on the same journey of discovering what it means to be powerful themselves and together start implementing this lifestyle of love over fear and punishment. It may take a few years, but you will get noticed, and you will get pushback, which is actually a good sign that you're having an effect. In my early years, I had teachers become angry at me because they were offended that their student behaved for me. Not everyone will be happy with your consistent grace, and yes, the students will actually like you, so very quickly you will find this may offend some people. If I had a dollar for every time someone complained that a student came back happy from speaking with someone in our team . . . that is when you know it is working and the cultural environment is changing. As you build a foundation of love, you will start to see results in your interactions with students and families, and with that you will notice that this slowly opens conversations with other staff and parents, even other schools. All while you increase in confidence, resilience, self-efficacy, and pleasure in teaching. You can and will enjoy teaching again.

You yourself may be questioning if we are letting students get away with too much and have given them too much freedom. But when we work together as a staff to be consistent, we set clear understandings about how we are going to respond to their behavior, communicate the process, allow them to choose, and ensure that they experience the consequences of their choices. We have strategies in place to help students on their learning journey, and we are comfortable reinforcing the limits with those clear expectations. Loving on purpose is not a free-for-all, boundaryless concept. Quite the opposite. I hope you feel empowered to set limits and boundaries as you learn what you will and won't allow in your classroom or school culture. Loving our Students on Purpose empowers our students and teachers to become experts in joyful responsibility.

The LoSoP vision is to provide educational systems with the tools and encouragement to build a culture of love as students joyfully take responsibility for their choices and teachers prioritize teaching without becoming weary from behavior management and disillusionment. Our students have thirteen-plus years to be immersed in a school culture of love that creates opportunities to develop internal honor and respect, manage freedom, and learn responsibility from the inside out, without the need for fear or punishment to enforce values and ethics. Our young people can change the rates of crime, divorce, suicide and mental health issues. They can bring communities together to protect our planet, preserve child innocence, and keep technology ethical. Imagine releasing young people encultured in love out into our communities around the world—young people who know how to be powerful people, who are not afraid, who can handle large amounts of freedom, who understand the importance of risk and healthy conflict, who honor differences, and who will teach all of this to the next generation.

Powerful teachers acknowledge that it is okay for students to keep making mistakes as they learn about life. They create safe places for repetitive learning to occur by setting clear boundaries and limits. Powerful teachers refuse to engage in disrespectful exchanges as they draw out the gold in each student. Through owning their choices over and over from prep to senior, our students are learning to make their freedom work for them, to manage themselves, and to become powerful people.

BIBLIOGRAPHY

Al-Ghani, K. *The Red Beast: Controlling Anger in Children with Asperger's Syndrome*. UK: Jessica Kingsley Publishers, 2008.

Arden, John. "Mind-Brain-Gene: Toward Psychotherapy Integration." Digital Webinar. USA: IAAN, 2022.

Badenock, B. *Being a Brain-Wise Therapist: A Practical Guide to Interpersonal Neurobiology*. New York, NY: W.W. Norton & Company, 2008

Beattie, Melody. *Codependent No More: How to Stop Controlling Others and Start Caring for Yourself*. USA: Hazelden Information & Educational Services, 1986.

Bowlby, John. *A Secure Base: Parent-Child Attachment and Healthy Human Development*. New York: Basic Books. Inc, 1988.

Brown, Brené. *Dare to Lead*. London, UK: Penguin Random House, 2018.

Brown, Brené. *The Gifts of Imperfection: Let Go of Who You Think You're Supposed to Be and Embrace Who You Are*. Center City, MN: Hazelden Publishing, 2010.

Cline, Foster & Fay, Jim. *Parenting with Love & Logic*. Colorado Springs, CO: NavPress, 2005.

Chapman, Gary. *The 5 Love Languages: The Secret to Love That Lasts*. Chicago: Moody Press, 2015.

Chud, Carla & Silk, Danny. *The Pathway to Powerful: Learning to Lead a Courageous, Connected Culture.* Sacramento, California: Loving on Purpose, 2018.

Coyer, H. "School Culture, Success and Sustainability." *Independent School Briefing.* 21, 8 (2017): 1-4.

Cozolino, Louis. "Our Social Brains." *The Neuropsychotherapist,* 9 (November 8, 2014): 22-32.

Cozolino, Louis. *The Neuroscience of Psychotherapy: Building and Rebuilding the Human Brain.* New York, NY: Norton, 2002.

Cozolino, Louis. *The Neuroscience of Psychotherapy: Healing the Social Brain,* 2nd edition. New York: W.W. Norton & Company, 2010.

Cross, D. "Teacher Well-Being and its Impact on Student Learning" [Powerpoint slides]. University of Western Australia, 2014). https://www.research.uwa.edu.au/__data/assets/pdf_file/0010/2633590/teacher-wellbeing-and-student.pdf

Dahlitz, Matthew. *The Psychotherapist's Essential Guide to the Brain.* Park Ridge, QLD: Dahlitz Media, 2017.

Epstein, Seymour. "Cognitive-Experiential Self-Theory" in L.A. Pervin (ed), *Handbook of Personality: Theory and Research.* New York: Gilford, 1990,165-192.

Epstein, Seymour. "Integration of the Cognitive and the Psychodynamic Unconscious," *American Psychologist.* 49, 8 (1994): 709-724.

Ford, Ed. *Discipline for Home and School, Fundamentals,* 3rd edition. Scottsdale, Arizona: Brandt Publishing, 2003.

Freud, Sigmund. *Beyond the Pleasure Principle.* New York, NY: W. W. Norton & Company, 1959. Original work published in 1920.

Gage, S. H. & Sumnall, H.R. "Rat Park: How a Rat Paradise Changed the Narrative of Addiction," *Addiction.* 114, 5 (2019): 917–922. https://doi.org/10.1111/add.14481.

Gardner, S. "Stress Among Prospective Teachers: A Review of the Literature." *Australian Journal of Teacher Education.* 35, 8 (2010): 2.

Geller, Shari M. & Greenberg, Leslie S. "The Mind-Brain-Body Connection, or How Emotional Styles Influence Health," In S.M. Geller & L.S. Greenberg, eds, *Therapeutic Presence: A Mindful Approach to Effective Therapy*. Washington, DC: Magination, 2012: 109-131.

Glenwright, Melissa. "How Samantha used neuroscience to build a pathway out of social anxiety disorder," in P.J. Rossouw, (Ed). *Neuropsychotherapy: Theoretical Underpinnings and Clinical Applications*. USA: Mediros Pty Ltd., 2014.

Grawe, K. *Neuropsychotherapy: How the Neurosciences Inform Effective Psychotherapy*. New York, NY: Psychology Press, 2007.

Greer, P., Horst, C., & Haggard, A. *Mission Drift: The Unspoken Crisis Facing Leaders, Charities, and Churches*. Australia: Baker Publishing Group, 2014.

Hasson, Bob & Silk, Danny. *The Business of Honor*. Loving on Purpose, 2017.

Henson C. & Rossouw, Peiter J. *BrainWise Leadership: Practical Neuroscience to Survive and Thrive at Work*. Sydney: Learning Quest, 2013.

Howard, S. & Johnson, B. "Resilient Teachers: Resisting Stress and Burnout," *Social Psychology of Education*, 7 (2014): 399-420.

Leaf, Caroline. *Switch on Your Brain: The Key to Peak Happiness, Thinking and Health*. USA: Baker Book House, 2015.

Levine, Peter A., in Ogden, Pat, Porges, Stephen, & Dana, Deb. *Clinical Applications of the Polyvagal Theory: The Emergence of Polyvagal-Informed Therapies*. New York, NY: Norton, 2018.

Lundquvist L. & Dimberg, U. "Facial Expressions Are Contagious," *Journal of Psychophysiology*, 9 (1995): 203-211.

MacLean, Paul D. *The Triune Brain in Evolution: Role in Paleocerebral Functions*. New York: Plenum Press, 1990.

Montgomery, Arlene. *Neurobiology Essentials for Clinicians: What Every Clinician Needs to Know*. New York: W.W. Norton & Company, 2013.

Ogden, Pat, Porges, Stephen, & Dana, Deb. *Clinical Applications of the Polyvagal Theory: The Emergence of Polyvagal-Informed Therapies*. New York, NY: Norton, 2018.

Porges, Stephen W. "Clinical Application of Polyvagal Theory." Digital Seminar. Wisconsin, USA: PESI Inc, 2019.

Porges, Stephen W. & Dana, Deb. *Clinical Applications of the Polyvagal Theory: The Emergence of Polyvagal-Informed Therapies*. New York: W.W. Norton & Company, 2018.

Powers, William T. *Behaviour and Control of Perception*. New York: Aldine, 1973.

Riley, P. *The Australian Principal Occupational Health, Safety and Well-Being Survey*. Institute of Positive Psychology and Education, Australian Catholic University: Melbourne, Australia, 2020.

Robinson, N. *Christine: An Adolescent and Social Anxiety Disorder*. In Rossouw, P. J. *Neuropsychotherapy: Theoretical Underpinnings and Clinical*. USA: Mediros, 2014: 73-90.

Rosanbalm, K.D. & Murray, D. W. "Caregiver Co-regulation Across Development: A Practice Brief," *OPRE Brief #2017-80* (Washington, DC: Office of Planning, Research, and Evaluation, Administration for Children and Families, US. Department of Health and Human Services, 2017). https://fpg.unc.edu/sites/fpg.unc.edu/files/resources/reports-and-policy-briefs/Co-RegulationFromBirthThroughYoungAdulthood.pdf

Rossouw, P. J. *Neuropsychotherapy: Theoretical Underpinnings and Clinical Applications* . USA: Mediros, 2014.

Schore, A. N. *The Science of the Art of Psychotherapy*. New York, NY: W.W. Norton & Company, 2012.

Schwarzer, R. and Hallum, S. "Perceived Teacher Self-Efficacy as a Predictor of Job Stress and Burnout: Mediation Analyses." *Applied Psychology*, 57 (2008): 152-171.

Silk, Danny. *Culture of Honor*. Shippensburg, PA: Destiny Image, 2009.

Silk, Danny. *Keep Your Love On*. Redding, CA: NewType Publishing, 2015.

Silk, Danny. *Loving our Kids on Purpose: Making a Heart-to-Heart Connection*. Shippensburg, PA: Destiny Image, 2008.

Silk, Danny, producer and director. *Loving Our Kids on Purpose*. DVD. Redding, California: Loving on Purpose, 2013.

Silk, Danny, producer and director. *Keep Your Love On.* DVD. Redding, California: Loving on Purpose, 2013.

Silk, Danny. *Unpunishable: Ending Our Love Affair with Punishment and Building a Culture of Repentance, Restoration, and Reconciliation.* Sacramento, California: Loving on Purpose, 2019.

Wilson, Claire. *Grounded: Discovering the Missing Piece in the Puzzle of Children's Behaviour.* CHEW Initiatives, 2018, Kindle Version.

Wise, J. "Well-Being and Educational Leadership," *Independent School Briefing,* 21, 8 (2017): 6-11.

RESOURCES & WEBSITES

- https://kids.loplifeacademy.com/
- www.heartsmart.school
- https://www.mylearningtoolbox.com/
- www.wimhofmethod.com
- http://kids.loplifeacademy.com/
- https://www.truwell.org/
- https://braingrow.com.au/

ABOUT THE AUTHORS

BERNII GODWIN

Bernii has a master's qualification in Social Work and a Graduate Certificate in Neuropsychotherapy, which complement her undergraduate study, Bachelor of Human Services/Bachelor of Arts in Criminology and Criminal Justice (majoring in youth and family justice). In addition, Bernii is a certified Loving on Purpose Trainer.

Bernii has worked in a broad variety of schools in various roles over the past two decades specializing in student well-being and behavior. Bernii is sought after by principals to consult on complex behavior and well-being issues, offer one-on-one coaching or supervision to educators and wellbeing teams, provide school-wide professional development, and insert hope into the life of "that kid or family." Her greatest passion is to see schools equipped with practical tools to increase student's engagement in their own academic learning journey by replacing fear and punishment with purposeful behavior education, safe connections, and powerful teachers. Bernii lives in Queensland, Australia with her husband, Jayden, and their son.

To connect with Bernii, please visit
www.godwinconsulting.com.au

DANNY SILK

As an author and speaker, Danny Silk offers life-changing books, conferences, and other resources drawn from decades of experience as a counselor, social worker, advocate, pastor, spouse, parent, grandparent, and leader. He is the President and Co-Founder of Loving on Purpose, a ministry to families and communities worldwide. Danny is also the author of multiple books covering subjects of building successful relationships, a culture of honor and strong families. Danny's passion centers around helping people build, strengthen, and heal their vital relationships. Danny and Sheri married in 1984 and have three children and three grandchildren.

To connect with Danny, please visit
www.lovingonpurpose.com

Printed in Great Britain
by Amazon

43102353R00165